FISCAL CHOICES

Canada after the Pandemic

The COVID-19 pandemic revealed that governments can quickly respond to a fiscal crisis without becoming mired in unproductive wrangling. But the pandemic has also revealed the limits of traditional policy instruments in stabilizing the economy, controlling inflation, and fostering economic growth. *Fiscal Choices* sheds light on the economic dimensions of COVID-19 and examines the state of Canada's fiscal policy and fiscal health following the pandemic.

The book covers a cluster of key fiscal policy topics: the overall capacity of government, the growth of inequalities, the management of sovereign debt, and the troubled institutions of federalism and parliamentary government. The book draws upon candid, in-depth interviews with over 70 former and current politicians, public servants, and academic experts who aim to establish a sustainable future within an accountable political system.

The book argues that although those who are entrusted with the instruments of power are intelligent and well meaning, they are reluctant to take risks or abandon well-known, if poorly performing, formulas. It concludes with a set of predictions and prescriptions rooted in a realistic interpretation of Canada's political economy. Ultimately, *Fiscal Choices* presents a sober assessment of federalism and parliamentary government as instruments of democratic accountability.

(Johnson-Shoyama Series on Public Policy)

MICHAEL M. ATKINSON is an emeritus professor at the Johnson-Shoyama Graduate School of Public Policy at the University of Saskatchewan and an adjunct professor in the School of Public Administration at the University of Victoria.

HAIZHEN MOU is a professor at the Johnson-Shoyama Graduate School of Public Policy at the University of Saskatchewan.

The Johnson-Shoyama Series on Public Policy

Taking a comparative and international perspective, the Johnson-Shoyama Series on Public Policy focuses on the many approaches to major policy issues offered by Canada's provinces and territories and reflected in their intergovernmental relationships. Books in the series each explore particular policy issues, and while research-based, are intended to engage informed readers and students alike.

Books in the series:

Fiscal Choices

Canada after the Pandemic

MICHAEL M. ATKINSON AND HAIZHEN MOU

UNIVERSITY OF TORONTO PRESS
Toronto Buffalo London

ISBN 978-1-4875-4578-9 (cloth)   ISBN 978-1-4875-5016-5 (EPUB)
ISBN 978-1-4875-4718-9 (paper)   ISBN 978-1-4875-4816-2 (PDF)

Library and Archives Canada Cataloguing in Publication

Title: Fiscal choices : Canada after the pandemic / Michael M. Atkinson
  and Haizhen Mou.
Names: Atkinson, Michael M., author. | Mou, Haizhen, 1977–, author.
Series: Johnson-Shoyama series on public policy.
Description: Series statement: Johnson-Shoyama series on public policy |
  Includes bibliographical references and index.
Identifiers: Canadiana (print) 20240281721 | Canadiana (ebook) 2024028173X |
  ISBN 9781487547189 (paper) | ISBN 9781487545789 (cloth) |
  ISBN 9781487550165 (EPUB) | ISBN 9781487548162 (PDF)
Subjects: LCSH: Canada – Economic conditions – 21st century. |
  LCSH: COVID-19 Pandemic, 2020– – Economic aspects – Canada. |
  LCSH: COVID-19 Pandemic, 2020– – Government policy – Canada. |
  LCSH: COVID-19 Pandemic, 2020– – Political aspects – Canada.
Classification: LCC HC120.E6 A85 2024 | DDC 330.971/074 – dc23

Cover design: John Beadle
Cover illustration: iStockphoto.com/Vadym Ilchenko

We wish to acknowledge the land on which the University of Toronto Press operates.
This land is the traditional territory of the Wendat, the Anishnaabeg, the Haudenosaunee,
the Métis, and the Mississaugas of the Credit First Nation.

This book has been published with the help of a grant from the Federation for the
Humanities and Social Sciences, through the Awards to Scholarly Publications Program,
using funds provided by the Social Sciences and Humanities Research Council of Canada.

University of Toronto Press acknowledges the financial support of the Government of
Canada, the Canada Council for the Arts, and the Ontario Arts Council, an agency of
the Government of Ontario, for its publishing activities.

 Canada Council
for the Arts Conseil des Arts
du Canada

 ONTARIO ARTS COUNCIL
CONSEIL DES ARTS DE L'ONTARIO
an Ontario government agency
un organisme du gouvernement de l'Ontario

Funded by the Financé par le
Government gouvernement
of Canada du Canada  Canadä

Contents

Figures

Tables

Preface

For most of us, the COVID-19 pandemic came as a shock, and shock is the word that best describes COVID-19's effect on the Canadian economy. Like most other countries, Canada plunged into recession in early 2020 and thankfully emerged rapidly the following year. In its wake COVID-19 has left a series of encouraging revelations: Biomedical research, in the form of new vaccines, can be applied much faster than anyone thought possible, and governments can respond quickly to a fiscal crisis without becoming mired in unproductive debate. But the pandemic also revealed limits both in public health expertise and in the ability of traditional policy instruments to stabilize the economy while controlling inflation.

This book takes a sober look at the economic dimensions of COVID-19, and examines the state of Canada's fiscal policy and fiscal health following the pandemic. Our analysis is a blend of three streams of interpretation:

- the academic literature on fiscal and monetary policy;
- the perspectives of elite players in the public sector; and
- our own opinions about the first two.

We try to be objective. Our own opinions do not show up in great granular detail. In fact, the most important opinion we express might be the topics we have chosen to highlight: the growth of inequalities, the management of sovereign debt, and the institutions of decisionmaking and accountability – federalism and parliamentary government. This blend of economic and political topics reflects our conviction that fiscal policy can be understood only by adopting a political economy approach.

Readers would be forgiven for thinking that political economy is what happens when you put a political scientist and an economist together. Not so, or at least not so simply. A country's political economy, for us, consists of the rules and norms used to solve the collective action problems standing in the way of creating and justly distributing wealth. One can adopt an entirely economic lens and concentrate on the role of markets in this process, or take a political science approach and focus on the exercise of political authority. But only by doing both, simultaneously, can one appreciate the range of policy choices available. And only by listening to decisionmakers can one appreciate how choices are made.

Academics have lavished attention, with good reason, on the institutions of policymaking, and we are equally committed to giving institutions and policies their due. But policies are made by people, and institutions require people to manage them. The people who populate the upper reaches of our fiscal policy institutions – politicians and their advisors – are the key players in this story. Clearly, they are human, and so suffer from the theoretical baggage and cognitive limitations familiar to everyone who has tried to understand the machinations of modern capitalism. Their task, however, is to do more than understand; they must thread the policy needles described here and change the content and conduct of politics such that a sustainable future within an accountable political system is within reach.

In the midst of the pandemic, we conducted interviews with many individuals who are or have been at the centre of fiscal policy choices. From these rich conversations, we can share verbatim only some of the opinions we heard expressed. But their influence on our own thinking extends far beyond those quotes. Every conversation produced nuanced insights, and several generated reading lists that helped us interpret our topic. We owe all of those with whom we spoke (academic economists, civil servants, and politicians) an enormous debt. We can say with certainty that, without their help, there would be no book.

The table of contents identifies the topics, but what did we learn and what do we want to convey? Here are some basic themes:

- Canada, like other developed countries, faces a series of policy crises: economic growth has slowed down; inflation is hard to control; income and wealth inequality are rising; environmental politics are polarizing; and demographic realities are beginning to bite. For some, this confluence of problems constitutes a "polycrisis": it is, at the very least, a set of compounding problems with serious economic and political implications.

- What makes this combination of problems especially challenging is our rapidly diminishing ability to anticipate the future. Our era is characterized by what some describe as "radical uncertainty." The effects of fiscal and monetary policy interventions are no longer certain, and the impact of technological changes are increasingly hard to predict.
- Economic growth, on which Canada relies for collective well-being, is becoming more difficult to generate, and the transition to a net-zero-carbon economy is especially threatening in a country that relies on natural resources to generate middle-class incomes. The idea that we are in the midst of a long-term "secular stagnation" is particularly sobering when we contemplate the difficulties Canada has had in preparing for inevitable economic changes.
- Most conventional indicators of well-being assure us that we live in the best of times, and there is no question that in absolute terms ours is a period of exceptional wealth. It is also a period, by no means the first, of exceptional and growing inequality. Our sense of justice and our expectations of continued growth demand more attention to emerging inequities and the question: "What should we expect from the economy?"
- Public trust in democratic governments and democracy itself is at a low ebb, and our political institutions do nothing to inspire confidence. Our leaders are increasingly reluctant to accept accountability for economic outcomes over which they have limited control or understanding, and our political discourse is dominated by performative posturing and blame avoidance.
- Those who are entrusted with the instruments of power show an understandable reluctance to take risks or abandon well-known, if poorly performing, formulas. Our economic elite is intelligent and well meaning, but fearful and conservative. Courage is in short supply, and the status quo has a strong grip on the imagination.

The set of challenges we are describing predate the pandemic, but the pandemic has had the salutary effect of drawing the details to our attention. It provides the fulcrum for our analysis, but we are well aware that there is an important pre-COVID-19 context and a challenging post-COVID-19 world, both of which need attention. As we look back on three extraordinary pandemic years, we hope that this book will promote awareness of these trends and challenges and encourage long-term, anticipatory thinking. We don't expect everyone to agree with our summary assessments, but we do hope that they will stimulate thought and even better ideas.

This book was funded by an Insight Grant from the Social Sciences and Humanities Research Council of Canada. We want to acknowledge and thank our collaborators in the SSHRC grant: Scott Cameron, Judy Ferguson, Mark Hallerberg, and Yilin Hou. In the process of writing the book, many colleagues and friends generously offered their time, despite the numerous challenges posed by the pandemic. The design of the interviews and a public survey benefited from the expertise of Loleen Berdahl, Paul Boothe, Dale Eisler, Don Drummond, Kevin Milligan, Doug Moen, Farah Omran, Marc-André Pigeon, and Geneviève Tellier. We thank the more than 70 former and current academics, politicians, and public servants who gave us their time and insights. A survey of more than 500 ordinary Canadians allowed us to probe the public's perception of fiscal policy priorities. We are more than grateful for their participation and thank Kyle Hanniman and Olivier Jacques for thoughtful suggestions on the survey itself.

Several colleagues took the time to read draft chapters. Daniel Béland, Ken Coates, Dale Eisler, Murray Fulton, Peter MacKinnon, Marc-André Pigeon, and Grace Skogstad offered us both encouragement and bracing commentary. We are also grateful to Mel Cappe, Ian Clark, Dan Perrins, and Harry Swain, all of whom read chapters and provided comments and suggestions that can come only from veteran public servants. They, and our academic colleagues, will be relieved to know that they are not responsible for the damage we might have done to their insights.

We received excellent support from our University of Toronto Press editor, Daniel Quinlan, who provided guidance in the entire process of the book. We want to thank the three anonymous peer reviewers for their very helpful comments. We especially appreciate the constructive comments of Reviewer 3, who brought us several useful references and offered sharp and fresh observations on every aspect of the book.

The preparation of the various versions of the manuscript greatly benefited from excellent professional editing by Heather McWhinney and Barry Norris. Data collection was assisted by students Iryna Laurynovich (Bajraktari) and Hayley Pelletier. Finally, the book would not have been possible without exceptional research assistance from our former student and assistant, Maritza Lozano, who was instrumental in the data analysis and production stages. Thank you to her and to everyone who has made this journey possible.

Michael M. Atkinson
Haizhen Mou
August 2023

Abbreviations

CBO	Congressional Budget Office
CECRA	Canada Emergency Commercial Rent Assistance Program
CERB	Canada Emergency Response Benefit
CERS	Canada Emergency Rent Subsidy
CEWS	Canada Emergency Wage Subsidy
CHT	Canada Health Transfer
CRA	Canada Revenue Agency
CST	Canada Social Transfer
EI	Employment Insurance
ESDC	Employment and Social Development Canada
FAO	Financial Accountability Office
GBEs	government business enterprises
GDP	gross domestic product
IFI	independent fiscal institutions
IMF	International Monetary Fund
LICO	low income cut-off
LIM	low income measure
MMT	modern monetary theory
OAG	Office of the Auditor General of Canada
OECD	Organisation for Economic Co-operation and Development
PBO	Parliamentary Budget Office
QE	quantitative easing
UBI	Universal Basic Income
WEF	World Economic Forum

FISCAL CHOICES

1 The Pandemic and After

In the space of little more than a dozen years Canada and the rest of the world endured two major economic crises: the Great Financial Crisis of 2008–9 and the Great Pandemic Crisis of 2020–2.

The financial crisis was a banking collapse fuelled by risky financial products and a profound relaxation of financial regulation. First diagnosed as a function of predatory lending in the US mortgage market, it proved to be much more than that. The Great Financial Crisis had its origins in the globalization of financial markets, which were regulated by national agencies. As banks purchased, repackaged, and sold toxic products to one another, they created a financial freefall when borrowers could not meet their credit obligations (Tooze, 2018). The resulting unemployment, which spiked in Canada at 8.3 per cent in the spring of 2009 (Statistics Canada, 2021d), was a global phenomenon. The world had not seen such a massive, synchronized recession since the market crash of 1929–30. It is no exaggeration to say the crisis almost brought down the neoliberal capitalist order. It certainly destroyed trillions of dollars in assets and set the stage for one of the longest recessions in history.

The Great Pandemic Crisis of 2020–2 was even more catastrophic in human terms. It killed millions worldwide, devasted public health everywhere, and shocked economies. As workers were banished from the workplace, economic activity slowed dramatically, standards of living fell, and supply chains unravelled. Years after the crisis first hit, the shortage of raw materials, semiconductors, and shipping containers threatened more economic tumult. Shocking as it was, the pandemic crisis was not what economists call a "black swan" – a complete surprise or unanticipated event. It was more like a grey rhino – a visible, predictable, coming-right-at-you crisis, with severe impacts and dire consequences (Wucker, 2016). We don't see black swans coming, so we

can't prepare. We know grey rhinos are coming, but we still don't prepare. Coronaviruses – viruses passed from animals to humans – have
been with us for a long time, and the 2003 outbreak of Severe Acute
Respiratory Syndrome showed that we would need severe measures to
isolate and extinguish a coronavirus if it ever got loose. These warnings
went unheeded, and the virus quickly exposed public health lassitude
and confusion.

Labelled COVID-19 in January 2020, in a deeply integrated global
economy the virus that emerged from China moved far more rapidly
than the Spanish flu virus a hundred years earlier. Canada's first confirmed COVID-19 case was registered on 25 January. Outbreaks had
already been reported in Iran and Italy, and on 11 March the World
Health Organization officially declared COVID-19 a pandemic. By then
a wide range of responses had already been launched, from outright
suppression via quarantines and travel restrictions, to contact tracing
and masking requirements. In a handful of countries, Sweden and
Japan being the most prominent, politicians determined that the best
response was to rely on herd immunity. They were in the minority. In
most rich countries, at least, accepting thousands upon thousands of
premature deaths was not an option.

On the economic front, reaction was swift and unprecedented in
scale and coordination. It also revealed startling vulnerabilities and
triggered a rethinking of some economic and political assumptions.
This book is a critical consideration of the character and content of that
rethinking. There are some reassuring messages about early-stage economic responses, but some disquieting revelations about our overall
preparedness, our understanding of fiscal policy, and our willingness
to face some basic economic and political realities. We want to believe
that our economic and political institutions are resilient and those who
manage them are competent. For decades they have provided enough
stability and resilience to allow a business-as-usual approach to economic management. And we are good at business-as-usual. But these
same institutions have built-in limitations that the pandemic, and our
response to it, have revealed.

First, our political institutions are not focused much on the future
except as an extension of the past. They are designed to produce stability. Threats to political order, such as economic crises, command almost all of decisionmakers' bandwidth. What is left is spent dealing
with political threats from competitors and critics. A four-year political
cycle means that policies with long feedback loops get less attention
than those crafted to respond to immediate pressures. Thus, politicians, who can be good at responding to crises, are uncomfortable

with hypothetical scenarios or too much speculation about the distant future. From the vantage point of early 2019, a worldwide pandemic looked quite hypothetical.

Second, political institutions take account of future generations mostly by protecting incumbents from the temptation of attempting to change too quickly. Political institutions rely on elite players with specialized expertise to craft workable policies. In the face of a crisis, senior public servants typically consult their prior assumptions and default to standard operating procedures even when the circumstances are far from standard. These senior officials are a heterogeneous lot – some are visionaries, many are capable managers, and most have a technical repertoire to tackle familiar problems. Unlike politicians, whose role in the policy process is linked to an electoral mandate, these players' legitimacy is based on their specialized knowledge and organizational skills. Their role when a crisis emerges is to estimate the scale of the problem, locate specific vulnerabilities, and fashion rational responses.

Risk is a central concept and risk management a preoccupation for all who operate the modern state. Of course, if political institutions focus on the immediate and are predisposed to invest in the familiar, some risks will go unrecognized and others will be misjudged. The COVID-19 experience is a reminder of how inadequate risk assessments can expose deficiencies in preparedness and capacity. During the pandemic, ordinary citizens were urged to assume unfamiliar roles as guardians of public health, while an economic elite assumed responsibility for unfamiliar policy interventions. Questions of sustainability arose quickly. How long would people abide by new restrictions? How long would pandemic initiatives delay the return to some semblance of economic normality?

Risk management sensitized both the public and elites to slightly longer-term risks as well. Managing the economic fallout from the pandemic meant inviting other kinds of economic fallout, especially inflation and debt. And other trends, which had been the subject of academic speculation – such as increasing levels of inequality – were now elevated by the unnerving spectre of massive job losses and huge public debts. Is the economy, as currently organized and imagined, sustainable? Can we continue on the same policy path without endangering future generations? The pandemic, and the government response, helped push these questions to the forefront of public debate.

Risk management implies that human interventions are worthwhile, but that there are choices to be made, responsibilities to be shouldered, and blame to be affixed to poor performance. In that sense risk management is highly political. True, it is in the nature of risks that they can be only partially apprehended, and the understanding of potential harms is always subject to critique and revision. Still, if we cannot locate responsible decisionmakers, then accountability is a pointless expectation. Going into the pandemic, trust in public officials was at a low ebb. Citizens had come to expect evasive language, and layers of institutional and organizational complexity made it difficult to locate responsibility among the vast array of those who are part of what is conventionally described as the decisionmaking process.

The pandemic was a short-term political, health, and economic crisis. It required rapid response, the mobilization of expertise, and coordination across organizational boundaries. On the economic front, early successes gave way to policy errors and eventually to a macroenvironment of rising inflation and sovereign debt that policymakers try desperately to avoid. Along the way, our sense of what is sustainable underwent some reconsideration. Or at least it should have. The pandemic gave us a chance to reconsider some basic policy assumptions. The same goes for our political institutions: the order they bestow makes sense to fewer and fewer people. Critical information on revenues, expenditures, and deficits is often obscure or unavailable, an especially serious deficiency during an economic crisis (Robson & Dahi, 2023). The result is a persistent accountability shortfall in which elites try to fix a system that few people understand and whose shortcomings have helped to unleash populist forces determined to uproot it entirely.

But let us begin with the pandemic itself. Our economic and political consensus is fragile, our institutions are not performing for the long run, and we have just received a wake-up call. In this important sense, the pandemic has been a gift.

Responding to the Pandemic

Initially at least, the pandemic's economic impact was on the supply side (Tooze, 2021). A supply-side contraction is very rare, involving a breakdown in the way goods and services arrive at the marketplace. Sometimes new technologies change production regimes and disturb familiar ways of producing and transporting consumer goods or providing services. These shocks are typically limited to specific sectors and specific countries. COVID-19's supply-side shock took the form of new rules for engaging in familiar economic activity, rules that made it impossible to accommodate everyone who wanted to travel safely or go to restaurants, retail stores, and cinemas. Restrictions on entry gave way to complete closures as economies locked down, consumers withheld their spending, and those workers who could afford to

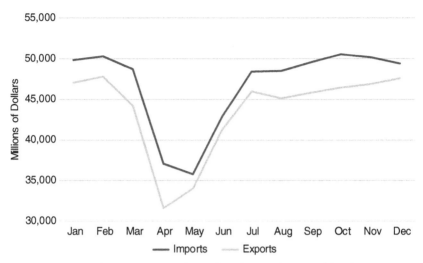

Figure 1.1. Canada's International Merchandise Trade, Monthly, 2020
Source: Statistics Canada (2021c). Contains information licensed under the Open
Government Licence – Canada.

do so abandoned the workplace in favour of toiling from home. The
knock-on effects – including changes in health care delivery, childcare,
and care for the elderly – were huge.

In Canada, the imposition of public health requirements – social distancing, masks, and business closures – swept thousands out of the workforce. By the end of 2020, 834,100 jobs had been lost (Statistics Canada,
2021d), most of them in service industries, which, pre-pandemic,
accounted for 79 per cent of the Canadian economy (Statistics Canada,
2021e). Customers vanished, discouraged by public health orders and
frightened by a virus that was said to be extremely contagious. Rental
car companies disposed of their fleets, airlines mothballed aircraft, and
container ships pulled into distant ports and remained there. Canada's
trade activity fell from $598 billion in annual merchandise exports
in 2019 to $524 billion in 2020, a reduction of 12.4 per cent (Statistics
Canada, 2021c). Annual imports in 2020 decreased to $561 billion,
8.5 per cent less than in 2019. The sharpest decline occurred in April
2020, at the outset of the pandemic, when exports decreased by 28.5 per
cent and imports fell by 24.5 per cent (Figure 1.1).

Throughout all the steps and missteps that were taken to contain
the virus and "flatten the curve," a debate raged about how much to
restrict economic activity deliberately. Decisionmakers conducted

implicit cost-benefit analyses with every measure aimed at harm reduction. The health of the economy and the health of Canadians were in the balance. Early hopes that Canadians would be relieved of these trade-offs by quickly arriving at herd immunity were set aside as the virus mutated, bringing fresh outbreaks to previously spared parts of the country. Premature openings, especially in the fall of 2020 and again in the summer of 2021, brought new pressures to hospitals and health care providers, obliging those who were overly eager to "open up" the economy to backtrack as cases mounted and intensive care units were stretched to the limit.

The list of vulnerabilities exposed by the pandemic is long. In Canada revelations began with the realization that our collective capacity to anticipate and respond to pandemics had recently been dismantled (OAG, 2021b). Having learned rather quickly – by March 2020 – that our virus antennae were not sensitive enough to a rapidly emerging threat, Canada began the arduous journey towards a set of measures to isolate carriers of the virus, educate the public on its transmission, and augment the equipment needed to expand hospitalization capacity. On the public health front, many mistakes were made. Canadians quickly learned that we had incomplete knowledge of contagion, insufficient supplies of personal protective equipment, and inadequate testing facilities. The pandemic revealed that Canada had highly vulnerable populations, limited vaccine research, and unreliable supplies of foreign-sourced vaccines. Most other countries experienced similar discouraging revelations. And throughout the pandemic, as disinformation slowed progress towards immunity, as Asian populations were targeted for abuse, and as hospital staff began exiting the health care profession, the vulnerabilities continued to mount. Those who suffered most were people who could not isolate themselves, pay for childcare, work from home, or afford broadband Internet service.

On the economic front, markets reacted by searching for safety. Anticipating a major contraction in economic activity and assuming that countless firms (and maybe even countries) would be unable to meet their debt-servicing obligations, financial institutions began liquidating their equity and junk bond holdings in a panicked dash for cash. In mid-March 2020, even the demand for US Treasury bills (government debt instruments), the one safe haven, had begun to dry up as bills were dumped on the market to raise cash (Tooze, 2021). The only source of reliable relief came from the very centre of turmoil during the Great Financial Crisis: the banking system or, more precisely, the central banks, led by the US Federal Reserve, commonly known as the Fed. As a lender of last resort, the Fed activated a loan facility for small businesses, purchased corporate debt directly, and indicated it would support fully governments' efforts to raise funds in bond markets. The latter step took the form of the purchase of public debt in a process known as quantitative easing,[1] a strategy pioneered during the Great Financial Crisis.

The Bank of Canada and other central banks joined in, first reducing interest rates (in Canada's case to 0.25 per cent) and then creating similar liquidity facilities to flood the market with cash. Central banks purchased government bonds that were issued to pay for major infusions of operating capital into Western economies. Between January and May 2020, the debt issued by member countries of the Organisation for Economic Co-operation and Development (OECD) was in the order of US$11 trillion (OECD, 2020). In Canada, in March 2020 the Bank of Canada started buying large amounts of bonds issued by the Government of Canada, worth about $5 billion a week (Bank of Canada, 2020). The upshot of this response was the shifting of large quantities of financial risk from private sector balance sheets to public sector balance sheets, an acknowledgment that financial markets remained vulnerable to liquidity crises even after post–financial crisis reforms (Hauser, 2021).

Central bank purchases allowed the release of fiscal policy tools – specifically, government spending programs – to reduce unemployment risk and allow employers to stay in business long enough to weather the restrictions on economic activity. These initiatives were pursued without the caution and reluctance that characterized the Great Financial Crisis. In March 2020, as governments realized the scale of the pandemic, the Fed's Open Market Committee indicated that it would purchase whatever Treasury securities and mortgage liabilities were necessary to create a market (Blinder, 2022). Economies inevitably would slow down, but they would not be allowed to plunge so deeply into recession that they could not recover. Governments might have underestimated the ferocity of the virus and overestimated their capacity to manage it, but monetary authorities, and the governments they supported, were not going to allow the pandemic to destroy the economy.

On 18 March 2020, Prime Minister Justin Trudeau announced the creation of the Emergency Care Benefit and the Emergency Support

---

1 *Quantitative easing* (QE) is a form of monetary policy whereby central banks purchase securities, mostly government bonds, which become available to commercial banks to increase lending and investment. QE is justified as a means of allowing the central bank to hit its inflation target when interest rates are already low, but it is often criticized as contributing to increased government debt.

Benefit and set aside $82 billion as an initial commitment (Harris, 2020). The monetary signals having been sent, this announcement marked the beginning of the federal government's fiscal policy response. It was followed by the Canada Emergency Response Benefit (CERB), which replaced two previously announced programs, a temporary additional payment to the Canada Child Benefit, a mortgage payment deferral, a temporary wage top-up for low income essential workers, changes to the Canada Student Loans program, the Canada Student Service Grant, the Canada Emergency Business Account Interest-Free Loans, the Canada Emergency Commercial Rent Assistance Program, the Canada Emergency Wage Subsidy, the Canada Emergency Student Benefit, and other economic support programs announced in late March and early April 2020 (Department of Finance Canada, 2020). As expected, spending levels increased dramatically. While the provinces spent on average 7 per cent more in fiscal year 2020/1 than in 2019/20, federal outlays were an astonishing 70 per cent higher in 2020/1 (Robson & Dahi, 2023, p. 4). Meanwhile, federal government revenues dropped from $973.5 billion to $943.2 billion in the twelve months following the advent of the pandemic. Hence the need for debt.

The Post-Pandemic Search for Stability

None of what the pandemic produced from governments could be described as normal. Normal – a kind of stable, predictable future – seemed to have taken a holiday. The laws of supply and demand had not been suspended, but the pandemic could not be met with standard assumptions about sound fiscal policy. What was sound in 2019 was no longer sound in 2020. In particular, standard finance shibboleths about the need to keep government spending in check and avoid large deficits seemed completely out of place.

Post-pandemic the short-term agenda was straightforward: first, deal with the inflation unleashed by clogged supply chains, income-support payments, and worldwide shortages; second, cope with very high debt levels as interest rates began to climb. Worries that had barely registered in the pre-pandemic era emerged with a vengeance as prices began to rise and real estate values began to fall. The search for some form of stability, if not predictability, was on. After two major financial crises and the outbreak of war in Europe, stability was a prized commodity. But how likely is it that a return to "normality" is in the cards? Or have we just been introduced to a new normal in which crises are more frequent and more disturbing and governments less capable of producing the conditions for stability, either economic or political?

We are not used to thinking that the economy is out of control. Since 1970 economists (literally those with PhDs in economics) have become policymakers on the promise that control is within reach. Complex models of both politics and economics offered the tools that politicians needed to create stability. Disagreements existed, of course, but the one thing economists could agree on was that stability was both desirable and possible. As Appelbaum (2019, p. 16) puts it, "[a]lthough nature tends toward entropy, [economists] shared a confidence that economies tend toward equilibrium."

Technically, equilibrium represents a relationship among actors in which the best response strategies have been deployed and no better outcome can be achieved. Equilibrium prices in markets represent a convergence of supply and demand that no single supplier or consumer can change unilaterally. In this classical model of the economy, factors of production experience a gravitational pull towards a particular steady state. The idea that such a state exists is reflected in concepts like the "neutral rate of interest" or the "natural rate of unemployment." Both are intended to convey the concept of a smoothly functioning market economy that, *ceteris paribus,* finds its own equilibrium path. Equilibria might change over time, but the key is that changes are predictable or at least not surprising.

Achieving equilibria typically requires trade-offs. The famous Phillips Curve describes the trade-off between inflation and unemployment: increases in one produce decreases in the other, until the 1970s when that relationship no longer held. The resulting period of stagflation – high inflation, high unemployment – represented a stable point that few, other than gold traders, wanted. Getting these trade-offs right can, in principle, foster stability. And for a while at least it seemed possible. In the period between 1984 and 2007, often called the Great Moderation, both inflation and output volatility declined significantly in most OECD countries.

At last macroeconomists were enjoying some success taming economic fluctuations and creating an economy on a stable growth path with (relatively) low levels of unemployment. There were still financial collapses and higher levels of unemployment than necessary to keep inflation at bay, but by the early 2000s some economists were convinced that the problems associated with macroeconomic policy had been more or less solved. In 2003, the then-president of the American Economic Association declared that the economics profession had figured out how to set macroeconomic levers – fiscal and monetary – in a way that reduced volatility. Any further attempt to cushion the impact of economic shocks would, he argued, purchase very little additional welfare (Lucas, 2003).

While some of the decline in volatility could be attributed to "luck," structural changes in the economy, particularly inventory management, clearly contributed to reducing output volatility. As for inflation volatility, deploying monetary policy, especially the adoption of inflation targets and "forward guidance" (Blinder, 2022, pp. 320–1), helped to reduce both inflation and inflation volatility. The relative importance of policy, as opposed to production changes in the private sector, is debatable, but it is safe to say that, during the Great Moderation, monetary policymakers could take some pride in their accomplishments (Bernanke, 2012).

Despite the victories of monetarism over inflation in the 1980s and over volatility after that, recent history has discouraged the idea that policy fixes are straightforward, let alone lasting, and that a return to the Great Moderation is at hand. As the pandemic exposed vulnerabilities and gifted the world a return to recession, optimism was evident in equity markets but almost nowhere else; then it disappeared there as well. Confidence in the economy's resilience declined precipitously (McKinsey & Company, 2022). Low interest rates, which had made public borrowing so attractive to governments and their advisors, had also helped push the cost of homes (and eventually mortgages) to new heights. Inflationary pressures, traceable in part to supply chain disruptions, threatened to undermine confidence in the ability of central banks to produce the one outcome to which they are uniformly committed: price stability. Behind inflationary signals lay the balance sheets of governments, now swollen by rescue packages to heights not contemplated since the Second World War. In the midst of this upheaval, pledges to achieve carbon neutrality clashed with renewed demand for fossil fuels, which remain vital to Canada's economy (Mousseau et al., 2021).

As if this were not enough, stagnation in the post–Great Financial Crisis world, particularly wage stagnation among the middle class in developed economies, unleashed a groundswell of support for populist voices in politics. The conceit that we had figured things out was lost on those left behind. The result was the by now familiar formula: endorsement of nationalism, rejection of science, search for scapegoats, and deep hostility towards elites, particularly the so-called globalist variety. The signs of a populist resurgence were everywhere before the pandemic. The policy response to the pandemic, particularly expanding and conflicting public health regulations, pushed all the populist buttons. By then a strong form of tribalism had already promoted polarization, undermined centralist parties, and curtailed consensus discourse (Potter, 2021).

So, is it reasonable to imagine that price and output stability can still be engineered in an economy riven with uncertainties and blanketed by political disenchantment? Consider the alternative: the very real possibility that our recent spate of economic crises is likely to continue and even get worse. In this view, crises are not a bug but a feature of capitalist production relationships. In the Schumpeterian version of economics, capitalism is a "dynamic disequilibrium system" (Skidelsky, 2018, p. 350). Finance capital, the global banking and credit system, is especially prone to generating crises far beyond normal business cycle effects (Minsky, 1986). In the Great Financial Crisis, the problem was global interpenetration of finance capital coupled with an insatiable appetite for new products. In the 2023 bank runs, the problem was the financial risks created by interest-rate increases and poor managerial decisions, combined with insufficient regulatory enforcement.

As for fiscal policy, the post–financial crisis record was not especially positive. The recession that followed the crisis lasted far longer than others and required unprecedented corporate bailouts. The lesson of 2008–9 was that one does not have to be the originator of a crisis, or a co-conspirator, to suffer its consequences. Those consequences included severe financial distress for major Canadian companies. The auto industry, already experiencing a cyclical downturn, accepted a $14.4 billion bailout from the governments of Canada and Ontario to help prevent the bankruptcy of Chrysler and General Motors. Nothing could prevent the subsequent restructuring of the industry and the loss of thousands of auto sector jobs.

Like most OECD countries, Canada emerged from the Great Financial Crisis hobbled and humbled. The new equilibrium was anything but universally benign. Convinced that a return to stability required austerity programs and the shrinkage of government's role in the economy, OECD countries, especially in Europe, embarked on a program that could be fairly described as starving the state (Alesina & Passalacqua, 2016; Blyth, 2013). In 2010, the US National Commission on Fiscal Responsibility and Reform (Simpson-Bowles) created by President Barack Obama recommended severe cuts to spending that would reduce the growth in the deficit by US$4 trillion by 2014 and reduce the debt by 60 per cent by 2023. Deficit and debt reduction was the order of the day. And although the Simpson-Bowles recommendations were never implemented, the austerity agenda they signalled helped slow economic recovery (Blinder, 2022).

In Canada, the Stephen Harper government, which had overseen the expansionary initiative of 2009–10, shifted priorities in 2011 to a low-tax/balanced-budget policy. This approach to the economy and to deficits lasted until 2015. By the second quarter of that year, the federal government's ratio of gross debt to gross domestic product (GDP) had retreated to about 46.1 per cent from 49.3 per cent in the second quarter of 2011. The objective was to reduce the federal debt, a goal that was largely achieved, but economic growth in the same period was anaemic. Informed observers concluded that the Harper government had sacrificed some economic growth to reduce debt, which was already at a relatively modest level (Dodge & Dion, 2016).

Will the post-pandemic future mean a return to austerity as governments seek to restore their balance sheets? This is an unlikely (but by no means impossible) scenario. Austerity is the imposition of aggressive reductions in levels of public sector debt. Reductions can be accomplished either by increasing taxes or reducing spending. Those prescribing austerity as a remedy for economic stagnation have argued that reducing public sector debt via spending cuts is far better policy than raising taxes (Alesina et al., 2019). Cuts to government spending could be expansionary, the argument goes, generating private sector investment that would more than compensate for short-term pain.

Evidence for these effects has been hard to come by, although Canada's retrenchment experience of the 1990s is sometimes cited as a case in point. More telling is the argument that austerity, far from inducing recovery, extended the post–financial crisis recession and made it harder for governments to manage their accumulated debt (Blyth, 2013). Critics of austerity also argued that reducing government spending when the source of the Great Financial Crisis recession was private sector speculation was misplaced targeting (Boyer, 2012). And anyway, not all countries have the same ability to absorb retrenchment or raise taxes, as Greece's experience illustrated.

In sum, as we argue in succeeding chapters, reaching for the standard tools to manage a swollen public sector balance sheet does not have much appeal in the post-pandemic world. The search for stability has not ended, but theorists and practitioners alike are obliged at least to consider whether it is time to make some fundamental changes.

What Kind of Change Is Required?

There are plenty of policy proposals. Conventional macroeconomic theory has not disappeared, although it is now largely trained on the problem of how to manage inflation and respond to enthusiasm for cryptocurrencies. Less conventional but highly public responses to the pandemic include the announcement, by the World Economic Forum (WEF), that COVID-19 has given us a chance to reconsider the entire neoliberal agenda. Sensing that we might be at an inflection point in the evolution of modern capitalism, or at least in the evolution of macro-economic theory, in 2020 the WEF offered a progressive agenda under the heading "the Great Reset." Where neoliberalism celebrated eco-nomic growth and prosperity achieved through the market economy, the authors of the Great Reset imagined a more sustainable, inclusive, and environmentally responsible world (Schwab & Malleret, 2020). The assumptions under which the pre-pandemic economy performed, in which market-derived efficiency was the most important value, would need to be replaced or augmented by a much broader set of considera-tions based on the well-being of the planet and its inheritors. Concepts such as "resilience" and "sustainability" would take centre stage and metrics such as GDP would need to share space with "environmental, social, and governance" criteria in evaluating both private investment and public policy.

One version of this new attitude, the "Cornwall Consensus," focused specifically on resilience as the organizing concept for the future in-ternational economy. Sponsored by the Group-of-Seven (G7) countries, the October 2021 report announcing this policy direction renewed a commitment to globalization, but concentrated on what are taken to be several serious deficiencies in the original Washington Consensus framework. Where the Washington Consensus advocated free trade, privatization, performance budgeting, and the like, the Cornwall con-sensus offers "diversification, co-dependence and public-private part-nerships within well-governed, open and integrated global markets" (G7 Panel on Economic Resilience, 2021). That these markets are not well governed is taken to be the core problem; the solution is said to be an imaginative investment in new institutions with new missions for a climate-challenged, pandemic-vulnerable future. New institutions are needed for new problems, including cyber security, vaccine distribu-tion, and, of course, climate change.

More institutions mean more rules, standards, and requirements, with all the attendant problems of compliance and enforcement. In this sense, the Cornwall Consensus is more of an update than a new international order. Cornwall is an early post-pandemic declaration; there will be more. These will be joined by admonitive pleas from oth-ers in the economic policy community who believe that it is time to get serious about liberal commitments. Or, more often, it is time to rethink what liberal commitments consist of. In an early contribution to the values side of the discussion, Mark Carney, former governor of both the Bank of Canada and the Bank of England, argues that we have overinvested in market definitions of value and failed to measure our collective progress in terms of public goods and well-being. His list of the values that need endorsement (or reinforcement) includes fairness, solidarity, sustainability, and, not surprisingly, resilience (Carney, 2021).

When central bankers argue that we need to shift our values to match the scale of our collective problems, it is fair to conclude that the global economic elite is on the move. Whether anyone will follow is an open question, although there are undeniable signs that the rhetoric and logic of resilience thinking are penetrating both public and private board rooms. In Canada shortly after the pandemic arrived, Prime Minister Trudeau spoke approvingly of the need to "build back stronger, more resilient, and greener economies" in a post-COVID-19 world (Prime Minister of Canada, 2020b). Suggesting how far the thinking of Canada's economic elite has evolved towards this agenda is a major objective of this book. Certainly, the new world order sketched out by the WEF is an unlikely place to start. It has been ridiculed in some circles, criticized in others, and has formed the basis for a resilient set of conspiracy theories. The fact that major financiers have signed on to this Davos-inspired change agenda has provoked deep distrust and contempt (Goodman, 2022). This does not mean change will not take place. It does suggest, however, that without strategies grand pronouncements are just words and that strategies are useless without clear goals. At best, these are merely emerging in the post-pandemic environment.

In this book, we offer a critical assessment of the idea that we are on the verge of a reordering of public priorities. We are cautious sceptics. A major change in public priorities would require a shift in policy and a renewal of democratic institutions, neither of which is easily managed. This kind of rethinking might be on the horizon, but the record of the response to the pandemic is not encouraging. The pandemic showed us how fragile our economy is and how the biological world can bring the economic world to a standstill. It drew attention (yet again) to massive inequalities and alerted us to the catastrophic consequences of myopic neglect. And yet, the pandemic response has been largely conservative. Very few will take governments to task for trying to stabilize markets and restore faith in the economy, but nothing in the pandemic policy mix suggests any plan to change the social order or address looming challenges.

The pandemic is an inflection point in the sense that it has drawn attention to the capabilities and deficiencies of modern governments. Even optimists will want to reflect on the challenges ahead, many of which were already well under way before COVID-19 burst onto the scene. They include digitization of all manner of services and the transformation of energy markets. Economic policy will need to adapt quickly to handle the fallout. Pessimists will suggest we prepare for failure. Demographic changes and their impact on labour markets will generate more inflation, challenging governments to chart a different kind of equilibrium path away from recession.

In Chapter 2, we describe the economic policy elite charged with navigating our fiscal future and discuss the importance of the roles they play. The remaining chapters lean heavily on their perspectives, not just to make sense of it all, but also to appreciate the intellectual tools they bring to the task (and the frustrations they feel). We then consider three major fiscal policy questions that all governments will need to confront. Chapter 3 asks how aggressive should governments be in trying to shape the future economy? Few dispute the proposition that, as the scale of global disasters increases, we will require governments with more foresight. But when it comes to taming the economic machine of capitalism, with its potential for creative disruption, there is clear hesitation. In Chapter 3, we describe a strong preference for steady, pragmatic, approaches towards the ultimate goal of economic growth.

Chapter 4 deals with the second major fiscal challenge: growing inequalities. We describe the magnitude of inequalities in Canada and the demand for policies that take us beyond tax-and-transfer programs. Prominent among those demands is the idea of a Universal Basic Income, a policy made more conceivable (and perhaps more palatable) by the income-support programs launched in the wake of the pandemic. The political implications of wealth inequality make the economic elite nervous, but so does fear that excessive taxation will stifle demand and discourage investment. In Chapter 5, we describe the debt challenge and outline two distinct positions on its importance. Canadian federal and provincial governments have experimented with fiscal rules, anchors, and guardrails. We discuss their utility and describe the options that governments confront when debt becomes onerous.

A stable and sustainable economic future is imaginable only if our institutions and the politics they engender are up to the task. In Chapter 6, we describe the reality of federal-provincial financial relations and the efforts made to create order out of the competing interests of sovereign governments. The task is critical because Canada, unlike most federal systems, has both a set of provincial governments with serious taxing and spending powers and central institutions, including the Bank of Canada, with their own priorities and agendas. Accountability, efficiency, and equity are all at issue. In Chapter 7, we assess the current state of budget accountability from the perspective of legislative scrutiny, bureaucratic oversight, and post-spending audit. Without fiscal accountability, public trust erodes, but the difference between what parliamentary democracy requires and what our current budgetary system delivers is not trivial. Close observers acknowledge the problems, as we show in Chapter 7, but there is no will within the political system to rebalance power, with the result that accountability is elusive and cynicism encouraged.

Keep in Mind

The pandemic has given us a chance to think about the future more deliberately than is our normal inclination. Chances are we will not do exceptionally well. As we discuss in Chapter 8, the future is extraordinarily difficult to imagine, and whatever we have learned from the pandemic will not translate automatically into superior responses to new crises. What we can do is reflect on the current state of thinking about fiscal policy and about how policy choices are (or are not) responsive to a system of democratic governance.

In the chapters that follow, we profile some basic operating assumptions derived from the academic and popular literature on fiscal policy, and survey the views of senior finance decisionmakers and Canadians themselves. Some of these operating assumptions are articles of faith; some are held rather tentatively. The Great Financial Crisis and the pandemic have taught us humility. They have also shaken our core understanding of how the economy works and of what policies we should adopt. Here are three assumptions that will need future attention.

- *Economic growth should be the overriding object of economic policy.* Although there are different growth paths with different outcomes, for most economists this assumption is bedrock. And while faith in the benevolent effects of economic growth is pervasive, our ability to engineer it is suspect and fading. The middle class in Canada has benefited enormously from our resource-extraction economy, but these benefits (which tend to be underestimated) are unlikely to continue to flow at the same pace. Slow growth or no growth might be welcomed by some, but not by those who are currently in charge of economic policy.
- *Policy can be shaped in a way that will bring stability to markets and resolve collective action problems.* This assumption is no longer held with much conviction. Instead, we are asked to consider the existence of "polycrisis" – a set of interconnected risks whose causal

relationships are hard to specify and whose outcomes are unpredictable (Homer-Dixon et al., 2022; Tooze, 2022). Despite the failure to confront these risks, neither abandoning policy nor arguing for "less government" is an especially appealing response.

- *Modern societies have deep talent pools that can produce the needed technological responses.* This optimistic assumption depends on a capacity to draw on and mobilize all the resources of a society. But ours, like many others, is beset by gross inequalities that inhibit innovation and foster political instability. Inequalities might be "natural," but that does not mean that increasing economic inequality can be tolerated. As market economies become subject to stagnation, they cannot be permitted to shrug off the distributive implications or steer a shrinking social surplus towards those who are already well off.

These contested assumptions circulate within institutions that are themselves in crisis.

- *Our federal institutions are creating more economic problems than they can solve.* Hardly anyone is happy with the current state of federal-provincial relations. Economic concerns aside, deterioration in fiscal relationships is having serious negative political effects. Decision-makers are open to change, but radically different provincial economies and contending interpretations of federalism itself are a drag on policy innovation.
- *Parliamentary institutions provide no serious safeguards against the abuse of economic authority.* The assumption that parliaments and legislatures are in control of the public purse strings is a holdover from textbook theories of parliamentary government. It collides with reality on a regular basis. Democratic accountability is weak and trust in government continues to decline.
- *Ambition and courage are in short supply.* While the destructive and destabilizing tendencies of capitalism are at the heart of the multiple economic crises we currently face, success in meeting them will depend on having the right people in positions of authority. An economic elite that is overinvested in the status quo is not going to be up to the challenge. In their place we need politicians, bureaucrats, and policy experts to be bold enough to propose new models and accept responsibility for outcomes they cannot entirely control.

Perhaps the most debatable assumption guiding economic policy is that we can learn from experience. We can certainly try. After all, the stakes are high. Not only our prosperity, but our very existence, is imperiled by a political economic system that rewards short-term gains and is populated by a policy elite with a strong attachment to the status quo. In Chapter 8, our final chapter, we trace the dimensions of this condition and the prospects for an economic policy that delivers a sustainable future. We discuss what sustainability currently means in terms of public finance and what it will have to mean in political economic terms in the future. We assess the willingness and ability of the current political economic elite to abandon, or at least seriously modify, its world view, and the scale of the challenge we face.

2 Making Economic Decisions

It should come as a shock to no one to be told that the economic policy decisions of Canadian governments are made by an elite composed of elected officials, appointed officials, and their advisors. The term "elite" has always carried connotations of conspiracy or manipulation, but now it is openly employed as an epithet, or an accusation, implying that elites are by definition an affront to democracy. That is unfortunate, if only because banning the term would simply force us to employ a euphemism to refer to the same phenomenon. And while the concept of an elite might be offensive to some, we use the term here in a neutral fashion simply to acknowledge that critical decisions of fiscal policy are made in close circles by small groups who are sometimes, but not always, working in concert with one another.

In pluralistic societies, economic elites tend to be located in complex organizational hierarchies comprised of people with skills, knowledge, and access, working in specific decisionmaking arenas. The fiscal policy elite described here is defined by the holding of positions of authority in federal and provincial policy hierarchies and, in the case of economists, by the possession of formal credentials. There is a reputational element to our definition, since we rely on those we initially interviewed to provide references and referrals. We do not explore specific relations among this elite, but they are clearly connected by a common concern for public finances: spending priorities, taxation, and the impact of fiscal policy on private decisionmaking. They frequently differ in their ideological starting points, but they share a common vocabulary, information base, and an awareness of what currently counts as economic orthodoxy, even if they do not endorse it.

Our working assumption is that the perceptions and perspectives of these elite players matter for public policy and that the decisions they take have important consequences. Of course, structural contingencies such as geography, technology, class relations, and inherited institutions have a big role to play in economic outcomes. They constrain choices, but they are not determinative. Understanding how elite players interpret constraints and fashion decisions is crucial to understanding both the triumphs and the disappointments of public policy.

Decisions are not singular events; they take place at several points in a complex social process (Simon, 1965). Decisions can be studied at the point when issues have been defined and alternatives outlined. Much decisionmaking research is focused here. But decisions can also be studied in their formative stages, when information is being gathered, interpretations compared, and attention focused. At this earlier point, decisions involve more than choice or technique. First, there are more fundamental questions: what should we be worried about? how should we think about a problem? what values are at stake? These kinds of questions do not yield easily to algorithms (at least not yet). They are qualitative, not quantitative, in character and they demand some creativity, not just calculation.

This book draws heavily on the interpretations of decisionmaking at this early, formative stage when the scale and impact of the COVID-19 pandemic was just coming into focus. Our conversations with key fiscal policy decisionmakers concentrated on values, agendas, priorities, and obstacles. But members of the economic elite often reflect on specific choices as well, particularly when these involve budget preparation. Their ideas about how the economic system works and where attention should be directed reflect the institutional framework in which they operate and the larger political culture. But decisionmakers are not preprogrammed and institutions do not create policies. It is the experiences and judgments of elite players that steer economic decisionmaking, and these are often neglected in contemporary interpretations of economic policy where it is sometimes assumed that options are already defined and actors are fully rational.

In surveying the major fiscal challenges that Canada faces in the post-pandemic era, we give voice to the opinions of members of this economic elite. We take a measure of their interpretation of the critical economic decisions that lie ahead and the steps that need to be taken to improve Canada's economic performance. We add to their judgments our own assessment of priorities and proposals, drawing on an ever-widening popular and academic literature that addresses our collective future. On some matters there is widespread agreement, on others predictable differences of opinion, and on still others something resembling confusion. We flag areas of consensus and dissensus on critical questions such as the role of government in the economy, the state of democratic accountability, and the problems of indebtedness and inequality.

We also canvas elite views on key institutions that structure, limit, and empower decisionmaking – specifically federalism and parliamentary government. The most important question is whether, based on the knowledge and opinions we hear, there is cause for concern or reasons to be optimistic about the direction in which the economy is being steered.

This chapter has three objectives: first, to describe the sample of politicians, bureaucrats, and economists we interviewed; second, to discuss what each group brings to the decisionmaking process; and third, to outline some of the limitations of elite decisionmaking. To anticipate what follows, the good news is that members of Canada's economic elite are intelligent, well versed in economic thinking, and well motivated. We could do much worse. The bad news is that there is only limited space for creativity, democratic expectations are seldom met, and there is little sense of urgency about fundamental change.

An Epistemic Elite

The elite whose views we are exploring consists of elected politicians, senior public servants (whom we call "bureaucrats" with no disrespect intended), public finance economists, think tank observers, and officers of Parliament. The offices they hold all bear on macroeconomic policy, conventionally divided into fiscal policy and monetary policy. Fiscal policy consists of the rules, norms, and decisions about spending, taxing, and debt. These topics are subject to continuous media commentary and partisan debate. Monetary decisions – interest rates, monetary aggregates, and now bond purchases – traditionally have been shielded from political contestation, but they loom large during crises and in an era of increasing debt.

Together fiscal and monetary policy create the macroeconomic climate for investment and consumption decisions. We use the term "economic policy" to cover both of these policy arenas, but note that boundaries are porous and economic policy involves more than the macroeconomy. Economic performance is tied to social policy – especially education and income support – and to industrial policy, including competition policy, trade, research and development, and selective subsidies to business. Although these latter topics are not our focal point, interviewees often insist on treating them as critically connected to monetary and fiscal decisions. That explains our reference in many places to "economic" rather than "fiscal" policy.

Some members of our elite are steeped in economic theory, but most combine a basic understanding of economic imperatives with a refined appreciation of contemporary political challenges. They are, in other words, expert practitioners playing specifically defined roles in an environment defined by politics. The question is: how do they imagine public resources should be deployed to maximize public benefit or minimize harm under conditions of risk and uncertainty? And beyond that, what criteria do they use to justify their advice and their decisions? These questions are at the heart of any evaluation of economic policy.

To get to that heart we conducted in-depth interviews with over 70 senior politicians, public servants, and public sector economists. The breakdown is as follows:

1 **Current and former politicians ("Politician," $n = 17$).** This group includes elected leaders at the federal level and from almost every province and territory. Most members of this group are or were either minister of finance or minister with senior economic portfolios that included finance and treasury responsibilities. Some were first ministers.
2 **Senior public servants ("Bureaucrat," $n = 30$).** This group consists of deputy ministers of finance, senior economic advisors in government, deputy ministers to first ministers, and parliamentary officers including auditors.
3 **Public finance economists ("Economist," $n = 24$).** Members of this group specialize in various aspects of fiscal and monetary policy. Most are located in public universities, but some are positioned in domestic or international organizations focused on fiscal policy, including credit agencies.

Potential participants were invited by email to participate in the study, with interviews beginning in November 2020 and lasting until May 2021. An initial 50 interviewees were selected on the basis of their role in the development of economic policy, and snowball sampling was used to augment the original cohort. Fewer than five of those we approached declined to be interviewed. The final sample size was 71, distributed over 66 interviews (one interview had three participants and three interviews had two). This type of non-random sampling limits the ability to draw reliable inferences to broader populations. For that reason, we refrain from any statistical analysis of various groups, but we do draw attention to areas of agreement and disagreement, particularly the former. Our selection of quotations is meant to be indicative of opinion, but we do flag minority views where these are important and occasionally reveal partisan affiliation where it is relevant.

Table 2.1. Distribution of Interviewees ($n = 71$)

Interviewees	n (%)
Category	
Politician	17 (24%)
Bureaucrat	30 (42%)
Economist	24 (34%)
Organization	
Government	42 (59%)
Independent agency	17 (24%)
University	12 (17%)
Region	
International/national	22 (31%)
Province/territory	33 (46%)
Sex	
Women	17 (24%)
Men	54 (76%)

Note: Independent agencies includes auditors, public accounting boards, federal independent agencies (e.g., Bank of Canada, Parliamentary Budget Office), think tanks, credit-rating agencies, and international organizations.

Table 2.1 describes the composition of our interviewees. Most interviewees were asked the same set of questions (see Appendix 1), which received prior review by experts and practitioners. All interviewees agreed to have their interviews recorded on the understanding that they would be given the chance to review the transcripts. Auditors, public accounting boards, and credit-rating agencies were asked a smaller set of questions, which excluded policy advisory issues. The sample included politicians and bureaucrats from most of the provinces and territories ($n = 33$) as well as the federal government ($n = 16$). Among the 13 provinces and territories, only Prince Edward Island and Newfoundland and Labrador are unrepresented.

While many of those we interviewed might bridle at being described as members of an "elite," few of those in the categories "Bureaucrat" or "Economist" would object to being called an expert. According to Scott Brewer (1998, p. 1589), "an expert is a person who has or is regarded as having specialized training that yields sufficient epistemic competence to understand the aims, methods, and results of an expert discipline." Senior public servants and public finance economists can all claim to have expertise, acquired through a combination of formal training and professional experience, in various aspects of economic policy.

Those in category 1, elected politicians, with few exceptions, have garnered their expertise in commerce, finance, or the political realm itself. Their knowledge base is different from that of bureaucrats and economists, but they have absorbed contemporary perspectives on fiscal and monetary policy, even when they are not always comfortable with them. Some of our respondents possess extensive knowledge that affords them the ability to speak with authority to a wide variety of policy issues. In other cases, their knowledge is limited to a specific terrain, and they sometimes declined to speak to questions that took them far beyond their training or the circumstances of their position.

All members of the economic elite that we are describing are "policymakers" in the sense that they contribute knowledge to decisions, even if these contributions seem small and often go unrecognized. The actual decisions might be made by a select group, sometimes exceedingly small, but those who contribute models, predictions, data, and briefings are policymakers for our purposes. It is knowledge, both the general familiarity with economic concepts and the specific knowledge of communities, programs, and methods, that makes this an epistemic elite. But it is not an exclusive club: the knowledge that policymakers possess is also found, in abundance, in the corporate elite, the media, and the academy. Economic policy debate is often a contest of expertise that extends well beyond the public sector itself. Specialized macroeconomic knowledge is no longer confined to those exercising political authority. Think tanks, for example, employ those with ample credentials and access to data and information that might once have been the preserve of finance departments or the Bank of Canada. And since the modelling tools of government agencies are subject to the same uncertainties that plague all forecasting efforts, governments seldom hold a significant advantage over outside specialists.

As this description makes clear, the economic elite we are concerned with does not include Canada's corporate elite: players from the commercial banks, insurance companies, major manufacturers, and industry associations. Many of those we interviewed have been employed at one time or another by private organizations and interest groups. None of them, regardless of their core assumptions, denies that they live in a capitalist economy where investment and consumption decisions are made by a wide range of players in a manner coordinated by the market. Business, with its privileged position in a capitalist economy, earns special attention, but not from every policymaker and only for some purposes. Only rarely do members of the public sector economic elite refer to good policy as policy that advances the interests of business, full stop. They cast their net much wider than that.

The economic elite becomes an epistemic elite when its members pool and share knowledge. In that process, two things are happening at once. First, all members of this elite are struggling to do the job they have been assigned. Doing their jobs well typically requires, at minimum, acknowledging one another's expertise and respecting boundaries. Economists are not politicians and will often declare a disinterest in the political process; politicians will steer clear of technical details and focus instead on the impact decisions have on the prospects of key constituents. These role distinctions are not always respected perfectly, but they act as constraints on the second process: making the right choices. The core deliverable in that process is the government budget. It represents the weight of past decisions, the trade-offs at the margins of new initiatives, and the overall direction of government policymaking. In one way or another, the members of the economic elite end up focusing on the budget process.

Distinctive Roles and Critical Relationships

The members of each of our elite categories bring something unique to the budget project. Politicians bring energy drawn from a competitive electoral process, bureaucrats bring equilibrium borne of an appreciation for the consequences of budget decisions, and economists bring expertise derived from a heightened appreciation of the macro effects that budgetary changes can induce (Aberbach et al., 1981). We describe these relationships in more detail to help locate the specific observations that are made about the topics in succeeding chapters. Questions about the role of government in the economy, about federalism, or about the looming problems of debt and inequality will be approached differently depending on roles and relationships. It is useful to sketch these relationships out in a preliminary fashion.

The relationship between those in categories 1 and 2 – politicians and bureaucrats – has been described in a variety of ways. One of the most popular, but least persuasive, descriptions portrays these two sets of actors as competitors in a struggle to bend policy in one or another direction. In this formulation, captured in the famous TV series *Yes Minister*, bureaucrats typically use their formidable knowledge of policy details either to thwart or redirect the aspirations of those at the political level. The bureaucrats are in charge.

A more accurate, if not entirely persuasive, interpretation also emphasizes distinct roles but suggests the relationship be interpreted as a bargain. Bureaucrats offer expert advice in exchange for anonymity and job security should that advice prove less than ideal (Savoie, 1999). Relationships change as the terms of the bargain shift over time and occasionally fall into disrepair, as when politicians blame bureaucrats for unhappy outcomes or bureaucrats blow the whistle on what they see as political corruption. This portrayal has the advantage of being rooted in the theory of parliamentary government, wherein politicians are replaced by the electorate, but senior advisors remain in place to provide continuity in the form of disinterested counsel to a new government.

It is helpful to be reminded about constitutional norms and practices because they form an overarching storyline to which all participants are expected to subscribe. But this storyline needs to be adjusted, sometimes substantially, depending upon the policy area involved. In line departments, where established programs are being delivered to specific clients, the distinctions between elected and bureaucratic roles are routinely respected. Programs are well established, ministers provide direction, and public servants focus on implementation. But at the centre of the political administrative apparatus – in the central agencies where broad policy initiatives are hatched and funding decisions made – these distinctions undergo modification (Atkinson & Coleman, 1985). Macroeconomic policy that feeds into budget decisions is a case in point. Politicians continue to bring the energy and bureaucrats the equilibrium, but there is also a clear community of interest.

In the case of economic policy, that community of interest takes the form of a commitment to economic growth, as we outline in Chapter 3. No expression of partisanship is required to persuade public servants that growth is good, and no apologies are necessary if economic growth turns into political advantage. Disagreements mostly take the form of whether proposed measures will make a significant contribution to the goal of economic growth or somehow impede it. Judgments here are based to some degree on (often ideological) interpretations of how the economy works, but also on the immediate environment: the business cycle, international competition, and looming threats. Because decisions have political consequences that must be appreciated by everyone, debates on all these matters are informed by the political context. As bureaucrats participate in these discussions, their advice becomes intertwined with the political instincts of the elected such that clear demarcations can become impossible to discern.

Which brings us to economists. They enter the conversation on economic policy armed with conventional models of the economy and economic policy and, occasionally, heterodox ideas of what drives change. It is probably safe to say that all professional economists are familiar with neoclassical models of the market, marginal theories of value, and assumptions about the rationality of decisionmakers. They subscribe to neoclassical propositions to differing degrees and endorse different theoretical positions on topics such as inflation and employment.

Although schools of thought provide a guide to their interpretative frameworks and to their advice, like all professionals, economists specialize. Those who focus on public finance are concerned principally with the role of government in the economy and the policy levers governments uniquely can pull. They are the economists who make up the bulk of the third group of interviewees, and they approach policy issues with an agenda that is sometimes different from that of either politicians or bureaucrats.

Let's first establish what the economists, public servants, and politicians agree on. Most public finance economists share with politicians and bureaucrats a commitment to economic growth as the most effective way of increasing public welfare. Tax and spending policies are evaluated initially from this perspective and only secondarily from the perspective of distribution. How to grow the economic pie precedes the question of how to share it, although some would dispute that it is possible to distinguish clearly between the two. Growing the economic pie means ensuring that the economy's assets are devoted to its most productive ends. For some this suggests a large positive role for government; others are devoted to policies that address market failures, narrowly defined. Most economists accept the need for a mixture of the two.

Whatever their other disagreements, public finance economists prefer public policies that minimize economic distortions. Frequently these distortions arise from monopolistic buying and selling power, but governments can create distortions themselves with spending, borrowing, and taxing policies that create perverse incentives relative to the objective of economic growth. The most fearsome distortion to be avoided is price instability, most recently experienced in the form of rapid increases in inflation. While inflation has its occasional defenders, public finance economists are eager to keep it within predictable bounds, principally to ward off the extreme policies required to quell inflation once it gets out of control. Deflation is even less welcome since it signals an economy working far below capacity.

Economists also agree with politicians and bureaucrats that politics plays a role in economic decisions – in all policy questions, in fact. At the heart of politics is the exercise of power, not the unrestrained exercise – torture, murder, and mayhem – but the ability to affect outcomes, sometimes (but not always) by compulsion. In democratic societies it is normal to suppose that politics will entail competition, compromise, and cooperation. Support must be mustered, coalitions formed, voices heard, and public judgments rendered. These are among the desirable, but not inevitable, features of democratic politics. They are intended to secure power and legitimacy – that is, the moral right to rule.

There are, of course, less reassuring by-products of the political process. Mark Warren sums these up by observing that "strategic maneuvering, duplicity, disingenuous speech, and compromised principles are likely to come with the territory of politics, even under the best of circumstances" (Warren, 1999, p. 222). We can safely infer that all members of the economic elite are familiar with a variety of political practices that structure public policy, including these more repugnant ones. No one we interviewed is naive about the work that must be done and the choices that must be made to exercise power in a democracy.

For many casual observers of public affairs, the importation of politics into public policy can sound inherently corrupting – something that should be resisted. The plea for "rational" or "evidence-based" policy is usually premised on the idea that good policy is threatened by ideological formulas or political calculations. For those who agree with this sentiment, the best way of handling the situation is first to imagine economic policy devised in the absence of politics. In other words, separate policy and politics from each other early on, concentrate on the policy part, and navigate the politics later. As Robin Boadway puts it, "the political process can be best informed about the desirability of alternatives if they are proposed on the basis of normative principles without being constrained by perceived political feasibilities" (2011, p. 167). This formulation, echoed by economists since Milton Friedman, presumes that there is a set of economic principles that have been tested for logical and empirical soundness and that their benefits have been found generally praiseworthy. Open markets, free trade, and vigorous competition are examples. They are often taken to be the hallmarks of neoliberalism, but these preferences align closely with classical liberal formulas for generating national wealth (Gerstle, 2022). For policy-oriented economists, the imperative is to devise policy consistent with these established propositions and to accept their dilution only after strenuous resistance.

Without much exaggeration, it is safe to say that most economists who are either drawn to public service or who comment on public affairs see politics as corrupting of good policy. The testimony of Alan Blinder, who served on Bill Clinton's Council of Economic Advisors, illustrates the point. In his experience, the requirements of politics are radically different from the requirements of business or science. Where business or academic debates turn on the merits of the case, political decisions must respect "the unholy trinity of *politics*, *message*, and *process*" (Blinder, 2018, p. 12). So, although economists might know too little about the economy, for Blinder and his colleagues the bigger problem is that politicians routinely ignore what economists do know. Add the confining shackles of ideology and the perverse effects of interest group politics, and good economic policy can be quickly sidelined.

An alternative approach to the politics/policy relationship, and one we endorse, is to assume a conceptual and practical overlap between them that cannot be dissolved. Policy and politics might not be precisely the same thing, but they share conceptual space. Both are purposeful, for example, although the purposes might not be identical. More important than overlap is their mutual dependence. Policy presumes politics: there are no rules (policies) without order and the orderly exercise of authority (politics). Politics requires policy, since the exercise of authority requires legitimacy, and policy is a key means of obtaining it.

In an important sense, politics frames all policy choices and initiates a feedback process whereby policy and politics interact with each other over extended periods (Pierson, 2004). Members of the economic elite will have different views on how much politics should influence policy and how much it actually does, but they are acutely aware that the management of public money is driven by both economic and political considerations. By economic considerations we mean a concern for the deployment of public and private resources for a flourishing, functioning economy. By political considerations we mean the various activities associated with capturing the high offices of the state, securing orderly change, and avoiding chaos. Most of our interviewees see policy as filtered through a set of shifting political imperatives, and members of all three of our elite categories – politicians, bureaucrats, and economists – express at least a tolerance for the role of politics in public policy.

The Limitations of Elite Decisionmaking

As we emphasized above, the elite we are describing is not a proto cabal. This is an elite based on knowledge, connected by experience, and located at critical places in the modern state. It is an epistemic elite, not a gang of conspirators. By the same token, even with their stores of pooled knowledge and the resources of the state, economic policymakers operate under limiting conditions. Three of these limitations deserve to be profiled.

Knowledge Is Imperfect, Uncertainty Abounds

Debates about economic policy are premised on the assumption of imperfect knowledge. If knowledge of the economy were perfect, there would be no debate. As it is, analysts will freely discuss risk and uncertainty as core elements in economic models and policy decisions.

As Frank Knight (1921) pointed out, risk is an expression of imperfect knowledge based on known conditions but indeterminate outcomes. Understanding risk entails an estimation of the likelihood of an event's occurring. It is a function of probabilities that, in principle, can be known or estimated in advance using historical information and standard inferential techniques.

Uncertainty is a more profound instance of imperfect knowledge. Events whose manifestations are uncertain have no known probabilities attached. The data-generating process is unstable, there are a lot of parameters to estimate, and relying on historical data is perilous. Uncertainty resists quantification because uncertain events, based on a multitude of interactions, present themselves as original phenomena. As a result, it is very difficult to make reliable predictions.

The term "black swan event" might not have originated with the Great Financial Crisis, but it acquired resonance then as a way of explaining how something that could not happen did. It was not technically impossible to predict when or if a stunning collapse of securitized assets would occur, but very few were able to do so. Although the COVID-19 pandemic was predicted, these predictions were largely ignored. A pandemic was always a risk, one to which probabilities could be attached, but without knowing its precise timing, location, and virulence, governments around the world preferred to cross the pandemic bridge when they came to it. When they did come to it, the impact was far more disruptive than most members of the economic policy elite could have imagined. The pandemic obliged governments to induce a recession in which economic activity was massively curtailed to avoid the even more deleterious effects of massive infections. That some governments reacted with more speed and effectiveness than others does not detract from the basic point: our imperfect knowledge about disease vectors and their likely arrival combined a predictable event with an array of uncertain outcomes.

So, when the pandemic was initially described as "unpredictable," this did not mean that it could never happen, only that the circumstances leading to its occurrence at a particular point in time were largely unknown. Predictability, in this sense, is a matter of degree: the more knowledge we have of the causal pathways, the more likely we will be to anticipate events. Sadly, humanity's track record in such matters is poor. Some developments are readily predictable – for example, the consequences of personal finance decisions – but changes in our collective condition are not so easily modelled. Reliance on probability estimation is standard practice in natural science settings, where underlying causal patterns are reasonably well known, but measurement error and modelling limits often preclude precise predictions. In social settings where causal mechanisms are not well known and strategic interactions complicate predictions, the future is even less likely to yield to precise forecasts. The harsh truth is that relationships within an economy can be modelled only by making bold assumptions about the underlying probability distributions of behaviours and events, and very few of these distributions are known with anything approaching certainty.

For economic policy, the traditional way out of this quagmire has been to place faith in complete and competitive markets. Markets send signals based on the choices of dispersed individuals, which, as a result, contain information that no central source can duplicate (Hayek, 1945). This strategy works well for familiar products in competitive markets. Unfortunately, perfectly competitive markets rarely exist and not all products are transparent. As Mervyn King (2016) has pointed out, it is not possible to organize an auction for goods and services that do not yet exist. Genuinely new products do not face existing markets, and consumers and producers have no preferences for products and services that have yet to be invented. Conventional ideas of risk management evaporate and insurance markets cannot form. King describes this situation as "radical uncertainty," and it places limits on efforts to anticipate the future simply by modelling existing market behaviour.

The realization that predictions are perilous is a good reason for caution in imagining how the world will unfold after COVID-19. In predicting the consequences of unique events, everyone confronts the paralysis of uncertainty. Elites confront it with the knowledge that, predicted or not, events generate demands for accountability. So, risk is not just a matter of the likelihood of something happening; it is also about the likelihood of getting blamed for it or getting blamed for not anticipating it (Weaver, 1986). This fear is, at bottom, the reason political and economic elites typically heed Nassim Taleb's advice to avoid engaging in large-scale predictions (Taleb, 2007, p. 203). By all means, he argues, use predictions about the likelihood of small scale, imminent events (like the weather), but avoid predictions about the solvency of the Canada Pension Plan decades from now.

Of course, avoiding predictions does not eliminate the need for decisions. In decision situations, experts use a variety of coping mechanisms, many of them based on heuristics – intuitive rules that can be employed without assembling masses of data or engaging in complex cost/benefit calculations. Speculating about the efficacy of heuristics has occupied behavioural economists over the past several decades. The results have not been especially encouraging. The "heuristics and biases" approach argues that decisionmakers are inconsistent in their decision preferences based on how options are presented. This framing problem is compounded by what has been called "the illusion of validity" – the belief that assessments are more accurate than they actually are (Kahneman & Klein, 2009). The result is overconfidence.

Against this rather pessimistic perspective on elite decisionmaking is the view that competence comes with repetition and the acquisition of tacit knowledge. Policymakers are constantly looking for patterns; intuition consists of the ability to recognize them (Simon, 1983). The fact that elites often fail in deploying their intuition to predict the future (Tetlock, 2017) might be more of a comment on the size of the task – truly enormous – than on the innate competence of those in authority. But it would be a mistake to overemphasize the sophistication of elite decisionmaking regardless of the scale of the challenge. Evidence suggests that elites are just as subject to framing effects and other choice anomalies as are ordinary citizens. They discount the future at an even more rapid rate than do voters, and they cannot resist trying to recoup sunk costs. Most important, elites have an attachment to the status quo every bit as powerful as the rest of us (Sheffer et al., 2018).

The Status Quo Has a Strong Grip on the Imagination

Status quo bias has been observed in a variety of decision environments, and is part of a much larger pattern of decisionmaking in which a reference point – in this case the status quo – anchors subsequent choices. This bias is not simply an expression of power relations, in which beneficiaries cement their advantages, and it is not simply a by-product of positive feedback, in which rules generate their own support. Both are classic impediments to change, but a bias towards the familiar is a cognitive predisposition shared at least to some degree by everyone. Uncertainty about the future bends our minds towards preservation of the devils we know. The assumption that the status quo has value, because it would never have been chosen if it didn't, can help us understand why families return to the same vacation spot year after year and why elected officials often enjoy an incumbent advantage independent of their performance (Samuelson & Zeckhauser, 1988).

In a similar fashion, public policies can acquire value regardless of whether there are preferable alternatives. Research on politicians has shown that they strongly favour existing policy "regardless of its content" (Sheffer et al., 2018, p. 316). This preference is rooted in what has been described as the endowment effect – the observation that it is more painful to give up something than it is pleasurable to acquire it (Thaler, 1980). In other words, decisionmakers, like the rest of us, are loss averse. They attach greater value than warranted to present conditions and strive to avoid losses that are traceable to their own decisions (Kahneman & Tversky, 1984; Mercer, 2005). They are also loathe to change course when they cannot be sure who the winners and losers might be once a reform is adopted (Fernandez & Rodrik, 1991). So, when policies and programs fail to reduce infection, curb inflation, or generate new housing starts, decisionmakers cannot be counted on to make the necessary policy shifts. Prior investments in policy beg to be justified regardless of their effectiveness.

These observations are directly relevant to the prospect of change in either fiscal policies or political institutions. Simply put, the initial obstacle to changing priorities and policies is blindness to the need to do so. Problems do not always come clearly into focus and data normally contain a lot of noise. When production, employment, and inflation are all changing gradually, the need to change policy is not obvious. Things are (or seem to be) under control, particularly if traditional measures of economic activity, such as GDP, suggest that the economy is healthy. When investment and consumption experience no sudden shifts, there is less precautionary saving and fewer episodes of financial risk taking to worry about. Recessions are avoided. And when recessions happen, an array of existing programs can act as automatic stabilizers, cushioning the effects of unemployment or putting the brakes on irresponsible loans and rapid financial manoeuvres. When things are going well, it is hard to describe attachment to the status quo as somehow irrational.

Prudence in the face of uncertainty might be a virtue, and protection against impulsive strategies is often welcome, but firm attachment to existing norms and practices brings its own risks. Chief among these risks is what Mark Carney (2021, p. 300) calls the Tragedy of the Horizon. Like the Tragedy of the Commons, on which it is modelled, the Tragedy of the Horizon is a writ large collective action problem that adds a temporal dimension. Its key observation is that the costs of not addressing pandemic threats or climate change are borne by those who are outside the decision process by virtue of being among the vulnerable but not the powerful. Doubts, delays, and deficiencies are visited on succeeding generations, most of whom have yet to be born.

Fiscal policy certainly has a short-term feel to it. The horizon for monetary policy is one or two years; for fiscal stabilization, a bit longer. The credit cycle, the business cycle, and the political cycle are all relatively short. The horizon for existential risk, on the other hand, is typically longer and can extend over decades. Under these conditions, existing norms and practices predictably will fail to produce the necessary collective adjustments. The pandemic appears as a short-term problem, but our response to it poses long-term questions that neither elites nor citizens are eager to acknowledge, let alone answer. Perhaps a major shift in the environment or an unanticipated mobilization of political forces will overcome status quo bias and oblige an economic elite to reconsider established doctrines and practices. Whether the pandemic qualifies as just such a major shift and whether decisionmakers are prepared to re-imagine policies and processes is a critical topic for the rest of this book.

Elite Policymaking Is Only Weakly Democratic

Democracy presumes that decisions on questions of public policy will respond, directly or indirectly, to public opinion formally expressed by citizens who enjoy equal political rights (Weale, 1999, p. 14). There are two justifications for preferring decisions that are democratically derived. First, some defenders of democracy argue that there are significant epistemic advantages to engaging the opinions of ordinary citizens as opposed to relying on the supposed expertise of an elite. The wisdom of the many, especially the diverse many, is expected to exceed the wisdom of the few. Even if individual citizens lack the knowledge required to pursue enlightened policy on their own, when their knowledge is pooled with that of a sufficiently large and diverse public, the likelihood of choosing the correct course of action improves significantly (Landemore, 2013). That's the theory. Second, it is easier to achieve compliance with decisions arrived at by a wide canvassing of opinion than with decisions imposed by a small elite. Democratic decision rules contribute to meeting the basic demand for legitimacy on which political order is said to rest (Williams, 2005).

The democratic arrangements Canadians are familiar with involve the election of representatives to sit in legislatures and deliberate on policies proposed by the political executive. Experiments with more direct forms of democratic decisionmaking, including referendums and deliberative assemblies, have been limited and not particularly consequential. For the past thirty or more years, political theorists have argued for a richer set of procedures that would better engage the public and help secure the putative benefits of widely dispersed knowledge. Despite much conceptual refinement, and the occasional attempt to implement deliberative democracy,[1] progress has been

---

1 *Deliberative democracy* is a form of political practice that posits public reasoning by free and equal citizens as vital to the legitimacy and hence acceptance of collective decisions. Sometimes contrasted with practices that emphasize voting and bargaining, deliberative democracy seeks epistemic improvements in the common good based on sharing information, clarifying argumentation, and promoting reflection.

confined almost entirely to the local level, where citizens can engage on issues with which they have some direct experience. Defenders claim that these "mini-public" decision forums demonstrate that ordinary citizens, when given enough information and time to deliberate, can make sense of complex, even technical, issues and come to "pertinent conclusions" about public matters (Pateman, 2012, p. 9). Others are sceptical: "A great deal of social psychological research suggests that individuals generally do not think in a logical, rational or reasonable way and do not evidence the communicative competence assumed by deliberative democratic theory" (Rosenberg, 2007, p. 344).

Whatever advantages might accrue to public decisionmaking in local matters, no serious attempts have been made to engage the public in macroeconomic decisionmaking. Deliberative enthusiasts concede that local councils have "a certain deliberative purity, which often gets lost in national legislatures" (Landemore, 2013, p. 215). In legislative settings, it is clearly the "indirect" influence of public opinion that is expected to satisfy the democratic standard. But here ideological posturing and interest-group pandering are often more in evidence than rational deliberation (Rosanvallon, 2011). Besides, the ranks of legislatures are seldom diverse enough that the opinions on offer reliably reflect those of ordinary Canadians. At the cabinet level it is only recently that conspicuous efforts have been made to achieve a gender balance. The economic elite as a whole is even more exclusive. Our own sample is male dominant (76 per cent), non-racialized, highly educated, and much older than the average adult citizen. In a descriptive sense it is not "representative" of the population at large.

These supposed democratic deficiencies, which are by no means limited to Canada, are joined by the argument that critical debates over the effects of neoliberal economic policies never take place inside democratic political institutions anyway. These institutions, critics argue, have been "hollowed out" for purposes of economic policy so that alternatives to a neoliberal economic order are never seriously considered (Crouch, 2004). Such debates as there are have been transferred to international policymaking arenas where institutions that are demonstrably non-democratic – the World Bank, the International Monetary Fund (IMF), the World Trade Organization, and the European Union – hold considerable sway (Mitchell & Fazi, 2017). An international rules-based order has an undeniable appeal even for those who lament globalization. Environmental and labour standards, for example, are most effective when they prevent an international race to the bottom. It is difficult to defend them, however, as exemplifying democratic decisionmaking.

These and other policies are created and/or negotiated by economic elites such as those we focus on in this volume. They are not the product of democratic deliberation.

For purposes of economic policy, Canada meets minimal requirements of democracy. Minimal democracy is democracy defined as a competitive struggle to rule in which the opportunity to dispense with the current rulers and replace them with an alternative is democracy's defining characteristic. Authority is exerted on behalf of the democratic public by virtue of success in this competitive contest, but those in authority seldom feel bound to follow the public's precise policy preferences, even if these could be clearly discerned. In the minimalist view, the critical requirement is that defeat entails a peaceful transfer of power – in other words, acceptance by all parties of electoral results (Przeworski, 1999). Governments are expected to pay attention to the interests of the public but not necessarily to public opinion. Promises are made (and sometimes kept), but the economic elite gives itself a significant operating margin and the right to reverse itself if conditions require a change in direction.

This rather stark, and decidedly unromantic, version of democracy has been described as "thin" since it asks so little of the democratic public and places so much faith in the capacity of elites (Barber, 1984). Still, it is minimalist democracy that disciplines decisionmakers in matters of economic policy. Outside prebudget meetings, which themselves are relatively new innovations and involve select members of the public, Canada's economic elite rarely turns to public opinion as a source of good macroeconomic policy. But public opinion can provide an indication of what might be acceptable or feasible and what would, on the other hand, imperil the government's political future. It is a constraining force, rather than a creative one.

Canadians can expect their views to constrain choices, but not on technical questions or on topics that governments have made central to their political appeal. The defence of these decisions takes place in Parliament and the legislatures of the provinces and territories, but, once again, the economic elite does not expect simply to take direction from voices in legislatures. The adequacy of democratic accountability procedures is a topic we take up in Chapter 6, where the presence of multiple governments complicates policymaking, and in Chapter 7, where we discuss budget processes and post-audit reviews. But to anticipate the conclusions of these chapters, democratic accountability is an elusive value that must compete with other values, including efficiency, discretion, and fairness.

Conclusion

A canvass of just some of the limitations of elite decisionmaking can be a bit depressing. Remember, though, that, although members of the economic elite are real people with the usual foibles and shortcomings, very few are motivated by purely personal agendas. Discussion of economic policy with Canada's public policy decisionmakers typically involves reference to the public interest, as amorphous and imprecise as this concept might be. Sometimes the public interest is defined in consequentialist terms, even as the product of an explicit cost-benefit analysis; sometimes it is employed as a means of simply blunting the claims of one or another set of private interests. Not that private interests fail to benefit from actions taken to benefit the public; on the contrary, they are often the principal beneficiaries. But rhetorically and tangibly, the concept of a public interest is ever-present. It invokes the spirit of the many who are not present in decisionmaking forums but whose claims haunt the deliberation on options that lie ahead.

In the chapters that follow we review some of these critical options. Most of these have been with us, in a silent state, for decades. The role of government in the economy, massive inequality, and debt overhang are not new issues. The strengths and weaknesses of our political institutions have not been revealed to us simply by the pandemic. There is a lot we already knew. Yet the pandemic has put them all in play. Policy elites are shaken and unnerved by the impact of the pandemic and uncertain that conventional strategies can cope with the challenges to come. Are they so susceptible to status quo bias and overconfidence that they are unable to imagine a response that takes us beyond the short-term fix?

We cannot claim that structured interviews yield direct answers to these questions. What they do show is that any willingness to rethink fundamentals, experiment with alternative policies, or imagine new institutional arrangements is hemmed in by considerations of political feasibility. Post-pandemic, the economic elite in Canada is caught between a desire to return the economy to a stable state – where variation in results is minimized, risk is managed, and uncertainty reduced – and a preference for making changes to policies and processes to address the vulnerabilities the pandemic has revealed. Many, probably most, are content to double down on what has worked in the past; in others, a minority, we detect a commitment to challenge the assumptions that have guided us to this point. We begin with an assessment of the role of the state in the economy, the subject of Chapter 3.

3 Governing after the Pandemic

The World Health Organization officially declared COVID-19 a global pandemic on 11 March 2020. By 2023 the world was still coping with its effects. By then most economies had endured a remarkable series of stop-and-go directives. In Canada, where provincial governments control most health and safety regulations, governments experimented with a variety of closures and openings of schools, entertainment settings, retail outlets, bars, and restaurants. These experiments affected hospitals whose ICUs were placed under extreme pressure as infection rates surged, declined, then surged again. The federal government's subsidy programs prevented widespread income collapse, but the business protection programs could not backstop all failing firms. By March 2022, 4,036 Canadian businesses had filed for bankruptcy (OSB Canada, 2022).

For more than two years the pandemic played havoc with supply and demand, and governments were whipsawed as they tried to respond to changes in both. Seeking to ensure both a high level of public health and a functioning economy, governments struggled to get the balance right. Supply chains were disrupted by lockdowns and problems in transportation. Food production suffered from input disruptions exacerbated by workplace configurations that fostered infection. Demand initially declined and then returned in a different form: more stress on goods and less on services, then a return to services, especially travel with its attendant restart challenges. The pandemic forced consumers to make adjustments and investors to navigate a highly uncertain future.

The pandemic might have been a relatively short-lived event, but the crisis raised longer-term issues, none more important than the credibility and competence of governments. For some, the economic response to massive economic shutdown was a lesson in why we need a strong and capable state. The income-support programs implemented in response to the pandemic stabilized the economy and the lives of millions of citizens who learned that economic order, like political order, has to be created and then managed. The scale of the pandemic's impact left little choice but to deploy a wide range of government instruments – from coercion to persuasion – to deal with its effects. Those who gave thanks for health directives and financial support – even those that seemed poorly crafted – were naturally predisposed to consider what else governments could and should do to keep us safe. The wish list is long: better infrastructure, stable supply chains, affordable housing, a Universal Basic Income, and green energy initiatives, among others.

On the other hand, as the initial effects of crises recede, so too does the demand for governments to become active players. At the outset of the pandemic there was relatively little debate over what the public interest demanded: protection from a public health hazard and from sudden income loss. As the pandemic dragged on, the early consensus on priorities and processes began to unravel, replaced by more established attitudes towards what government could or should do. These attitudes, sometimes described as "priors," are often well rooted, hard to move with evidence, and sometimes the product of motivated reasoning (Epley & Gilovich, 2016). As we argue in this chapter, early on in the crisis a return to the previous normal (not a "new normal") was already the preferred option for the large majority of the economic elite we interviewed.

We begin with a consideration of what reasonably can be expected of governments facing the kinds of uncertainties we discussed in Chapter 1. Using data from our interviews, we then offer an elite perspective on the income-support programs launched in the immediate aftermath of the pandemic. The generally positive assessment of these programs raises the question of how the economic elite envisages the role of government in the post-pandemic period. On the assumption that the pandemic should prompt at least some reflection on the role of government in society, we ask whether fundamental changes are afoot and what the future might look like. The answers reveal a willingness to experiment but also a lack of clarity on direction and misgivings about the wisdom of making significant change. When we turn to the question of priorities, we uncover a strong, if not always clearly articulated, assumption among members of the economic elite that government's principal job is to encourage economic growth. The problem, however, is that growth is elusive and very few of our elite members have worked out a plan to achieve it.

Can Governments Do Good?

It is natural to wonder whether a crisis like a pandemic will alter fundamentally the way markets are permitted to work and the way we govern ourselves. Before we offer some answers, consider the fact that the pandemic came at a time when many changes were already under way. The technological innovations of the twentieth century have been deeply absorbed into the economy, and we have become used to extended supply chains even though few people understand their intricacies. The market was delivering different products, including financial ones, at a remarkable pace, but when crisis arrived either in the form of exogenous threats – natural disasters, for example – or endogenous ones – a collapse in markets themselves – the natural response has been to look to the state for a reprieve.

In the past, the response to threats has been to suspend or modify the operation of markets and invest in a centralized response in which resources are mobilized and focused on the immediate threat. Wars provide the best example, but pandemics clearly qualify. A collapse in the global financial system, as occurred during the 2008 Great Financial Crisis, required a remarkable amount of collaboration among central banks and governments, with little or no track record for heroic intervention. The pandemic provided a second example. It was not just the speed and size of the response that impressed, but also the willingness to set aside textbook distinctions and conceive of fiscal policy and monetary policy as part of a policy continuum. The idea that banking independence requires that banks refrain from monetizing debt[1] was shelved, perhaps permanently. Governments must be able to borrow to engage in fiscal rescues and income support; central banks must be willing to monetize that debt. The fact that the central bank cannot go out of business any more than the government can helps obviate the distinction between them and remind us that the central bank is a public institution. Finance departments and the Bank of Canada worked together because, in a crisis, neither could afford an economy deprived of liquidity.

Was this the beginning of a return of the idea that governments could, and should, play a constructive role in shaping markets to the

---

1 Central banks are said to monetize government debt by purchasing government bonds or extending a direct line of credit, thereby relieving governments of the obligation to raise taxes or sell bonds on financial markets. Critics consider *debt monetization* to be a form of direct monetary financing equivalent to governments' "printing money," and have sought to discourage the practice by championing central bank independence.

advantage of all citizens, not just the owners of capital? A popular narrative covering the latter part of the twentieth century describes the post-war period, up to and including the 1960s, as one in which our collective energies were harnessed to major projects of rebuilding and reconceptualizing Western economies. The state played a large role in an economy that, while it retained its market capitalist fundamentals, was directed towards broad projects of social emancipation and innovation that would yield long periods of economic growth. The traditional role of the state – internal peace and external security – was augmented by the expectation that governments would invest in the foundational requirements of economic growth: a transportation infrastructure, an accessible health care system, and an education system capable of supplying the growing demand for human capital.

In his 1971 Nobel Prize speech, Simon Kuznets observed that the countries that made the biggest investments in these kinds of public goods were the ones that grew the fastest (Hacker & Pierson, 2016, p. 64). But it was not just spending that created paths to growth. The mixed economy included the idea that economic regulation of anticompetitive behaviour, competitive contracting, and robust governance regimes are all predicates of sustained economic growth. A market properly restrained and augmented by public investment was the key to prosperity.

Until it wasn't. In the 1970s faith in governments' ability to supply the foundational requirements of market-based prosperity began to wane. The proximate cause was a period of stagflation – a combination of inflation and high levels of unemployment – that signalled the effective end of Keynesian-style management of the business cycle. New supply-side theories that did not depend on active state intervention received a hearing in the United States, while other countries sought ways to rein in government spending in general. This historical turn in macropolitical economy came to be called "neoliberalism," to summarize the view that governments are an impediment to economic well-being and that the deregulation of markets, the privatization of public assets, and the compression of social programs will hasten economic growth. Since its introduction into academic parlance, "neoliberalism" has undergone a conceptual stretching to the point that it is used almost exclusively by its critics to describe an "overarching dystopian zeitgeist" (Venugopal, 2015, p. 165). Economists avoid the term but they have supplied much of the intellectual firepower behind tax cuts for the rich, deregulation, and austerity (DeLong, 2022; Gerstle, 2022; Madrick, 2015).

The language of governance shifted as well during the 1980s. Governments began to be described as rent-seeking operations dedicated to the opportunistic extraction of surplus value for the benefit of political intermediaries – lobbyists, bureaucrats, and politicians themselves (Krueger, 1974). Regulations were viewed as costly tools of interference in market exchange and spending characterized as bribes offered by politicians to supportive constituencies. The election of Ronald Reagan in the United States, Margaret Thatcher in the United Kingdom, and Brian Mulroney in Canada signalled a political shift, in rhetoric if not in reality, towards lowered expectations of government and heightened expectations of market exchange.

Of course, despite their supposed inherent deficiencies, governments did not go away in any of the Western democracies. Rather, governments actually grew, but now they were obliged to engage in deficit financing to maintain public programs (DeLong, 2022, p. 444). What also changed was a newfound willingness to embrace the idea that the boundary between the state and the market needed to be redrawn and the internal affairs of government made subject to market discipline. Entrepreneurship in government needed to be celebrated, waste eliminated, and privatization pursued. Above all, governments needed to demonstrate competence. Competence is a standard well suited for democratically elected politicians and most other public decisionmakers. It does not presume the wisdom of Job or the insights of philosopher kings. It does, however, imply an ability and a willingness to search out policies that are welfare enhancing and deliver on them.

Unfortunately, many examples of the opposite come easily to mind. A short, illustrative list of prominent Canadian failures would include cost overruns, like British Columbia's Site C dam, spending scandals, like the Sponsorship program, misguided projects, like residential schools, and internal fiascos, like the Phoenix payroll system. Post-pandemic, the federal government's inability to manage the demand for passports cut close to a function that is central to the expectations of citizenship.

Governments, it is alleged, display these deficiencies for a variety of structural reasons, including incompatible incentives, information asymmetries, implementation hurdles, and bureaucratic infighting (Light, 2014; Schuck, 2014). In Canada they stand accused of failing to respond to the public interest, make evidence-based decisions, adopt internal reforms, and implement programs effectively and efficiently (Savoie, 2015). As if to confirm these suspicions, the Trudeau government launched its political agenda in 2015 under the banner of "deliverology," with its uncontested assumption that governments simply are not effective service providers.

Whatever good all of this unrelenting critique might have accomplished in terms of spurring reform, it fed the already substantial negativity bias that accompanies public affairs. Negativity bias has its roots in the cognitive predisposition to value losses more than gains (Kahneman & Tversky, 1984). This tendency to key on losses, personal or societal, is amplified by news media trained to focus on pain – in the argot of the trade, "if it bleeds it leads." The result is that success is largely ignored and failure gets the spotlight treatment. The effects do not end there. When journalists, academics, and social media influencers focus their attention on mistakes and misadventures, those in authority spend considerable effort avoiding responsibility for choices and outcomes (Hood, 2011, pp. 9–12). Public speech becomes over massaged, elliptical, and devoid of much content, while governments are careful to conceal any information that might reflect negatively on their stewardship. It is little wonder then that trust in government has eroded. Using data from the 2020 Gallup World Poll, the OECD (n.d.-g) reports that on average only 51 per cent of people in OECD countries trust their governments.

This historical arc from embrace of government post–Second World War to high scepticism since the 1980s could be described crudely as the rise and fall of the state. Will the state rise again? Possibly, at least if the past 50 years can be interpreted as part of a natural pendular swing in values and/or enthusiasms. In this reading, an enormous investment in collective aspirations eventually leads to disappointment and a hankering for increased levels of personal consumption. This is the dynamic described by Albert Hirschman (1982), who observed that humans, unlike other animals, are never satisfied. Their dissatisfaction manifests itself in a pattern of preferring collective goods provision to private consumption until such time as disappointment with the products (or costs) of public-spirited investments gives way to an emphasis on private satisfactions. The latter eventually runs its course in turn, and a demand for public goods regains priority.

There is no way to be sure that such a cycle is inevitable, but exogenous shocks such as wars, climate change, and pandemics can sometimes create the conditions for a major rethinking of what we value and set off a reconsideration of fundamentals. Some reformers pin their hopes on just such a dynamic in their calls for a reconsideration of our values (Carney, 2021). But as we have already observed, there are strong impediments to wholesale reconsideration of policies and many positive returns to carrying on with the same practices and priorities. A display of competence presumably would help, and the pandemic provided governments with just such an opportunity. Deciding on whether competence marked the COVID-19 policy response is, of course, a matter of judgment, and not all policies are likely to pass the test in a retrospective assessment. But what about the economic response to the pandemic? Does it pass the competence test?

Stabilizing the Economy: Program Design and Delivery

By spring 2020 it was understood that the COVID-19 pandemic would be a heavy blow to the Canadian economy. By the end of June 2021 Canada had had more than 1.4 million COVID-19 cases and more than 25,900 deaths (Worldometer, 2021). In a short time, real GDP shrank by about 12 per cent (Statistics Canada, 2021g), and unemployment shot up from 6 per cent in January 2020 to almost 14 per cent in April 2020.

The federal and provincial/territorial governments implemented a series of public health measures, such as lockdowns and restrictions, and provided economic relief programs to mitigate the negative effects of the pandemic on individuals and businesses. By 1 July 2021, Canada had spent $435.2 billion, or 19.7 per cent of GDP, on spending and tax measures in response to the crisis created by the pandemic. About two-thirds of the rescue package went directly to affected individuals, households, and firms via subsidies and benefits. Key policy responses included: i) $60.3 billion (2.7 per cent of GDP) to the health system to support increased testing, vaccine development, medical supplies, mitigation efforts, and greater investment in Indigenous communities; ii) about $290 billion (13.2 per cent of GDP) in direct aid to households and firms, including wage subsidies, payments to workers without sick leave, access to Employment Insurance (EI), an increase in existing goods and services tax credits and child benefits, and a new Indigenous Community Support Fund; and iii) around $85 billion (3.9 per cent of GDP) in liquidity support through tax deferrals (IMF, 2021a).

Figure 3.1 shows the economic impact of the pandemic compared to recent economic shocks. COVID-19 mitigation efforts produced an economic contraction about six times larger than the one suffered during the 2008 financial crisis. Canada's discretionary fiscal responses were significant, but, as Figure 3.2 shows, they ranked only about average compared with other developed countries.

In the early days of the pandemic, shortly after the launch of the Canada Emergency Response Benefit (CERB) and the Canada Emergency Wage Subsidy (CEWS), there was considerable criticism in some quarters about the scale and generosity of these programs. The Fraser Institute objected to CERB eligibility for young people (ages 15 to 24) who lived as dependents in families earning $100,000 a year. A 2020 Fraser Institute report made this observation: "In almost every case, the benefits CERB provides to these young Canadians – almost one million

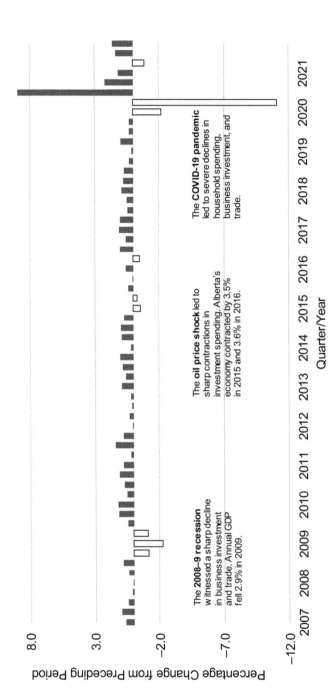

Figure 3.1. The Pandemic's Impact on Economic Activity: Gross Domestic Product and Change from Preceding Quarter, Canada, Q4 2006–Q4 2021

Note: Real GDP in constant 2012 dollars.

Source: Statistics Canada (2021g). Contains information licensed under the Open Government Licence – Canada.

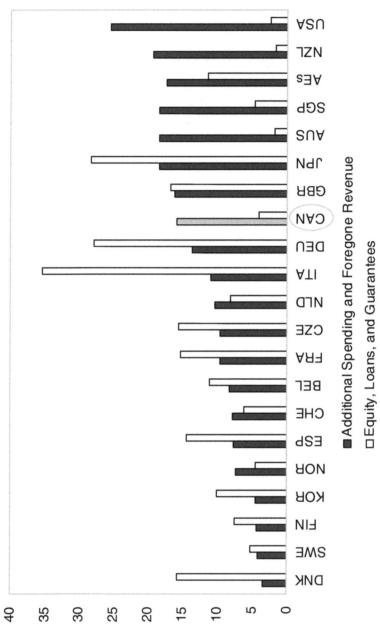

Figure 3.2. Discretionary Fiscal Response to the COVID-19 Crisis, Selected Economies
Note: The country group average of advanced economies is weighted by GDP in US dollars adjusted by purchasing power parity.
Source: Data from IMF (2021c).

of them – exceed their monthly earnings in 2019, actually making them better off now, during one of the worst recessions in Canadian history" (Clemens et al., 2020). The report also complained that eligibility for seniors should have been limited to those receiving the Guaranteed Income Supplement. The report concluded that $22.3 billion had been "poorly targeted," approximately one dollar in every four. Philip Cross (2020), writing in the *Financial Post*, went further, arguing that the employer programs were much more onerous than the CERB in terms of eligibility requirements and paperwork. Several months later, John Ivison (2021) echoed these sentiments, suggesting that, by going beyond simply replacing lost income, the government was either attempting to reap a political reward or was simply being incompetent.

Within a few weeks of these negative assessments, the auditor general reported on the programs and their rollout. The report emphasized the speed with which the programs had been created and the strategies employed to address the risks of invalid claims made by ineligible applicants: "The unprecedented nature of the global pandemic in mid-March 2020 meant that developing policy, conducting economic analysis, drafting legislation, preparing communications products, and ultimately putting the Canada Emergency Response Benefit in place occurred very quickly. Turnaround time for key steps was often a few hours or overnight" (OAG, 2021a, pp. 6–7). There were no precedents for the pace with which this kind of program was developed, and managers were aware of the possibility of error in the absence of prepayment controls. In fact, approximately $500 million was dispersed to people who had already received support from the Canada Revenue Agency (CRA) or Employment and Social Development Canada (ESDC). Corrections were quickly made and post-payment verification began in earnest. The auditor general had more to say about Canada's state of readiness for the pandemic, but the overall assessment of the financial support programs was positive given the time constraints. This positive assessment included the observation that ESDC had addressed "many key areas in the benefit's initial design" (OAG, 2021a, p. 7).

Although the auditor general had little to say about the actual delivery of funds to recipients, swift identification and dispersal would not have been possible without the data systems operated by the CRA. As one of our respondents put it: "The EI computer system stank; the one from the CRA was a supercomputer that could handle the CERB. In the absence of that, we would have been toast" [Economist 13]. Among other things the CRA was able to confirm automatically that applicants had a valid social insurance number, were not deceased, were at least 15 years old, and not in a federal prison. Still, the CRA declined to filter out companies and individuals with a history of fraudulent behaviour. Time constraints are the most likely reason. But cybersecurity experts also observed that, as the CRA became involved in typical banking functions, paying out billions of dollars in electronic transfers, it became a juicy target for cybersecurity attacks (Brethour, 2021). In August 2020 the CRA shut down its website and in February 2021 and again in March of that year suspended hundreds of accounts on the strength of hacking threats.

None of the CRA's difficulties, or the news about overpayments and poor targeting, had much of an effect on the views of the economic elite. With very few exceptions, our respondents praised the federal government's rapid fiscal response to the pandemic and ignored shortcomings in delivery and deficiencies in design that were later confirmed by the auditor general. The Office of the Auditor General (OAG) identified $4.6 billion of overpayments and $27.4 billion that need further investigation (OAG, 2022b). At the time, however, criticism was muted. Among politicians, Conservatives were as willing to credit the Liberal government as the members of other parties. A Conservative politician put it this way: "I don't think it was perfect, I think it was too much and, I think it was badly targeted, but I think given the amount of time that they had to design it, I'm impressed with what they did. I think that the folks at finance proved that they have a policy capacity that I didn't know was there before" [Politician 2].

That is a somewhat grudging, backhanded compliment to be sure, but it is in keeping with the auditor general's initial report. More effusive praise came from the public servants among our interviewees, none of whom was involved directly in the design or execution of the program. Their astonishment at the speed and execution of the program is perhaps an even more impressive comment on the government's responsiveness. As one interviewee said, "The fact is the federal government came out flying. Obviously, they had the playbook ahead of time. I was super impressed. To have anyone criticize their targeting or anything like that, that's nonsense. Particularly since the CERB is taxable, so we'll get it all back in if it wasn't supposed to be handed out. The risk of somebody getting too much or something happening – those are like minor risks in the whole system" [Bureaucrat 2].

As for the programs' being poorly targeted and overly generous, the public servants among our interviewees often placed the programs' commitments in a broader context. The funding, they suggested, was not overly generous – "It seemed reasonable, kind of minimal. It's really difficult to live on the amounts that were given out" [Bureaucrat 8] – and, most important, it prevented a bleak recessionary experience for thousands of workers and students: "I look at the aggregate effect and how the economy was still able to keep chugging along, how there wasn't a massive series of foreclosures and how the breadlines didn't quintuple overnight" [Bureaucrat 7]. From this perspective, the programs were literally disaster relief. As one economist observed, "What was 'poorly targeted and overly generous' in 2020 is playing an extraordinarily useful role in sustaining the recovery. We should stop whining about the 'poorly targeted' programs of 2020, given that they are playing a useful role in 2021" [Economist 17].

The speed with which these programs brought relief was a revelation that led some of our interviewees to anticipate their continuation in some form or other. The rationale for this kind of funding rests on the premise that it constitutes an automatic stabilizer. Not that the program was automatic when it was launched; it had to be invented and quickly. But the lesson drawn by several of our elite respondents is that the CERB and its successor programs might be seen as blueprints for a guaranteed annual income, a topic we take up directly in Chapter 4.

To understand how opinion might constrain some options and define what is politically feasible, we commissioned a random sample survey of Canadians and posed questions directly related to several of the topics we covered with members of the economic elite (see details in Appendix 2). It was conducted in January 2021, at the height of the second wave of the pandemic. Our 563 respondents resemble the population in the 2016 census in terms of age, gender, province of residence, urban/rural mix, and income groups. (The survey has a margin of error +/− 4.3 per cent, 19 times out of 20.) The programs themselves were met with overwhelming support among survey respondents, but their precise character – immediate relief or harbingers of a change in social policy – left our respondents divided. Answering in January 2021, long after the programs had begun but well before they were wound down, about 38 per cent of our sample wanted to see the programs wrapped up quickly "after the pandemic," while 35 per cent disagreed, and the rest chose the category "neutral." As will become evident, the economic elite was similarly conflicted.

Governments' Role in the Economy: Will Anything Change?

The Canadian federal government might have passed the initial competence test set by the pandemic, at least in terms of income protection, but this does not mean that the economic elite is necessarily willing to reconsider its basic assumptions about government capacity. As we observed in Chapter 2, the forces of inertia are formidable. Whatever impact a singular event might have, there is a strong tendency to revert to the familiar or at least look for reasons to do so. Besides, income-support programs were widely appreciated in part because they were universal in design and they built on a social consensus that is not likely to be replicated across other policy areas. So, as profound a shock as the pandemic has been, we should not be surprised to learn that, for many members of the elite group, it is safer and more satisfying to imagine things as they used to be rather than how they might be given our new collective experience.

This tendency to revert to the way things were might be why, when asked whether governments will take a more active role in shaping and steering the economy in a post-pandemic world, about 30 per cent of our interviewees responded in the negative. It was a nuanced no, mixed at times with regret and at other times with relief. But then, at the other end of the spectrum, there were those who saw the pandemic and the policy response it engendered as signalling a paradigmatic shift in the role governments play in society. About 18 per cent of our interviewees thought that governments' role will expand and things will never be the same again, while another 29 per cent believed governments' role will increase but there are limits to change.

First, let's consider the view that the economy will return to a previous equilibrium. In the "back to normal" camp are those who stress that the pandemic was an exogenous shock, not something that emerged from internal contradictions or limitations in the economy. Nor was the pandemic the product of poor political choices. Here is how a bureaucrat and an economist described the pandemic: "It's a very unusual kind of shock ... The world is different but not so radically different that we have to change the way we think about things" [Bureaucrat 18]. An economist put it this way: "I don't think you see the present situation or the future situation any different from what it was a few years ago" [Economist 10]. From this perspective, the pandemic is not the route to major changes. As one politician said, "It's not really clear to me what the link between COVID-19 and some kind of utopian outcome really would be" [Politician 10].

To be sure, some patterns of behaviour do seem destined to change, if only because they have been redefined as part of that collective experience. Working from home, or at a distance, is now imaginable on a scale that would have surprised, or more likely astonished, our pre-COVID-19 selves. This disruption to established patterns of work was made possible by rapid application of technologies. Enticing workers and students back to the office or the classroom proved to be a challenge in some locales, especially where the virus emerged or revisited.

For those without the bandwidth to participate fully in the world of Zoom or Teams, the pandemic heighted their sense of isolation and sharpened demands for better access to the Internet. Those obliged to work in tight quarters – slaughterhouses, fulfilment centres, assembly lines – felt a deepened sense of grievance beyond the reality of higher rates of infection. Adding new vulnerabilities to already existing inequalities set the stage for renewed demands for improved compensation and better working conditions.

For most of the economic elite, fixing these problems does not require an active or intrusive state intervention. What is required is policy tweaking and attention to stabilization. This view was prominent among senior public servants, many of whom argued like this one that "government has a stabilization function – it's always had that function. It should continue to follow that. If some people are thinking that, well, this is an opportunity to change our entire policy universe, I'm not quite there" [Bureaucrat 25]. For those who suspect that public servants are eagerly anticipating the opportunity to expand the role and reach of government, most of our bureaucrat interviewees took the opposite view. The federal government might be uniquely positioned to supply the credit required to see the economy through a shock, but in the view of most public servants, it is not well suited to do much more. Here's an example of this perspective from a senior provincial public servant: "Government can get more things wrong than right, in terms of steering [the] economy … Government will have a role to play but part of the success of public policy lies in successfully transitioning government out of being a very active steerer in the economy because I don't think the governments in Canada are kind of set up to do that kind of thing over the long term" [Bureaucrat 20]. A former federal public servant echoed this scepticism: "Identifying necessarily specific areas where you as a government believe we've got to put money because that's the future? I don't know if there's reason to believe that that's been successful in the past or that it would be successful in the future" [Bureaucrat 9].

Scepticism turned to cynicism at the political level. There, Conservative ministers sensed a risk that the pandemic will be used as an excuse to expand the reach of government, something that would be "perverse," in the words of a former finance minister: "To suggest when we are weak that we should do something to make us even weaker, is perverse reasoning" [Politician 12]. And yet the pandemic might provide the rationale for intervention: "I think this idea that we should be telling people to build a wind farm instead of an oil rig is a bad idea. But I actually think that's where governments are going to go" [Politician 2]. From this end of the political spectrum, the thought that the pandemic could be an excuse for an expansion of government into private enterprise brought a shudder: "When I hear the statements, and we all heard them in recent months, that governments will have a really significant role, a much greater role of importance in reshaping the economy, it scares me" [Politician 15]. It is not that government has no role to play, but for small "c" conservative politicians its role is to create a broad-based competitive environment and allow entrepreneurs and investors to allocate capital based on perceived opportunities. COVID-19 should not change that.

Several of our interviewees were confident that the pandemic would not foreshadow an expanded role for government simply because public attitudes had not shifted in that direction: "It's possible that activists will see this as an opportunity to reshape government in certain ways, but I don't see any sign that Canadians are more interested in that than in the past, but that could be me" [Economist 21]. The experience of the Spanish Flu in 1919 suggests a relatively rapid return to an economic normal. There might be new health measures, but as one public servant observed, "people are quick to forget" [Bureaucrat 15].

Certainly, the details of the virus's spread likely will fade, but the experience of vaccine development and deployment might linger. Much depends, as a former minister observed, on how government management of the crisis eventually is assessed: "There's always scepticism about government's ability to do things, but a lot of people have seen through this period of time that many things in fiscal policy and otherwise had to get done and nobody else could possibly have done it" [Politician 9]. But is the public's perception positive? A senior economist was not so sure: "Basically government has not performed very well as an institution and I would say we in the West as a populous we have really not performed as well as we might have" [Economist 3]. Our willingness to accept direction on managing our own health status (wearing masks and observing social distancing) was far from universal, and while vaccine procurement likely earned governments some credit, the health care system as a whole appeared vulnerable, especially as COVID-19 cases pushed other testing and surgical interventions to the side, seriously exacerbating wait times.

What all of these observations have in common is a presumption that policy is responsive to public attitudes. This causal sequence is at the heart of much theorizing about how policy is made, and it has a reassuring normative core. Politicians, in this view, tailor their electoral appeals to voters who choose the policy package that best meets their needs. At the centre of this theory of policy lies the median voter theorem[2] and the image of political parties adjusting policy to fit with median voter preferences (Hacker & Pierson, 2014). This theory depends crucially on the assumption that elites can perceive public preferences accurately and are willing to act on them. Notwithstanding democratic expectations, neither of these assumptions is a given.

An alternative perspective reverses the sequence. Politicians and other political actors are motivated by the desire to make policy changes rather than simply respond to the median voter. Policy is the prize (Hacker & Pierson, 2014, p. 645). It breaks through stalemates, proposes new ways of thinking, and shapes preferences. Policy locks in advantages for some and imposes losses on others. Organizations respond politically, trying to bake in rights, mitigate losses, or reverse policy itself (Trebilcock, 2014). The key to success is organized mobilization and adept institutional management.

In this "policy affects politics" model, feedback is key (Pierson, 2004). When the feedback is negative, organizational players mobilize against it, while policymakers make adjustments to improve a policy's appeal or reduce its effects on those experiencing losses. In the case of the pandemic, positive feedback was the more interesting dynamic. Assuming, as some of our elite members do, that governments' handling of the economic effects of the pandemic conferred credibility on policy, then the issue is whether positive feedback will be cemented into future spending and taxing decisions. Some are convinced it will, if only because, in their view, this is how governments grow. As one economist noted: "After these types of crises, governments tend to basically start getting involved and once they're there, they usually will not retreat for some time to come" [Economist 2]. And expectations change, or become more refined. If governments are willing to take significant risks with their balance sheets once, the expectation is that they will do it again: "I think people are going to come out of it expecting more from policymakers. I think there is bound to be a bigger role for government in the new 'normal'" [Economist 17].

Positive feedback has been described as "a self-reinforcing process that accentuates rather than counterbalances a trend" (Baumgartner &

---

2 When an odd number of voters is arrayed along a single dimension (left versus right, for example) according to the intensity of their preferences, the median voter will occupy the central position such that an equal number of voters is found on either side. According to the *median voter theorem* (sometimes referred to as a theory), political parties (or candidates) typically will craft appeals premised on attracting the support of median voters, since their vote, when combined with those to their left or right, will constitute a majority.

Jones, 2002). In the punctuated equilibrium[3] version of policy change, positive feedback requires a shock to get started – the kind of shock that a pandemic provides. Change then acquires momentum as governments capitalize on the opportunity to move forward on specific items – such as enhanced childcare support – that might be only tangentially related to immediate economic relief. For many of our interviewees, the problems revealed by the pandemic have been with us for some time; governments have simply either failed to prioritize them or to figure out what an appropriate response might look like. Consider the list proposed by one economist:

> I share the view that we are entering a period in which governments should play a larger role in rebuilding and steering the economy. However, this view has nothing to do with the pandemic. Global warming, rising monopolies, inequality and poverty, rundown infrastructures, latent xenophobia, the aging of population, digitalization, unregulated social media, volatile international capital markets, the loss of firepower of monetary policy, et cetera, are all huge problems that were blatant very much before the pandemic. [Economist 6]

So, the pandemic was a moment when the need for change was accentuated, but the pandemic has not made policy problems more tractable. In other words, don't expect too much change. Governments might grow in importance and play a role in facilitating change (or ensuring that it is not too slow), but many members of the economic elite we spoke with doubt that governments in Canada will be playing a new leadership role in the economy. It will be more a matter of tweaking existing policies to keep up with developments elsewhere, especially in the United States, where, as one interviewee noted, "shifting electricity generation, shifting different manufacturing technologies, retooling the auto sector; this is going to take up a lot of what the federal government can do" [Economist 22]. The realism that attends these kinds of assessments is based in part on Canada's size and the vulnerable position in which we find ourselves whenever policy changes in the United States. The impact of US subsidies for green energy, for example, dwarfs what

---

3 *Punctuated equilibrium* is an idea borrowed from evolutionary biology (where it remains controversial) that describes a pattern of gradual adjustments in equilibrium interrupted by a sharp burst of change tied to specific events. In public policy the concept refers to smooth, incremental adjustment to policies and budgets punctuated by occasional outbursts of rapid policy change within a stable institutional environment.

can be expected of governments in Canada. As a former premier put it, "we are not the United States" [Politician 2].

While the body of opinion among our interviewees suggested we rein in our ambitions, a minority expected governments to act boldly to seize opportunities that a crisis presents. This portion of the economic elite sees major technological developments – artificial intelligence being a prime example – as clearly in need of government steering, and not simply for regulatory purposes. They imagine a much more active state taking equity positions in domestic start-ups with an eye on the "triple bottom line." A senior provincial finance official explained the idea this way: "It's the idea of the triple bottom line, you're achieving social objectives and are also helping start-up companies to mature and become fully grown companies earning a financial return for government" [Bureaucrat 29].

This approach would represent a turn to more aggressive industrial policy. Canada has always had industrial policies in the form of selective subsidies to business, training programs, procurement policies, research and development funding, and public ownership. But in a neoliberal era, many of these policies were often framed as exceptions, treated as transitional, or were openly retaliatory in the case of trade disputes. That might be changing with shifts in geopolitical strategy. Adherents of this perspective also point south of the border, this time arguing that, "what Biden is doing is essentially formulating an industrial policy for the United States" [Politician 1]. Again, this was a minority perspective, but in Canada and elsewhere governments are already major funders of innovation (Mazzucato, 2018). Should they do more?

Certainly, at the federal government level the appetite for industrial policy has increased post-pandemic. In the 2023 federal budget, a variety of subsidies for green energy was announced, at least in part to offset the impact of US subsidies contained in the deceptively named *Inflation Reduction Act* (Department of Finance Canada, 2023). Some of these measures are familiar cash incentives intended to match commitments from specific companies, but the bulk of the spending took the form of tax incentives employed to expand electricity capacity regardless of source: wind, solar, nuclear, even natural gas could qualify. The problem is that in Canada neither government nor the private sector has demonstrated an ability to foster major product and process developments regardless of the policy instruments employed. Direct subsidies attract the criticism that governments are trying to pick winners, while tax incentives, which are among the least intrusive means of steering economic development, have uncertain payoffs. Canada does have significant socio-economic advantages, but underinvestment in private sector research and development, a lack of scale in business, and the absence of strategic direction and implementation strategies from governments have hobbled efforts to match comparator countries (Phillips & Castle, 2022).

It merits emphasizing once again that imagining a more activist state does not require a pandemic. With the conspicuous exception of vaccine manufacturing capability, very little of an industrial policy program arises naturally from a rampant infectious disease, and very few members of the elite we interviewed thought the pandemic would spawn an era of high protectionism. What they did see was significant fiscal and monetary intervention at the macro level, and that prompted speculation about the future of governments as active economic players. Others have been more aggressive: the Leroux Report, from the Industry Strategy Council (2020), linked the pandemic to economic development by arguing that the federal government should go beyond "response" and "restore" to "reimagine." For the Council, the task ahead, post-pandemic, is to "develop a made-in-Canada industrial strategy to ensure that our leading industries will help Canadians prosper in the new post-COVID-19 world" (Industry Strategy Council, 2020, p. 10). Industrial policy of the type imagined in the Leroux Report would take government well beyond orthodox economics and would be resisted by most of the economic elite. But once an equilibrium has been upset, agendas can be reconstructed. Policymaking is not an election, and the median voter will not necessarily determine future steps.

Finally, we must note that a sizable minority of our economic elite, comprised primarily of women, were eager to press home the point that the economy is more than income and consumption. For them, the lesson drawn from the Great Financial Crisis is that priority will be given to investors. As one commented, "the global financial crisis was the most in-your-face socialization of risk and privatization of profit with Main Street bailing out 'too big to fail' Wall Street/Bay Street" [Economist 24]. The pandemic was a wakeup call that the family is part of the economy and that community development, in its broadest sense, is as important to economic growth as is finance capital. Education and job training are important, but an even more appropriate response to the pandemic was policies that supported caregivers. These kinds of policies were both socially responsible and economically sound: "We know we're losing billions of dollars of productivity because women can't get into the workforce, and there are women who have left their jobs in droves or have moved to part time as result of COVID" [Politician 17].

Behind these admonitions lies a view of the economy as embedded in a wide array of social relations, particularly familial and kinship, but also religious and community ones (Booth, 1994). Requiring governments to be attentive to these relationships as they endeavour to shape the economy could be simply a plea for a more inclusive idea of what counts as an economic priority. If the survival of banks has been a priority, why not the working conditions of women? Posing this kind of question is the equivalent of asking, "whom is the economy for?" This question is at the heart of a more radical (if also more ancient) moral-economy approach to public policy. With few exceptions, it is a question that was never directly addressed by any of the elite members we interviewed. Some of them, however, were clearly searching for a way of dislodging, or at least modifying, the standard narrative regarding economic priorities.

The Growth Imperative

In the standard narrative of macroeconomic priorities, employment and inflation loom large. In the early stages of the pandemic, the collapse in employment was top of mind for elites and the rest of the country. Inflation barely registered as a problem. So, what should our priorities be in the post-pandemic era? Naturally, Canadians wanted to get back to a public health normal, but what should an economic normal look like? Creating jobs and controlling inflation have been traditional goals of economic policy, but what about the admonition (or pledge) to "build back better"? In a post-pandemic Canada, how important should income protection programs be? What about reducing government debt? To gauge Canadians' sense of the relative importance of different goals, in the midst of the pandemic we asked our random sample of Canadians to rank the following five economic policy priorities in order of importance:

- protecting the income of citizens;
- controlling increases in the cost of goods and services;
- reducing the level of government debt;
- reducing income inequalities; and
- creating jobs.

Figure 3.3 presents the results. It shows that our respondents were particularly sensitive to income issues – and not just their own. While 20 per cent thought that "protecting the income of citizens" should be the most important priority, an even larger proportion endorsed "reducing income inequalities." Almost 30 per cent of the respondents ranked reducing income inequality as the most important policy

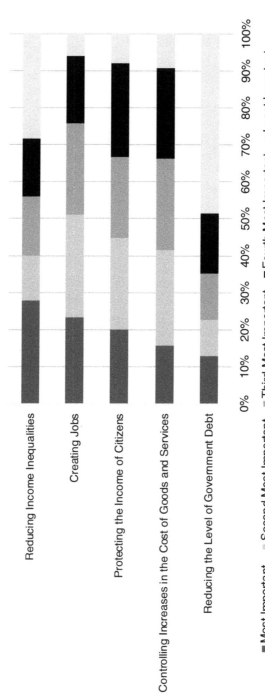

Figure 3.3. Ranking Survey Respondents' Economic Policy Priorities
Source: Atkinson and Mou (2021).

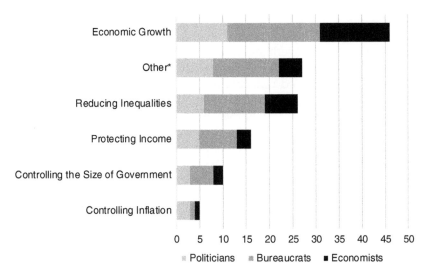

Figure 3.4. Policy Priorities Mentioned by Interviewees
* This category includes the environment and climate change; female participation in
the workforce (childcare); education and training; industrial policy (supply chains,
productivity, competitiveness); and health and well-being.

priority. The traditional dual goals of economic policy – "creating jobs" (employment) and "controlling increases in the cost of goods and services" (inflation) – received about 23 per cent and 16 per cent of votes, respectively.

If we combine the votes for the most important and second-most important policy priorities, "creating jobs" received the support of more than half (51 per cent) of our respondents. These findings are in accord with estimates of the substantial direct and indirect (negative) effects of unemployment on subjective well-being (Helliwell & Huang, 2014). In contrast, 40 per cent of the respondents chose reducing income inequality as the most or second-most important priority.

These preferences, registered at the height of the pandemic's initial waves, signal a willingness to contemplate active government involvement in shaping market outcomes. The venerable public finance goal of "reducing the level of government debt" received support from less than 15 per cent of the respondents, and was deemed the least important of the five proposed priorities.

The economic elite shares a concern with income inequality, but for most of our elite interviewees nothing is more important than economic growth. For them, the formula is simple: economic growth will solve most of the problems that have emerged on the heels of the pandemic, including the debt overhang. In posing the question of priorities, we offered them a number of possibilities, including reducing inequalities, protecting income, and reducing the size of government – and coded all mentions. As Figure 3.4 shows, stimulating economic growth was the option that received by far the strongest endorsement from all three groups of interviewees.

Growth has been the key to rising standards of living. It allows for increased investment and consumption, and ultimately for improvements in well-being. For many, perhaps most, economists and other members of the economic policy elite, it is the ultimate collective goal. Growth has been described as necessary for both freedom and peace and for the welfare of people around us, to say nothing of personal happiness (Cowen, 2018). Even more essential, the future of the species appears to depend on expanding opportunities.

Conventionally, growth is understood in terms of productivity. The deployment of labour and capital to their most rewarding returns generates an increase in the national income, a portion of which can be reinvested – ideally in people as well as in innovative products and processes. The result is more economic activity: more production and more consumption. The problem is that economic growth does not respond to simple economic formulas (Banerjee & Duflo, 2019), and disputes persist about whether political variables such as democracy are an asset or a liability (Acemoglu et al., 2019; Przeworski & Limongi, 1993). What we do know is that, over the course of human history, economic growth is itself highly unusual. Until the Industrial Revolution, economic growth was virtually unknown. By the twentieth century, steady growth had become a reasonable expectation. And growth, even modest annual growth, has produced an unprecedented and substantial increase in overall wealth. The economic historian Brad DeLong estimates that, at a growth rate of about 2.1 per cent a year, by 2010 we were collectively 8.8 times as wealthy as we were in 1870 (DeLong, 2022, pp. 4–5).

Growth has not been even, of course. Not all countries have grown at the same pace and there have been episodes of serious decline. But beginning in the 1950s, Western economies experienced the "Glorious Thirty" years of significant and sustained economic growth that only came to an end with the first oil crisis in 1973. Not that growth ended: what ended was the rapid pace of growth (Vollrath, 2020). Although the nominal growth rate slowed down, growth in real (inflation-adjusted) GDP per capita, an indicator of living standards, was about as large as it had been in earlier years. Real GDP per capita in Canada was 19 per cent higher in 2019 than it was in 2000.

Because growth is seldom theorized directly, the impression is often left that growth means more – particularly more choices, more technology, and more consumption. And conventional measures of economic growth focus on the market value of all goods and services produced –in other words, gross domestic product. From the beginning of its dominance, this measure has attracted critics, particularly those who contend that GDP is a production measure and not equivalent to well-being, which is presumably the purpose of the economy in the first place (Stiglitz et al., 2009). Nor does GDP measure the depreciation or the depletion of natural assets, so shifts in wealth go largely undetected. These problems are compounded by the difficulty of measuring whether a growth path is sustainable or self-defeating. It is one thing to determine the current rate of growth, but how do you measure, using a tool like GDP, whether this rate can be sustained (or is even self-defeating) in the future (Coyle, 2014, p. 139)?

It is not hard to see why critics of capitalism treat growth as a major threat to survival, since capitalism seems bent on using up resources without replacing them (Homer-Dixon, 2020, p. 196). This critique of growth, however, will need to confront the evidence that growth and resource consumption are no longer so tightly connected. Rich countries are now growing without using more and more of the planet's precious resources, such as fresh water or land. Technological innovation has played a major role in "dematerializing" our investment and consumption, taking less and less from the planet while constantly improving our living standards (McAfee, 2019). Still, there are major distributive issues to face, since not all countries are "rich" and the development path that many are on is not especially benign.

None of these concerns about the negative consequences of growth weighed heavily on the minds of members of the economic elite we interviewed. For them, growth is highly desirable, and very few offered any caveats to this assessment. Some interviewees suggested economic growth would solve most of the other problems that we identified. One put it like this: "If we can get the economy growing north of 3 per cent on a sustained basis, it won't solve all of our social and political issues, but it will help solve them" [Economist 2]. This perspective came from all quarters – politicians, economists, and bureaucrats. And while those with conservative credentials were enthusiastic about a growth agenda, so were those with roots on the political left.

The economic elite in Canada worries less about the specific pace of economic growth in any given year than about the possibility that growth will grind to a stop or go into reverse. Still fresh in their minds is memory of the Great Financial Crisis. In 2009 the Canadian economy contracted by 2.9 per cent and maintained only a meagre rate of growth in the succeeding ten years. The problem with a slow growth rate is that it compounds over time. As our ability to harness human and physical capital to develop innovative projects recedes, the worry is that momentum is drained from the economy. The dynamism that has sustained confidence slowly erodes and fear of the future increases. When a negative economic expectation settles in, the expectation could be self-fulfilling, and the economy might move into decline. Needless to say, the 2020–1 pandemic stoked these concerns.

Having economic dynamism in mind, some of the economic elite were laser-focused on the country's productivity challenge: "If the investments that are made now into the future, if they are productivity enhancing, these measures can give you economic growth" [Economist 11]. The problem is that Canada has not made the kinds of investments required: "We have been underinvesting in the productivity performance in Canada on the part of government. That ought to change or else we're going to continue to drift into a mediocre economic performance unless we pay attention to what is needed to promote productivity in Canada" [Bureaucrat 13]. So far, the kind of change that these observers were calling for has not surfaced in Canada's response to the pandemic. Much more attention has been paid to ensuring incomes are protected and demand sustained.

While giving the federal government credit for its huge fiscal stimulus, former Bank of Canada governor David Dodge offered the view that our current account deficit is an unaddressed cause for concern: "If Canada is to fully recover from the COVID crisis, we need to articulate and promote a medium and long-term plan to restore ourselves as a favoured destination for investment and to use that investment to enable forward-looking industries and entrepreneurs to make and sell what the rest of the world wants to buy from us" (Dodge, 2020).

From 2009 to 2021, Canada's current account was in deficit, a situation that cannot be sustained indefinitely without undermining our attraction for foreign investors. Worse, oil and gas have done a disproportionately large part of the work associated with strengthening the current account balance. The positive balance in 2022 was a product of surging demand. That will change as demand for fossil fuel products is expected to decline after 2025 if countries are to meet their net-zero pledges (International Energy Agency, 2021). In fact, if we are to meet net zero by 2050, governments should be investing now in clean technology. If G7 economies returned to the investment ratios of the 1970s, half of the global shortfall in investments in clean technology would be filled (Sandbu, 2022).

Those who are prepared to predict the future are not particularly bullish on Canada's prospects. On the contrary: based on a comprehensive OECD assessment of market economies, David Williams concludes that "Canada can at best achieve real per capita GDP growth of only 0.7 per cent per annum over 2020–2030" (Williams, 2021). The 2023 federal budget confirmed this pessimistic assumption, at least over the short term. Canada will not be the only advanced market economy to experience deceleration over the next several years, but it is disconcerting to learn that the country is expected to be the slowest in the G20 (OECD, 2021c). Mind you, not all projections are quite so glum. The IMF predicts that Canada's growth rate will decline to around 1.5 per cent by 2025 – not much different than that of other G7 countries and substantially better than that of Italy and Japan. Data in Figure 3.5 suggest that, if previous trends continue, Canada's growth rate will be similar to that of the OECD as a whole. Still, this growth rate is considerably lower than the rate in the first years of the twenty-first century, until the 2008 Great Financial Crisis, and there is no guarantee that the future will resemble the past.

Growth deceleration can be traced to a relatively small number of factors operating at different rates across the economically developed world. On the supply side, the biggest contributor to slowdown is demographic: a reduction in fertility rates and an aging population (Bricker & Ibbitson, 2019). In 2014, over 6 million Canadians were ages 65 and older, representing 15.6 per cent of Canada's population. By 2030 Canadian seniors will number over 9.5 million, making up about 23 per cent of the population (Canada, 2014). Canada's baby-boom generation (born between 1946 and 1966) is relatively large compared with the same cohort in other OECD countries, and its exit from the workforce will aggravate supply-side issues and increase dependency ratios.

The prospect of a declining labour supply has already prompted pleas to increase the age of eligibility for Canada Pension Plan recipients to encourage longer working lives. Demands for more immigration to offset these effects have come from several sources, including the Advisory Council on Economic Growth (2016), which suggested a target of 450,000 immigrants per year, and from popular writers who envisage a "less claustrophobic and more spacious" maximum Canada (Saunders, 2017, p. 228). Whatever the merits of more immigration and a larger population, neither will completely offset the effects of aging or compete with extended working lives as a spur to economic growth (Robson & Mahboubi, 2018).

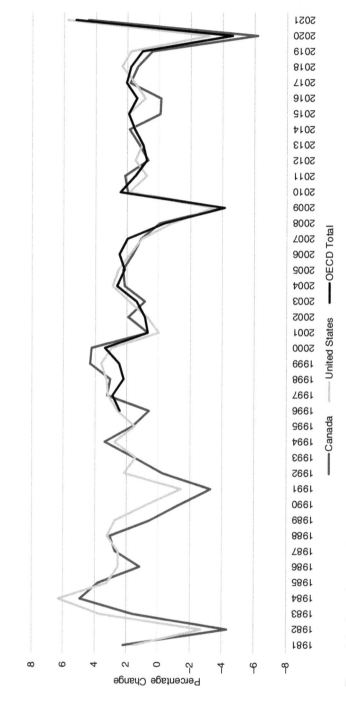

Figure 3.5. Growth Rate of Real per Capita GDP, Canada, the United States, and Total OECD, 1981–2021
Note: Data for total OECD are available only from 1996 onward.
Source: Data from OECD (n.d.-b).

Investment in worker knowledge and human capital can raise productivity and so offset some of these effects, but the impact of investment policy on endogenous growth is difficult to predict without some strong assumptions about labour force productivity. In Canada total labour force productivity traditionally has lagged the rate of productivity growth in the United States, and Canada's rate has declined in the past decade, in part because of a growing mismatch between education achievement and labour force needs. But human capital is only part of the productivity picture. Competition – especially exposure to industry leaders – and economies of scale are also critical, and so is organizational technology such as Toyota's manufacturing systems. The removal of stifling regulation would also help (Baily, 2023). A massive improvement in productivity would be welcome, but it is not going to happen magically. And while governments have a role to play, "more government" is far too simple a proposition. "More smart government" is closer to the mark.

Low productivity discourages capital investment, which in turn reduces aggregate demand (Gordon, 2015). The result has been described as "secular stagnation" – a protracted period of slow growth. The secular-stagnation thesis, advanced by former US treasury secretary Larry Summers and endorsed by other neo-Keynesians, argues that advanced economies have begun to settle into just such an equilibrium (Summers, 2018). Secular stagnation is characterized by a high level of savings – a "savings glut" encouraged by increased longevity – but low levels of investment. The result is a persistent output gap – the difference between actual GDP and potential GDP if all factors of production are employed to their full potential.

For some, secular stagnation is essentially a supply problem. As the demand for and the price of capital equipment decline, we see less borrowing and less investment. Safe assets, like government bonds, become more attractive and corporations begin to prefer stock buyback programs to investing in new plant and equipment (Summers, 2014). For others, stagnation is a demand problem. For post-Keynesians, growth depends on real wage increases, which simultaneously promote productivity gains. These critics argue that, when wages stagnate and jobs are outsourced to other countries, a declining wage share of economic output means demand for consumption goods and economic growth both slow down. More debt, both public and household, is required to sustain economic activity (Baccaro et al., 2022, pp. 9–13).

Whatever its source, a major manifestation of stagnation is a decline in the real rate of interest, which is something economists have been observing over the past several decades until the pandemic's economic effects changed the calculus. But a return to low interest rates will not necessarily increase investment or stimulate aggregate demand. The problem is that monetary policy loses its stimulative capacity when interest rates reach zero bound. Neo-Keynesians respond by urging governments to borrow at low interest rates and spend on productive projects, infrastructure being among the most obvious. The objective is not only to boost consumption, but also to strengthen aggregate supply. Increased debt levels are an obvious risk, as we discuss in Chapter 5, but the alternative is a feeble growth rate, something with which the economic elite in Canada has had limited experience.

Not everyone endorses this gloomy outlook or the secular stagnation thesis, but few expect a rapid return to the days of strong growth in developed economies. In fact, some economists welcome what has come to be called a "stationary economy" in which the equilibrium we achieve is one dictated by the limits of our natural capital (Daly, 1996). For them, a slower pace of growth need not represent a reduction in living standards. Consider why growth rates have been high in the first place: because countries like Canada were starting from a low point in terms of available goods and services, so that significant increases were possible by employing Fordist means of production,[4] with their capital intensiveness and economies of scale. At first these innovations are transformative (think cars and airline travel), but eventually the pace with which these technologies produce marginal improvements in productivity and living standards begins to slow down. Robert Gordon argues that this deceleration has been going on for some time as we exhaust the benefits of early twentieth-century innovations and begin to shift our investments from durable goods to services (Gordon, 2016).

In the 1980s, Canadians' spending on services – for example, education, legal services, accounting, and entertainment – was already approximately 25 per cent of total household consumption (Statistics Canada, 2022c). The rest was largely made up of durable goods – for example, dishwashers, cars, and televisions. By 2018, the ratio had changed dramatically. Now we spend about 33 per cent of our income on services, many of which (think streaming, coaching, and fitness) did

---

4 Fordism, a label inspired by the economics of Henry Ford, is a term used to describe a particular form of industrial organization characterized by the mass production of standardized products using large-scale repetitive processes. A *Fordist means of production* implies relatively unskilled workers whose wages are sufficient to purchase low-cost products. Fordist production is frequently contrasted with tailored, niche-market products generated by processes that rely on worker ingenuity, localized advantages, and flexible specialization.

not exist (at least in their current form) in 1980. This shift in spending is a positive signal in the sense that we have reached a point at which our basic material needs are being met, and enhancements in living standards have begun to assume a different form. Unfortunately, it is a form that does not translate easily into higher growth levels.

William Baumol was among the first economists to reflect on the importance of different levels of productivity growth in different sectors of the economy (Baumol, 1967). The technologically advanced capital goods sector permits productivity growth through scale economies, innovation, and the substitution of labour for capital. In what Baumol described (rather unfortunately) as the "stagnant" sector – which includes legal services, insurance, the arts, and most of education and health care – productivity growth is much slower given the "handicraft" character of the supply process (Baumol, 1993, p. 624). Slower growth, in this reading, is a result of the time and attention services demand, not a failure of technological know-how. In fact, it is an acknowledgment of our economic success (Vollrath, 2020).

For the public sector, however, stagnation poses political problems, especially as governments manage unprecedented levels of debt. A slowdown in economic growth means that governments will be urged to provide income support while simultaneously experiencing slower revenue growth. Most members of the economic elite in Canada are aware of these dangers. And while our interviewees expressed support for income-support programs, they worried that from the outset of the pandemic the economic response of the federal government was focused heavily on replacing income and cushioning pandemic shocks rather than developing a robust growth strategy. As welcome as income-protection measures are, they do not constitute a growth agenda, as Canada's former minister of finance has argued (Morneau & Reynolds, 2023).

From the provinces, a senior public servant offered the following less than enthusiastic assessment: "I think stimulating economic growth is going to be critical ... We're not where we want to be in the innovation economy and the Trudeau Liberals have just not paid attention to that in the broader set of issues that they've been advancing for the last four or five years" [Bureaucrat 19]. Until they were prompted, not a single one of our interviewees mentioned one of the federal government's major innovation efforts, the Innovation Superclusters Initiative (now called the Global Innovation Clusters) (ISED Canada, 2021), and then only grudgingly. More than one interviewee repeated the clichéd admonition to avoid picking winners, a mantra that seemed to be used to ward off ambition as much as guard against overreach. And to be fair, there is limited appetite for hands-on business development among Canadians at large. Over half (54 per cent) of our survey respondents agreed or strongly agreed that "governments should not be expected to help private companies become more competitive."

The economic elite's hesitation regarding an active industrial policy does not mean they believe government should avoid subsidies, tax expenditures, and other transfer policies, or that governments should refrain from regulating economic activity. None of our interviewees was prepared to place all faith in the spontaneous and benevolent effects of the unregulated market. Then again, the idea that governments can act as benevolent planners is equally unattractive, even though early versions of public finance theory often would make this convenient assumption. There is, in short, a palpable tension between government as a constructive force and government as a chronic bungler, and few members of the economic elite we interviewed were prepared wholeheartedly to endorse either one of these images. But a large number were willing to argue that governments can and should do more to offset the negative effects of capitalism, especially those revealed by the pandemic: precarious incomes, uneven labour market participation, and increasing levels of asset inequality.

It is possible to take this view even further and endorse a "degrowth" position that challenges the idea that government promotion of growth is a good thing (see, for example, Hinkel, 2021). Although a distinctly minority point of view among our interviewees, it is worth considering the perspective of one former finance minister: "I may be the most unique finance minister in history because I'm a little sceptical about the goal of economic growth. I personally don't think we have to always be in an economic growth mode" [Politician 13]. That perspective does not mean that growth is necessarily bad, only that other concerns matter at least as much. This person added, "I would like to see growth of the economy balanced with other indicators of well-being like human development, equality of life factors, health and gender empowerment" [Politician 13]. But the idea implicit in these remarks, that growth does not equate to increased well-being, is a view the large majority of our economic elite would find difficult to accept.

Conclusion

The pandemic has not altered the fundamental realities of the Canadian economy. Canada still has a chronic current account imbalance, an aging population, a low level of productivity, and a heavy reliance of commodities to generate national income. The unprecedented intervention of governments to reduce the negative impact of the COVID-19 recession was a necessary shift in the neoliberal approach to economic policy, but it has done little to dislodge existing elite ideas about the role of government in the economy or about the overall importance of stimulating economic growth. Just how economic growth is to be achieved is no clearer post-pandemic than it was before. Only a few elite observers appear to believe that the vulnerabilities revealed by the pandemic are a signal that even more vulnerabilities lie in store and that governments should gear up to meet them. Most yearn for a return to normal, even if the normality produced by globalization has proven more fragile than expected. The invitation to imagine an economy more shaped and steered by government than it was prior to the pandemic was largely declined.

The one exception to this overall rejection of a larger role for government involves investments in human capital. Most of our interviewees were aware of, and sensitive to, growing levels of economic inequality. They would like to see these tendencies reversed. In the next chapter, we explore how far they are prepared to go. Meanwhile, our survey respondents chose income inequality as a top priority, but did not privilege childcare or other human capital investment opportunities – job training or support for post-secondary institutions. Elite players read signals and, in the aftermath of a pandemic, have a natural desire to do something – in Canada's case, just not something too radical.

4 Confronting Income and Wealth Inequalities

Only relatively recently have income and wealth inequalities in Canada begun receiving intense attention. Poverty has been a topic of periodic concern, but inequality in general has been slow to pierce the consciousness of the economic elite. Before the 1980s, inequality was something that seemed to emerge naturally from the workings of a market society. Now, the topic is attracting much more attention. The reason is simple: inequalities have been growing. A persistent pattern of inequality might be a cause for lament, but increasing inequality, without apparent limit, is a cause for concern. As Osberg (2018, p. 9) points out, it is one thing to ask Canadians to live with a stable, if unequal, distribution of economic resources and quite another to be content with the prospect that, in the future, inequalities will get progressively worse.

For a variety of reasons, the 1980s – specifically, the era of Reagan, Thatcher, and Mulroney – has been singled out as the moment when a relatively stable set of inequalities began to shift in the direction of substantial gains for the very top of the income pyramid. During this period, when the neoliberal agenda of free markets began to take hold, the gap between those at the top – the 1 per cent and the 0.1 per cent – and the rest of the population began to grow. By 2019, the top 1 per cent of individuals in Canada were earning at least $275,000, while the average income earned by the remaining 99 per cent was $39,500, and the average income made by the bottom 50 per cent was a mere $9,500.

For years, economists and political scientists typically assumed that democracies eventually would encourage income equality and so close the gap between the most and least affluent (Galbraith, 2012). Simon Kuznets (1955) famously posited an inverted U-shaped curve in which the transition from an agricultural to an industrial economy would exhibit rising inequality followed by a more equitable distribution of income. This reassuring portrayal of economic development began to be challenged in the early 2000s as research revealed that degrees of income inequality in advanced economies were becoming larger, middle incomes were stagnating, and vast fortunes were accumulating. Thomas Piketty's widely praised 2014 volume, *Capital in the Twenty-First Century*, provided a sweeping assessment that pointed to structural sources behind income and wealth inequalities (Piketty, 2014).

Although the pandemic did not constitute an economic transition of the kind that Kuznets contemplated, the transition to an information economy and to the increased deployment of artificial intelligence solutions to all manner of economic problems (Brynjolfsson & McAfee, 2014) had begun well before the pandemic. If anything, the public health threat and response reminded people that those with high incomes were vulnerable (if not as vulnerable as everyone else) and that they would need to await a summons to be vaccinated along with the rest of Canadians. High incomes doubtless allowed some escape from general restrictions, but the pandemic was a reminder that, in liberal societies, income and wealth have their limits in crisis situations.

Still, the pandemic appears to have sharpened the sense that major societal problems are to be confronted, not avoided, that inequalities in income and wealth are divisive, and that society-wide interventions could yield better outcomes. Of course, income and wealth inequalities have been the subject of reformist campaigns since at least the nineteenth century. Without inheritance and income taxes, pioneered in the early twentieth century, inequalities would be much greater. And, from time to time, pledges to introduce confiscatory tax policies or place limits on executive incomes surface in political debates. Yet public policy has not responded with particular zeal to demands for the amelioration of gross inequalities.

The mood, however, is changing. In this chapter, we discuss the size and scale of inequalities in Canada and other OECD countries. How important, or threatening, are these inequalities? Respondents to national surveys, including our own, are inclined to consider inequalities a major problem and one that deserves immediate attention. Fiscal decisionmakers in Canada are concerned with the political ramifications of growing income gaps and are sympathetic to efforts to address the needs of specific constituencies – especially children and the elderly. But they display little appetite for more radical reforms, including wealth taxes or a Universal Basic Income. Here, we consider the arguments and the reasons for the apparent reluctance to embrace significant change.

Why Is Inequality a Problem?

Market economies produce inequalities in income and wealth. These inequalities are not inevitably a problem, but they do need to be justified. The standard, neoclassical justification is to portray market outcomes as the products of free choices among individuals who enjoy equal access to property. Those prepared to make the necessary investments and take the necessary risks are the direct beneficiaries and assumed to be the most deserving. But because market economies that secure property rights are able to generate unprecedented levels of national wealth, even those who are not among the wealthiest still benefit from their enterprise. That's the theory. The resultant inequalities, by this measure, are not only just, but also globally beneficial.

If inequality is attributed to individual choice, the product of wise and unwise decisions, then it is likely that even large inequalities will be deemed morally acceptable. This interpretation of inequality presumes that individuals have high levels of agency; their economic condition is a matter of personal responsibility (Mounk, 2017). This idea, especially in this unvarnished form, strikes many economic historians as preposterous (Piketty, 2020), but towards the end of the twentieth century it became increasingly acceptable, even obvious, to assign responsibility for economic success or impoverishment to personal choice. Politicians such as Bill Clinton and Tony Blair began invoking the need for personal responsibility just as their predecessors Ronald Reagan and Margaret Thatcher had championed the idea that each citizen needed to take ownership of their own decisions. Even those prepared to acknowledge the role of "luck" – the natural lottery of talents and disabilities (Frank, 2016) – are at pains to distinguish between bad luck accompanied by deliberate gambles and bad luck that is purely fortuitous (Dworkin, 2002). The latter qualifies for amelioration, but the former, "bad bets," are much less deserving.

The alternative to this "responsibility as accountability" ethic is the argument that inequalities are not simply the result of individual choices but are instead structural in nature: they emerge from the character of capitalism itself. Piketty (2014) famously argued that returns to capital, if greater than the rate of growth in the economy, will outpace rates of return to wage income. His exhaustive empirical study found that the larger the initial capital investment, the greater the rate of return. In other words, wealth inequality tends to be self-reinforcing: inherited wealth grows more quickly than wage income, and the wealthy become wealthier over time. This interpretation of inequality traces its origins to property rights regimes that are fundamentally political constructs (Piketty, 2020). The inequalities they produce are in no sense "natural," inevitable, or the product of personal choices.

These starkly different interpretations of the origins of inequalities – personal responsibility or structural determination – influence attitudes towards their amelioration. Those who emphasize individual choice are devoted to increasing incentives to work and invest; those who focus on structural conditions argue that impediments to greater equality are the problem and we should focus on their removal. Impediments range from denial of access to productive participation in the labour market to the extreme insecurity of the gig economy to outright exploitation. As long as personal choice is constrained by oppressive conditions beyond an individual's control, the resulting inequalities undermine the implicit social contract that capitalism proposes (White, 2000). Jobs that fail to produce a living wage, for example, deprive even the most willing productive participants of the opportunity to address inequalities on their own. Disabilities, family care duties, and other restrictions curtail participation in the labour market, while lack of capital discourages investment in education and training. Equally worrying, the employment risks engendered by a capitalist economy are increasingly borne by families through personal credit markets (Hacker, 2019; Wiedemann, 2021).

Granted, capitalism generates structural impediments, but do they qualify as policy problems? Inequalities rise to the level of policy problems for both philosophical and political reasons. Philosophically, they engage and challenge our sense of distributive justice. Modest differences in welfare are tolerable, particularly when they are traceable to natural endowments of talent, but gross inequalities threaten the liberal ideal of politically free and equal citizens cooperating in the solution of shared problems. John Rawls proposed cutting through these problems by focusing attention on the worst-off individual. According to his "difference principle," the cause of economic justice is served by making changes to the distribution of income and/or wealth to achieve a level of inequality that benefits the least advantaged members of society (Rawls, 2005). Inequalities could be quite large and still justifiable as long as these inequalities produce a more advantageous outcome for the poorest among us.

A focus on the poor has policy implications. Those who concentrate attention on the dispossessed and interpret economic inequalities from their standpoint are more likely to propose policies that meet the needs of the demonstrably poor, rather than policies that reduce differences among the relatively rich. This perspective does not do away with considerations of responsibility, but it insists, on egalitarian grounds, that the social contract include everyone, even those who bear some personal responsibility for their economic condition.

Utilitarians have a different idea. Rather than focus on the worst off, they propose that inequalities are acceptable if they produce the maximum benefit for the population in aggregate (Sen, 1973). Utilitarians draw our attention to differences among all citizens and to whether those differences work to everyone's advantage. This is a more morally neutral perspective in which matters of personal responsibility are nudged aside in favour of a focus on overall prosperity. While there are valid objections to the utilitarian world view, in the matter of public policy utilitarians can claim to be non-judgmental about personal choices. Their concern with inequalities is whether they produce desirable or undesirable outcomes for everyone. Redistribution is acceptable, indeed required, as long as gains and losses produce net benefits in welfare.

Considerations of distributive justice might seem rather abstract, but they help us understand why governments often ignore inequalities or adopt policies that are not premised on strictly egalitarian principles. There is, however, another, overtly political, reason that inequalities are problematic from a public policy perspective: they generate distrust and discontent. Economic inequalities, especially if they are perceived to be growing, drive voters away from mainstream political parties and towards right or left populist extremes and leaders who promise miracle cures. The defining characteristic of populism is the assumption that society is divided between elites and "ordinary people." Elites are perceived as eager to preserve and expand their privileges and to use public and private institutions to promote their interests, whereas ordinary people are expected to follow rules that elites ignore and to accept outcomes they are powerless to affect.

Growing inequality enters the picture as a stimulus to this "us-and-them" kind of thinking. As disposable income declines or stagnates for the majority while expanding significantly for the fortunate few, feelings of relative deprivation, lack of upward mobility, or increasing risk fuel populist responses. These reactions do not take the same form in different occupational classes (Han, 2016) or at different income levels (Engler & Weisstanner, 2021), but they contribute to a radicalization of politics by reducing trust and social solidarity. Put simply, as inequality grows, trust in government declines (Stoetzer et al., 2021).

Complicating the growth of political alienation is inequality based on race. European- centred policy, and the norm of liberal universalism, has relegated race to an incidental feature of inequality, rather than recognizing the central experience it is for racialized communities

(Banting & Thompson, 2021). Yet, in reality, race is correlated with income inequality. In 2015, the poverty rate of racial minority groups in Canada was 30.6 per cent, compared with 23.4 per cent for non-minority groups. In addition, existing tax-and-transfer programs are less redistributive for racial minority groups than for the rest of the population (Banting & Thompson, 2021, p. 877). The starkest income inequality is between the Indigenous and non-Indigenous population. Canada's Indigenous population is one of the most economically disadvantaged groups, with 24 per cent living below the poverty line (a market-basket measure) in urban areas, almost double the 13.3 per cent poverty rate for the non-Indigenous population (Statistics Canada, 2020). On top of this long-standing income-inequality problem, the pandemic added disproportionate negative impacts on the economic well-being of the Indigenous population, making the Indigenous inequality problem even worse.

The political implications of excessive inequalities are accumulating, and the social mobilization efforts of interest groups and civil society organizations have amplified these pressures. There are three policy responses to these income-inequality problems. The first is to make the tax-and-transfer system more progressive and redistribute income towards the less well off. Research from the United States cautions that public support for progressive taxation is limited and that top tax rates have not changed much even as inequality has increased (Scheve & Stasavage, 2016). While it might seem rather paradoxical, research on a variety of countries reveals that, where income inequalities are perceived as large, there is actually less support for redistribution. What has come to be called "system justification motivation" posits that information about inequities prompts adjustment in what is deemed legitimate: if there are major inequities, they must be there for a reason (Trump, 2017). This form of status-quo thinking is not impervious to change. Significant shifts in tax policy are often the product of major crises – raising the intriguing possibility that COVID-19, much like wars and depressions, might prompt a compensatory rationale for redistribution: those who are harmed the most deserve special consideration. But these effects are rare. To persuade decisionmakers that compensation is justified would require "a compelling, concise, and unifying argument that succeeds in capturing the multiple inequalities that COVID-19 has exacerbated" (Scheve & Stasavage, 2020). So far, that argument has not emerged in Canada.

A second response to inequalities, one which has gained considerable traction, is to invest in the human capital and labour market preparedness of lower-income groups and so improve their ability to participate in the economy. The concept of "just transitions" is an implicit acknowledgment that the resource economy, which has buttressed the Canadian middle class (Milligan, 2018), will not be available forever. Which brings us to a third response – namely, to use tax-financed investment as a direct spur to growth, and hope that a growing economy will naturally improve, or even out, the incomes of different groups. Each of these strategies has strong advocates among Canada's economic elite, and each has appeared in recent federal budgets.

Much of what we recognize as ideological division in Canada turns on the relative importance of these options. Of course, they are not mutually exclusive. Note, however, that advocates of economic growth – including almost all members of the economic elite – are inclined to argue that dedicated growth strategies are the most attractive on the grounds that growth raises welfare levels for (just about) everyone. Put another way, it is easier to confront the challenge of dividing the pie if the pie is growing. but is it growing fast enough and in a way that will reduce inequalities?

The Complicated Relationship between Inequality and Economic Growth

For years, many economists accepted that increases in efficiency would result in less equality. The "big trade-off" was assumed to be inevitable; the real question was what kind of trade-off is politically acceptable? If rapid growth requires higher incomes for the highly productive, so that entrepreneurship is rewarded and economic dynamism nurtured, then inequality is the price we pay for prosperity. We are back to the neoclassical justification. And some research does suggest that the larger the share of income that goes to the highest-income earners, the higher the level of economic growth (Cingano, 2014; Voitchovsky, 2005).

In theory, high-income earners, who cannot consume all they earn, invest the remainder, and so generate benefits for the entire society. But low levels of income at the other end of the distribution are negatively correlated with economic growth. Those with extremely low incomes are deprived of the capacity to expand household demand or make human capital investments (Cingano, 2014). Weak household demand means firms lack the necessary motivation to invest in new technologies, while underinvestment in human capital reduces upward social mobility and dampens the economy's dynamism (Chetty et al., 2016).

Empirical assessments of the relationship between inequality and growth turn up contradictory findings. Depending on the time frame selected, the countries sampled, and the functional form of the model

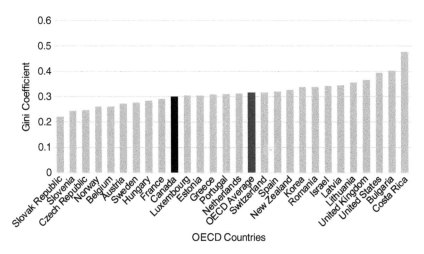

Figure 4.1. Gini Coefficients, Canada and Other OECD Countries, 2019
Source: Data from OECD (n.d.-d).

specified, researchers find that inequality is a spur to growth, inhibits growth, or has no effect at all. Barro (1999), for example, shows that from 1960 to 1995 higher levels of inequality reduced economic growth in relatively poor countries but encouraged growth in richer countries. It appears likely that relationships are non-linear, as Kuznets originally suggested, but finding the right, or unbiased, model for the relationship is exceptionally difficult (Banerjee & Duflo, 2003). Besides, inequality is at least partially endogenous to growth: changes in skill levels or improvements in capital markets will affect both inequality and growth. And growth is not just a function of inequalities. Natural endowments (like oil and gas) can be either positive or negative for growth. Much depends on the country involved and the measures taken to redistribute income.

Income inequality is commonly measured by the Gini index, also known as the Gini coefficient. A Gini index summarizes the distribution of income in an entire population and ranges between 0 in the case of perfect equality and 1 in the case of perfect inequality. The higher the Gini index, the higher the inequality of income distribution in a population. Compared with other OECD countries, income inequality in Canada is modest: in 2019, Canada's Gini index (0.301) was slightly below the average of the 27 OECD countries (see Figure 4.1) and much lower than that of the United States, which had a Gini index of 0.395.

These results might be somewhat reassuring, but it is shifts in income shares, not just overall levels of inequality, that are problematic for future growth and stability. The shift that has drawn the most commentary, both popular and academic, is the startling increase in incomes at the very top of the distribution, the so-called 1 per cent. Thomas Piketty and Emmanuel Saez (2003) outlined a pattern of growing income inequality in advanced economies beginning in the 1970s, particularly in the United States, which could be traced to significantly higher wages among those at the top of the income scale.

In Canada in the late 1970s, the top 1 per cent received approximately 8 per cent of total income; by the 2008 Great Financial Crisis that figure had blossomed to 14 per cent (Fortin et al., 2012). Well before that crisis, in the 1980s and the 1990s, incomes for the top 1 per cent, 0.1 per cent, and 0.01 per cent had surged (Veall, 2012). The share these high-income earners commanded began to increase in 1985 and, with a brief pause from 2008 to 2009, continued to rise in the years following. Much of the change in Canada's Gini index – from 0.395 in 1985 to 0.421 in 2019 – can be traced to the exponential rise in these high incomes.

The higher one ascends the income ladder, the faster the rate of increase – the growth rate for the 0.1 per cent, for example, is higher than for the 1 per cent (Osberg, 2018, p. 93; Yalnizyan, 2010). Apart from the eye-popping plutocratic paradise that has been created for the ultra-rich, the biggest systemic impact might simply be the instability that these upper-level gains have introduced into the income-distribution system as a whole. Before 1980, income shares across deciles were unequal but change was relatively stable. That stability has gone. We are now living in a period in which some incomes increase substantially while those of the majority languish. The gains generated by economic growth have gone heavily to a tiny sliver of the population.

This growth in income among the highest earners is not easy to explain. What is clear is that in Canada most of those in the top 1 per cent are older men who earn their income from work rather than investment. Looking at data from 2007, Yalnizyan (2010, p. 15) concluded: "Today the income of the richest 1% is due mostly to the lavish sums they are paid for the work they do." In the United States, economists speculate that weak corporate governance combined with a massive finance industry has driven up the highest incomes (Banerjee & Duflo, 2019), but in Canada high earners are a diverse group that includes senior managers, professionals, and, in all likelihood, some hockey players (Fortin et al., 2012, p. 128).

The explanation for changing patterns, not just at the highest levels but also among those in the stagnant middle, takes us into the realm of technological change and industrial organization. On the technology front, the rise in the premium for education, particularly post-secondary, accounted for about 70 per cent of the income dispersion in the United States between 1980 and 2005 (Goldin & Katz, 2007). In a modern, technology-driven economy, as the demand for cognitive skills increases, so too do the rewards. This simple formula is not an iron law, but it holds up well across OECD countries and helps explain rising levels of inequality in general (Autor, 2014).

But the bigger picture is the evolving economics of production in which capital substitutes for labour and competition is suppressed. Since 1988, growth in the economy has disproportionately advantaged corporate shareholders (as opposed to labour) (Greenwald et al., 2019). The labour share of income has remained low thanks to a combination of technology, globalization, and outsourcing. Machines and technologies improve efficiency in resource allocation but they also replace low-skilled labour. Technological advances tend to increase return on investments, but, coupled with globalization and outsourcing, they reduce the need for labour and hence the political power of unions. A growing concentration of market power among a few larger firms also leads to slower productivity growth and an increase in income inequality (Furman & Orszag, 2019). Companies that use online networks such as Amazon and Facebook attract millions of users to their platforms and eventually generate network effects and a demand for superstar employees whose compensation is far higher than it would be in a more competitive economy.

Capitalism is often modelled as a self-equilibrating system, but in recent years its disruptive and destructive propensities have been on full display. The resulting growth in income inequalities is a testament to the limitations of simply "growing the pie." For one thing, the pie isn't growing fast enough to reduce substantially relative differences in earned income. According to Osberg (2018, p. 233), it would take "an implausibly large acceleration of middle-class income growth" to get back to the inequality levels of 1982. Back then social mobility was a reasonable expectation. Now it is a promise that has become increasingly hollow.

The trick, then, is to keep inequality relatively low in the first place and avoid stranding those from low-income families in situations they cannot improve. Growth itself is unlikely to accomplish this task, so what about redistribution of income?

Traditional Programs that Tackle Inequality

Redistribution has had its enthusiasts, defenders, and critics, most of them organized around the different interpretations of inequality's origins discussed earlier. The question here is, can redistribution, as currently conceived, stabilize inequalities at a level tolerable from a moral perspective and efficient from an economic perspective?

Taxes, Transfers, and Gini Indexes

Gini indexes can give us the big picture of income distribution based on both market returns and income distribution before and after government policies aimed at sharing the benefits and the burdens of the modern economy. In Figure 4.2, the initial Gini index (the dark grey line) is based on adjusted market income. It includes pre-tax (or "pre-fisc") incomes derived from activities in the formal economy (salaried and hourly earnings, investment income, business and farm income, pensions) and excludes government transfer payments. The second Gini index (the lighter grey line) is based on adjusted total income that includes both market income and government income transfers but does not include the effects of taxation. The third Gini index, called the post-tax (or "post-fisc") Gini index, is based on income after the effects of both transfers and taxes (the dashed line).

In Canada, the pattern in these three Gini indices followed similar trends from 1980 to 2019. They rose at the beginning of the 1990s (indicating increasing inequality) and slightly declined from 2013 to 2019 (indicating slightly decreasing inequality). The difference between the pre- and post-fisc Gini indices reflects the level of income redistribution attained through tax- and-transfer programs. In 2019, the post-tax Gini index was at 0.30, much lower than the initial Gini index based on only market income (the dark line), at 0.42. A 0.12 difference between the two Gini indices indicates a substantial (29 per cent) income redistribution effect from Canadian tax-and-transfer systems. As Figure 4.2 shows, income transfers play a bigger role than progressive taxation in redistributing income and reducing income inequality. Of the 29 per cent reduction in income inequality, twice as much was attributable to the effects of income-transfer programs (the distance between the dark grey and the lighter grey lines) than was attributable to taxation (the distance between the lighter grey and dashed lines).

What can we infer from the overall pattern? First, tax-and-transfer programs make a real difference in reducing income inequities, but despite numerous changes to eligibility criteria and program generosity, there has been little progress over several decades in closing the remaining inequality gap. Second, some things have changed. For example, there has been a general retreat from universalism in the delivery of social programs and greater support for targeted assistance (Boadway & Cuff, 2013). Targeted assistance is generally an employment initiative, not a welfare strategy: it is intended to remove impediments to labour

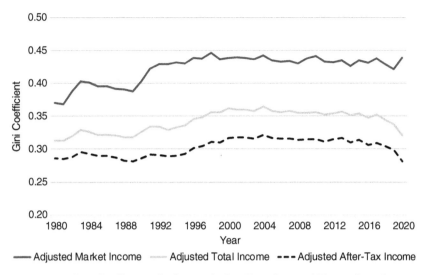

Figure 4.2. Gini Coefficients before and after Transfers and Taxes, Canada,
1980–2020
Source: Statistics Canada (2021b). Contains information licensed under the Open
Government Licence – Canada.

force participation and the acquisition of skills among specific groups
in the population.

As for taxes, the graduated marginal income tax rate in Canada flat-
tened in the 1980s as protections for savings – for example, registered
retirement plans – increased. Inheritance taxes largely disappeared,
and the top marginal tax rate for high-income earners dropped steadily
from 80 per cent in 1971 to 57 per cent in 1987 and to a low of 55 per cent
(depending upon province of residence) in 2019. Meanwhile, Canada's
social spending – "cash benefits, direct in-kind provision of goods and
services, and tax breaks with social purposes" (OECD, n.d.-f) – remains
below the OECD average. As a share of GDP, Canada's social spending
was 17.2 per cent in 2012 and grew to 18 per cent in 2018. The OECD
average in 2019 was 20 per cent (OECD, n.d.-f).

A second observation concerns the most recent decline in market
inequality and post-fisc inequality reflected in the slight dip in Gini
scores since 2016. Effective 1 January 2016, the Liberal government implemented a series of tax-and-transfer reforms, including the creation
of a new top-income bracket above $200,000 taxed at a marginal rate of
33 per cent. Meanwhile, the marginal federal tax rate was reduced from

22 per cent to 20.5 per cent on incomes between $45,282 and $90,563 (Canada, 2015). Most important, a new Canada Child Benefit was introduced in July 2016 to replace a suite of child- and family-related benefits including income splitting, the Universal Child Care Benefit, and several boutique tax credits (Prime Minister of Canada, 2016). The federal government also reduced the tax shelter room available to high-income earners by returning the annual contribution limit to Tax-Free Savings Accounts from $10,000 to its previous level of $5,500. These measures made the tax-and-transfer system more progressive and contributed to a reduction in both poverty and income inequality.

Gini indexes give an overall impression, but what effect did these policy changes have on incomes at the very top, the middle, and the bottom? Appreciating the impact of tax-and-transfer policies on specific income categories requires assumptions about tax incidence, units of observation (families or individuals), and the comparability of data sources. That said, most countries have made multiple changes to their tax-and-transfer programs to blunt the impact of increases in pre-tax income inequality. Across the wealthy democracies, with the exception of the United States, the rich are paying more taxes, while government transfers to those with middle and lower incomes have increased (Elkjær & Iversen, 2022). Recent work on the United States finds tax-based redistribution erases some of the differences in income growth among the lowest 50 per cent, but does not touch the upper reaches of the income distribution, where imputed tax rates are lower than they are for many low-income earners (Piketty et al., 2018).

In Canada, from 1995 to 2005, taxes restored some equity in incomes for those at the bottom of the distribution, but at the top taxes failed to close the gap between high-income earners and those in the middle (Milligan, 2013). A more recent analysis of average tax rates shows that Canada's income tax rates are progressive overall, with some significant caveats at different income levels. The Buffett rule – Warren Buffett should pay more taxes than his secretary – is respected: high earners have higher tax rates than middle-income earners (Milligan, 2022). But the details, especially the effects of taxes on the 1 per cent and 0.1 per cent income categories, show an uneven impact.

The final column in Table 4.1 reveals that, in Canada from 2005 to 2019, both pre-tax and post-tax Gini indices declined. The post-tax Gini index decreased more than the pre-tax index, suggesting that taxes and transfers were more progressive in 2019 than in 2005. But from the fiftieth to the ninetieth percentiles, the impact was in the opposite direction: The tax-and-transfer system left those in the fiftieth percentile worse off than those in the ninetieth. Both the top 0.1 per cent and the top 1 per

Table 4.1. Income Inequality and Degree of Income Redistribution, Canada, 2005 and 2019

Income Inequality	Pre-Tax	Post-Tax	Pre-Tax	Post-Tax	Pre-Tax	Post-Tax	% of Changes in Pre-Tax Gini, Undone (−) or Added (+) by Taxes and Transfers
	2005		2019		Change		
Gini	0.44	0.32	0.42	0.30	−0.01	−0.02	+29
P90–P50	0.54	0.39	0.52	0.38	−0.02	−0.01	−33
Top 1% share	13	9.3	11.6	7.9	−1.4	−1.4	0
Top 0.1% share	5	3.4	4	2.6	−1	−0.8	−20

Source: Statistics Canada (2021a). Contains information licensed under the Open Government Licence – Canada.

cent of income earners in Canada had a smaller share of total income in 2019 compared with 2005, suggesting no growth in income concentration at the top over this period. But again, note that the tax-and-transfer system undid 20 per cent of the improved income concentration at the top 0.1 per cent level. Put differently, after the effects of the tax-and-transfer system, the top 0.1 per cent income earner group had a larger share of total post-tax income than total pre-tax income (Milligan, 2022).

There is good reason for paying attention to the top 1 per cent of income earners: over the past 20 years this is where changes have been the most acute and where the tax-and-transfer system seems least effective from an inequality mitigation perspective. Here, at both the federal and particularly the provincial levels (Quebec excepted), the tax-and-transfer system has become less progressive and more selective. For example, despite rate increases on the highest incomes in 2016, research shows that revenues from the wealthiest taxpayers actually declined following the reforms. Why? Because it is these taxpayers who are most able to reduce their taxable income by legal tax planning and tax-avoidance measures (Deslauriers et al., 2020).

Protection of the income of high earners has been a de facto policy. What about the neediest in society? Have concerns about growing inequality resulted in policy responses aimed at them?

Poverty-Reduction Measures

The relationship between poverty and inequality is not as straightforward as it might appear. Although inequality has been growing in Canada, poverty levels have not. Popular means of defining poverty typically rely on income measures, but because income-inequality measures are dominated by the non-poor, in principle it would be possible to eliminate poverty without reducing overall inequality (Osberg, 2000). Alternatively, efforts to reduce income inequality will not automatically reduce poverty. Poverty-reduction measures need to be targeted, generous, and effective. They depend on the conviction that, rather than simply reducing Gini scores, the most pressing moral imperative is to relieve those who are either comparatively, or absolutely, among the most needy in society.

Still, the state of poverty in most countries is estimated using metrics such as Statistics Canada's low-income cut-off (LICO) and the low-income measure (LIM) to establish how many people are below the poverty line. The LIM, for example, is adjusted for family size and set at half the after-tax median income. In 2020 13.3 per cent of Canadians lived below this poverty line (Statistics Canada, 2022a). Compared with other OECD countries, Canada is at about the mid-point, but this level of poverty has been harshly criticized, and Canada has been described as "stuck near the bottom of the pack in combating poverty" (Banting & Myles, 2013, p. 29). Real welfare incomes do not rise to the level of these poverty lines, and minimum wage laws do not guarantee a living wage.

The provinces, in particular, have embraced what has been described as a "tough love" approach based on welfare-to-work programming (Richards, 2010). While there are provincial differences in levels of support, minimum-income policies in the provinces are among the least generous in the OECD. And it does not matter which party is in power or whether formal poverty-reduction strategies are in place (Noël, 2020). Small changes, such as increased support for lone parents, have been successful in reducing poverty rates, but the overall picture is far from optimistic (Richards, 2010). Among the major impediments that remain is inadequate housing for the mentally ill or addicted.

Of course, incremental program additions and adjustments can have a cumulative effect. Public contributory pensions, Old Age Security, and the Guaranteed Income Supplement have gone a long way towards reducing poverty among the elderly (Béland & Marier, 2022). In the 2000s, child poverty rates in Canada were two to four times higher than in Scandinavia and continental Europe. Those rates have come down significantly with the introduction of the Canada Child Tax Benefit in 1997 and its extension, the Canada Child Benefit, in 2016. In 2017, the first full year of the benefit, about 9 per cent of children under 18 years of age lived below the poverty line, representing a significant

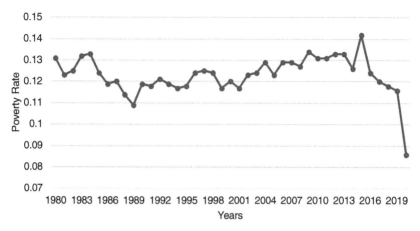

Figure 4.3. Poverty Rate, Canada, 1980–2020
Source: Data from OECD (n.d.-e).

drop from 11 per cent in 2016 (Statistics Canada, 2019). Described as "super-progressive" (Boadway & Cuff, 2013, p. 353), refundable tax credits contributed to a decline in poverty rates among children from 17.5 per cent in 1995 to 10.6 per cent in 2018 (Statistics Canada, 2022b). Although income-redistribution programs have not kept pace with increases in market-based inequality, they have had an impact on poverty rates overall. Figure 4.3 shows that the poverty rate (LIM) in Canada declined in the 1980s, climbed after 1990, and has declined sharply since 2016.

But poverty is not simply a fiscal policy problem. Much of the mitigation of poverty requires the provision of supports for vulnerable populations as well as augmentation of their incomes. Here, Canadian liberalism is of limited assistance. The retreat from universal programs does not mean retreat from universalism as the ideational foundation of the Canadian welfare state. Special arrangements for Indigenous peoples, for example, are met with a measure of hostility in the non-Indigenous community (White et al., 2015) and attitudes towards welfare support are conditioned by negative racial stereotypes (Harell et al., 2014). Because racial inequalities are not the object of income-redistribution policies, racialized communities are left with relatively weak policy instruments (Banting & Thompson, 2021). Meanwhile, social policy advocates continue to take aim at broad distributive justice problems, including one that has often been overlooked: expanding differences in wealth.

Inequalities in Wealth

The idea that concentrations of wealth are part of the dynamics of capitalism and that returns to capital normally will outpace returns to labour (Piketty, 2014) has renewed interest in the accumulation of wealth and its consequences. Wealth is measured as the net worth that an entity possesses – that is, individual or family financial and non-financial assets minus total liabilities. As with income inequalities, wealth inequalities need some justification. From the neoclassical perspective, voluntary exchange in competitive markets should place assets in the hands of those who can best use them, regardless of their wealth. As long as that happens, wealth concentration need not be a problem. But this fortuitous outcome is seldom realized. If wealth concentration limits access to credit, for example, fewer productive projects are undertaken. And if the owners of wealth create barriers to its redistribution, by offshoring assets in tax havens or lobbying sympathetic politicians to secure tax advantages, resources are used up rent seeking rather than innovating or investing.

What seems more settled is the idea that increasing wealth concentration is a political phenomenon as much as an economic one. Wealth inequality, in other words, is unlikely to decline as a result of market exchange. Politics in the form of institutional impediments to change and incentives for the rich to exercise their influence mean that the affluent have far more impact upon policy change than do average citizens (Gilens & Page, 2014). The cumulative effects show up in the growth of wealth inequalities across a wide range of countries over the past several decades. Although this growth has been described as "mild" (Zucman, 2019, p. 21), it has been accompanied by an increase in offshore holdings that makes it difficult to estimate overall concentration.

Reporting gaps make reliable wealth data difficult to come by, but wealth survey data show that in Canada the shares of the top 0.1 per cent, 0.5 per cent, 1 per cent, and 5 per cent all increased from 1970 to 2012 (Davies & Di Matteo, 2021). Wealth inequalities in Canada have been on a similar trajectory to those in the United States, but the levels of inequality are different. Wealth inequality in the United States is much greater than in Canada and other OECD countries. Figure 4.4 shows both income inequality in adjusted disposal income (that is, post-fisc income) and inequality in net wealth among households in Canada compared with selected OECD countries that have comparable data.

In this case, inequality is measured by comparing the ratio of mean to median income (or wealth) in each country. When income (or wealth) is concentrated among a smaller share of households, the mean is

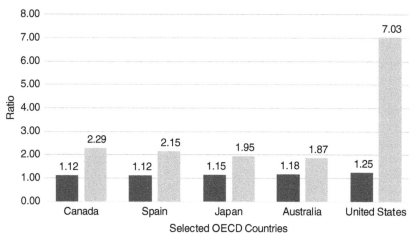

Figure 4.4. Inequality in Income versus Inequality in Wealth, Selected OECD Countries, Fiscal Year 2018/19
Source: Data from OECD (n.d.-c).

normally greater than the median. The higher the mean-to-median ratio, the greater the degree of inequality. Figure 4.4 shows that, in fiscal year 2018/19, Canada had the lowest post-fisc income inequality among five comparator countries, but inequality in net wealth in Canada was slightly higher than in Spain, Japan, and Australia. The United States is the outlier: there, inequality in net wealth was more than three times wealth inequality in other countries.

One consequence of inequality in income and wealth is reduced intergenerational mobility – that is, the ability of individuals to move up the social ladder from the rung occupied by their parents. As inequality increases, intergenerational mobility decreases – the so-called Great Gatsby curve (Nolan & Valenzuela, 2019). The phenomenon is not uniform across all countries (Corak, 2013). In the United States, intergenerational mobility has declined since 1940 (Chetty et al., 2016). At age 30, around 90 per cent of people born in 1940 earned more than their parents when they were the same age, but this rate fell to 50 per cent for people born in the 1980s. In Canada, the intergenerational mobility for individuals born between 1970 and 1984 has remained relatively stable (Ostrovsky, 2017). At age 30, about 59 per cent of people born in 1970 earned the same as or more than their parents at the same age.

For those born a decade later, from 1979 to 1984, this rate increased slightly, ranging between 64 per cent and 66 per cent.

Although the effects of the COVID-19 pandemic are only now being estimated, the fiscal response to the pandemic likely affected both income inequality and wealth inequality in Canada. Some households survived the pandemic only because of government income assistance. More than one-quarter (28.3 per cent) of Canadians ages 15 to 69 reported having received some kind of federal income assistance since the beginning of the pandemic and claimed that these pandemic relief benefits offset the decline in family income (Statistics Canada, 2021i). On the other hand, some households' income and assets emerged largely intact or even expanded during the pandemic. Many properties changed hands, and house prices soared during the initial stages of the pandemic, eroding affordability for potential buyers.

Alternative Proposals on Inequality

Tax and transfers and investments in human capital are the major policy tools to battle income inequality. But traditional tax-and-transfer programs based on pre-tax income levels are not sufficient to address all of the emerging inequality problems. For example, while the real value of the minimum wage increased between 1998 and 2018, the proportion of employees earning the minimum wage in Canada grew from 5.2 per cent to 10.4 per cent (Dionne-Simard & Miller, 2019). More than 30 per cent of households in Canada live "hand to mouth," and about two-thirds of these households belong to the middle class (Hotchkiss, 2014). Plus, the labour market is changing, and the management of income and wealth in households is taking new forms. To be effective, policies aimed at reducing inequalities need to reach beyond post-market income redistribution and pay attention to the dynamics of the labour market, lifecycle needs, and patterns of wealth distribution.

As the economic consequences of the pandemic came into sharper focus, two long-standing ideas about mitigating inequalities – a wealth tax and a Universal Basic Income – received renewed attention. The sudden reversal of economic growth was a reminder that trickle-down prosperity was an unlikely path to greater equality, at least in the short term. Perhaps those at the very top of the prosperity pyramid might offer more to everyone else. And perhaps everyone else should be given some form of certainty about their economic future, rather than rely on rapid-response efforts from the state.

A Universal Basic Income

At the beginning of the pandemic, the universal Canada Emergency Response Benefit protected incomes and reduced income inequality. The process of claiming and receiving the CERB gave individuals a taste of a universal, unconditional welfare program. It also ignited speculation that the CERB would pave a road towards a permanent Universal Basic Income (UBI). A senior public servant we interviewed observed that "the CERB, that's $2,000 a month, and that's a basic income that's probably going to end up staying. It's very efficient. It was very fast, it's almost as automatic as you can get ... if they created it in an elastic way, it's only as big as the economy needs it to be. Which is exactly what you'd hope for [in] an automatic stabilizer" [Economist 17].

Enthusiasm about the concept of a basic income has been growing for several years. To be clear, a UBI is an income paid unconditionally to every individual in society. There is no means testing and no work requirement. On the surface it appears rather hard to justify. For the able-bodied to live off the efforts of the industrious offends some commonsense ideas of distributive justice. And yet many efforts have been made to justify just such an arrangement. Some are prudential, arguing that opportunities for full-time employment will become increasingly scarce as robots and artificial intelligence reduce the need for all but the most refined of technological skills. According to some predictions, in the "second machine age" (Brynjolfsson & McAfee, 2014), the right to income will need to be divorced from the need to work to avoid massive inequalities (Straubhaar, 2017). Put this way, a UBI appears as an efficient response to the growing gap between those with valued human capital and those relegated to "bullshit jobs" (Graeber, 2018).

Philosophical justifications for a UBI are more elaborate and seem to unite social critics from a variety of ideological perspectives. One of the most influential arguments is based on the libertarian idea that individuals should be empowered to decide the kind of life they want to live. A UBI would facilitate this kind of freedom. In terms of distributive justice, Van Parijs (1991) argues that a guaranteed income would meet a Rawlsian maximin criterion, "giving real freedom to those with the least of it," including careless Malibu surfers (Rawls's example of the undeserving). This argument has little to do with eliminating poverty. Whatever inequalities might be reduced by a guaranteed income for all, it "is not exclusively nor ultimately about the distribution of income or consumption power. It is about the power to decide what sort of life one wants to live" (Van Parijs, 2013, p. 174)

In Canada, the economic elite is not persuaded. In discussing the idea of a UBI, most of our interviewees rejected the concept on economic grounds or argued that it is politically infeasible. Chief among the economic objections is the view that a UBI would create serious labour disincentives. Here is one example: "The Quebec government had announced that they would give money to students that would accept to go and work in the field instead of these foreign workers that could not come in [because of COVID-19 restrictions]. Suddenly the federal government announced that they were going to give money to students anyway, whether they worked or not. Nobody went and worked in the field" [Bureaucrat 18]. And in an echo of the careless surfer meme, another respondent combined economic and philosophical objections: "Always in the back of my mind is: why should we give money to some guys who are just playing guitar, smoking dope somewhere in their rooms with a couple of friends? That makes me a bit annoyed" [Economist 10].

In the same vein, members of the economic elite, along with others who prefer a job guarantee to an income guarantee, are typically pro-work: "The notion that – and you see a lot of this coming out of Silicon Valley – basically, we're going to take the peasants' work away from them. Let's mollify them with a UBI, and I just think it's a terrible implicit philosophy. People don't get their meaning from life from a cheque in the mail. They get their meaning from making a contribution to society" [Bureaucrat 30]. The idea of a meaningful contribution as a condition of receiving a guaranteed employment is central to Anthony Atkinson's proposal for a "participation income." "'Participation' would be defined broadly in terms of social contribution, which for those of working age could be fulfilled by full- or part-time waged employment or self-employment, by education, training, or active job search" (Atkinson, 2014, p. 633). In other words, participation, not citizenship, would be the requirement. And because employment might be difficult to acquire, a participation income could be augmented by an offer of guaranteed employment at a living wage. A contribution requirement would meet some of the philosophical objections to a UBI, and its defenders argue that a job guarantee would help stabilize the business cycle, reduce inequalities, and strengthen the hand of labour (Kelton, 2020).

It would not, however, meet all the objections to a UBI, one of which is its affordability, or lack thereof. Assuming a UBI were set at a level sufficient to address poverty concerns, for some the high cost of the program would be enough to rule it out, even if benefit reduction rates were imposed. As one economist put it, "If we had economic growth like the nineteen fifties, sixties, maybe that would be doable, but if you look at the projections ... that's not really there" [Economist 2]. The most extensive assessment of a UBI in Canada, carried out under the auspices of the British Columbia Expert Panel on Basic Income, concluded that, even if all the (many) objections to it in principle could be answered, the province was not in a sufficiently robust fiscal position to take on what the Panel believed would be substantial extra costs. As the report puts it, "even a modest UBI would be very difficult to accommodate fiscally" (Green et al., 2020, p. 365). For example, to absorb the entire cost of a UBI high enough to reduce poverty significantly, personal income tax in British Columbia would need to double. A strategy of eliminating tax credits to help defray the costs would introduce distortions and still leave some citizens in need of special assistance.

As much as the universal character of a basic income is an attractive feature, targeted funding in the form of specific assistance for at-risk groups would still be needed. Without these assists, a UBI would dilute the income assistance received by those in need, who could likely end up receiving less support under a UBI than under current targeted programs. In addition, a UBI, as an income-replacement program, could not provide the in-kind transfers or other forms of assistance that serve specialized needs. One of our respondents expressed the concern in these terms: "Many people argue against basic income for lots of reasons, it costs too much, it's inefficient, whatever. Those might all be true but to me the fundamental argument against it, is it's a bad deal for those who are in greatest need. If you were a kid that has a disability, under provincial social assistance programs, you can get disability support, you get a wheelchair" [Economist 13].

Critics of Canada's response to inequalities describe current efforts as piecemeal, fragmented, and uninspired, but most of our interviewees do not share this view. In fact, the incrementalism decried by some is seen by others as an asset: "Canada's governments have always been incremental in their approach, and we elect politicians who are incrementalists, if not less than incrementalists. From the left to the right, we elect institutional conservatives. That's my opinion. Nobody's going to blow up our system" [Economist 21]. The myriad programs designed to provide relief to particular communities and cohorts in distress act as insurance against wholesale change. Federalism does the same: "I don't think we will ever have [a] guaranteed basic income, fundamentally because we are a confederation. It is so hard to get consensus at the FPT [federal, provincial, territorial] level ... What share of the cost of that program should be federal versus provincial? What about the territories? ... Have or have-not provinces? ... Those constant battles at federal-provincial level complexities make it so hard" [Bureaucrat 15].

In short, members of Canada's economic elite are disinclined to wander too far from the status quo. They offer a host of objections to a UBI, most of them practical and several of them fiscal, and suggest that much the same (positive) effects could be achieved by expanding refundable tax credits and improving the coverage and conditionality of existing programs, including Employment Insurance. This does not mean the push for a UBI has failed to stir some rethinking. Although the conversation about a UBI might not have persuaded decisionmakers to jump into a major overhaul of social welfare, it has prompted active consideration of how the existing tax credit system might be redesigned to make a dramatic impact on poverty and income inequality (Stevens & Simpson, 2017). As one of our interviewees observed, "We could do an awful lot of good by taking a look at the systems that we've got and thinking about what are the elements of UBI that people like? It's sort of its simplicity, its non-stigmatizing entry points, its adequacy of benefit levels, its autonomy of the beneficiary recipients, its reduction of some of the conditionality in terms of ... what the income is supposed to be used for" [Economist 18].

A Wealth Tax?

Much like the idea of a Universal Basic Income, wealth taxes have acquired new currency. They featured prominently in the 2020 US presidential campaign, and they are being debated in several European countries where they were previously abandoned. Taxes on assets are not uncommon. Many jurisdictions tax the sale of capital assets, for example, and inheritance taxes are common in most OECD countries. These taxes are progressive, and a wealth tax would be even more so, in part because a wealth tax is normally a recurrent tax on a stock, which means the same assets are taxed every year. And the idea is very popular. In 2020 an Abacus poll found that 80 per cent of Canadians surveyed supported a 1 per cent tax on assets of more than $20 million (Anderson & Coletto, 2020).

Despite their current popularity among members of the public, and in certain political parties, wealth taxes do not exist everywhere. In a sample of 45 countries, researchers found wealth taxes had been tried at one point or another in half of them, unlike income taxes, which are found everywhere (Limberg & Seelkopf, 2022). Wealth taxes appear to augment income and consumption taxes, rather than invariably join them in a comprehensive tax system. They also wax and wane in popularity. Both Denmark and France, for example, employed wealth taxes for years, but abandoned them in the 1990s, just as other countries were introducing them. Their introduction is typically prompted by "emergency" fiscal needs brought on by a recession. If the alternatives – more borrowing or expenditure reduction – are difficult or unpopular, wealth taxes, with their highly progressive qualities, suddenly become politically attractive (Papadia & Truchlewski, 2022).

The economic case for wealth taxes takes us back to the dynamics of inequality in capitalist systems. Since income and wealth inequality are endogenous in an economy, the market cannot be expected to fix the inequality problem itself. And if rapid income growth and wealth accumulation of the top 1 per cent income earners impede economic growth (Piketty, 2014), a tax on wealth acquires new legitimacy. Thomas Piketty has recommended a globally harmonized wealth tax that could be as low as 0.1 per cent or as high as 2 per cent – "global" because of the incentive to move wealth to low-tax jurisdictions.

Such a proposal likely would appear radical and utopian in Canada, which has never experimented with the concept. Certainly, it appears to offend a basic principle of a market economy – namely, the sanctity of property rights. Economists Persson and Tabellini (1994, p. 617) make the theoretical case that wealth taxes are harmful because they "do not protect property rights and do not allow full private appropriation of returns from investment." Others object on practical grounds: a wealth tax would discourage capital investment or prompt capital flight, although there is limited evidence of this kind of effect (Jakobsen et al., 2019). In any case, collecting data on wealth is difficult and subject to strenuous efforts to exempt certain asset classes. Administration and compliance issues are said to be at the heart of European decisions to abandon wealth taxes, although avoidance and evasion patterns likely depend on compliance effort.

If these problems could be overcome, would a wealth tax make sense in Canada? Given their lack of enthusiasm for a UBI, it will not come as a surprise to learn that among members of Canada's economic elite, there is also little enthusiasm for a wealth tax. The objections are partly on principle: once income is taxed, it should not be taxed again as wealth. "Income earned is taxed by income tax. Once income is earned and taxed, individuals should be able to make decisions on how to use the income. A wealth tax is levied on the accumulated savings and will distort decisions" [Economist 11]. The practical objections are also familiar: wealth is difficult to estimate and wealth taxes are easy to avoid. Here is how one interviewee summed up the case: "Wealth taxes have largely been failures in almost every country they've been rolled out in ... They are easy to plan around, very easy to plan around in most countries. The assets are very difficult to value in many cases. You're talking about things that are often luxury assets, like artwork, that are very difficult to come to a specific price on" [Economist 5]. Although estimates are hard to come by, a wealth tax starting at $20 million might not raise large amounts of money, especially if principal residences were exempt. Again, the point is made: "Canadians have wealth, in the form of their house and their retirement assets ... If you exclude those you're not left with a lot. The revenue to be secured is actually quite modest, but the main issues are around the fact that the assets are illiquid and for most people an annual wealth tax is a real hardship because you don't have any liquidity associated with those assets" [Economist 5].

For these and other reasons, economists in Canada have responded to the idea of wealth taxes with proposals for reforming the existing tax system instead. In much the same way that the economic elite has suggested alternatives to a UBI, tax specialists have suggested reforming the capital income tax and introducing an inheritance tax (Boadway & Pestieau, 2019). In Canada, capital gains are heavily concentrated among high-income earners: between 2014 and 2018, about 72 per cent of capital gains went to families in the top 10 per cent of the long-run income distribution and 41 per cent to those in the top 1 per cent (Smart & Jafry, 2022). Because the top 1 per cent has a large share of capital gains in their income, the actual average tax rate for that group bends down – that is, the average tax rate on the top 1 per cent of income earners is actually lower than the average tax rate of those who earn slightly less than the top 1 per cent earners.

In this context, simply increasing the top marginal income tax rate on the top 1 per cent would not improve the progressivity of the tax system, but reforming the tax treatment of capital income could. The inclusion of only 50 per cent of capital gains as taxable income costs $35 billion annually in forgone government revenues. If the inclusion rate were raised to 80 per cent, governments could raise more tax revenue than a 1 per cent wealth tax on individual wealth portfolios in excess of $20 million (Smart & Jafry, 2022). In short, there are other ways to raise revenue that might be more effective and less distortionary than a wealth tax.

As for the politics of a wealth tax, despite its obvious popularity in the abstract, there are political risks. One interviewee put it bluntly: "The only way the Liberals could lose Toronto is putting a tax on capital gains on homes without putting a million- or two-million-dollar floor" [Politician 12]. The same respondent also pointed out that a wealth tax with a politically acceptable floor would not generate much revenue.

In sum, for practical purposes at least, the economic elite is open to reform of taxes on capital gains, but nervous about, and even hostile towards, wealth taxes.

Social Investment

If inequality is not to be tackled with a new Universal Basic Income program or confiscatory wealth taxes, is there no room for innovation? That would be too bleak a conclusion, and on the strength of Canada's track record of policy change, a premature one. An unmistakable sense of policy drift accompanies incrementalism, but recessions, even brief pandemic-sparked ones, can create opportunities for new programs, especially if they can be connected to labour market needs and life-course transitions. But new opportunities require new ideas about inequality and Canada's social architecture. Rather than framing inequality as a problem of redistribution in the here and now, a more encompassing approach would focus on resilience and sustainability over a lifetime in a competitive knowledge economy.

This approach to inequality has been described as a "social investment paradigm" (Banting, 2006; Hemerijck, 2018). It emphasizes human capital formation with attention to lifetime education and critical transitions – from school to work, from work to child rearing, from one job to another, from employment to retirement. This social investment focus places less emphasis on ameliorating existing inequalities and more on stifling inequalities that emerge from lack of attention to future capacity. Of particular importance are policies aimed at children – not just poor children, but also parents who are experiencing employment instability, work-life imbalance, and inadequate income (Jenson & Saint-Martin, 2006). This shift in the framing of social policy, it must be emphasized, did not originate with the pandemic, although its stresses undoubtedly underscored the need for long-term, holistic approaches to work and family. Even during the days of redistribution retrenchment, a social investment agenda had been established in Canada and other OECD countries (Jenson, 2013), where it appealed to those interested in reducing, or trimming, income-support programs in favour of a human capital strategy that places more responsibility in the hands of recipients (Banting, 2006).

In keeping with the spirit of social investment, the Trudeau government, in its first post-pandemic budget in April 2021, announced spending up to $30 billion over five years to create a national childcare system. Creating a mega social program in the midst of a recession is the policy equivalent of defying gravity. It is also, however, part of an emerging pattern that clearly connects social policy to economic development. As a national program, it is designed to provide Canadian parents with, on average, $10-a-day regulated childcare spaces for children under six years old. Under such a program, parents can save between $2,600 and $9,400 per year per child, depending on the province in which they reside (Department of Finance Canada, 2021c).

The program, supporters and critics note, shares many of the features of the Quebec childcare program. In 1997, the Quebec government introduced a childcare program that heavily subsidizes licensed childcare providers. Initially, parents paid a daily fee of $5 per child, increased by 2021 to $8.50 per child. In major cities outside Quebec, parents pay as much as six times the Quebec rate. In 1998, Quebec had the second-lowest labour market participation rate for women with young children (ages 3–5) in Canada, with just 67 per cent working outside the home. By 2014, this number had risen to 82 per cent, the second-highest in the country (Mohamed, 2022). Research confirms that the Quebec daycare program has had a statistically significant and positive effect on maternal labour supply and earnings (Baker et al., 2008; Lefebvre & Merrigan, 2008).

Some of our interviewees observed that the federal childcare initiative, because it is modelled on Quebec's program, represents a windfall for the province: "Quebec's happy to take the money. Why would you want to create another program where the provinces deliver the goods and you have to collect the taxes to pay for it when you've already got in hand a direct federal government transfer to households in the child tax benefit" [Politician 10]. This objection – more federal programming in difficult fiscal times – was met by the argument that Quebec's fiscal turnaround had its roots in precisely this kind of social investment. One of our interviewees pointed out: "Look at Quebec and the way they have dealt with daycare. They made it available, inexpensive, and boosted female [labour] participation hugely. That economic growth is what made their fiscal situation so much stronger than everyone else's. It'll do it for Canada, too ... It's going to cost billions, right? It will pay for itself in no time" [Economist 17].

In our interviews, few criticized the basic goal of subsidized daycare given the country's weak track record on childcare. Here it seems is an idea whose time has come. Put differently, the post-pandemic electorate was judged to be in the mood for a major investment in human capital. As one interviewee put it, "Women in the work force, that's been a real takeaway from this crisis. That's where you've seen a bit of a policy shift. The childcare package that came in through the recent budget was something that Paul Martin had tried to do in 2005 and there just

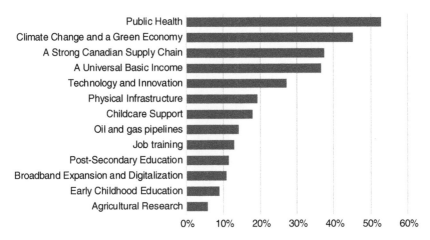

Figure 4.5. Survey Respondents' Top Three Spending Priorities
Source: Atkinson and Mou (2021).

wasn't the appetite for it. Now, public sentiment has shifted, and the government's priorities have shifted" [Bureaucrat 21].

Mind you, governments are not simply reflecting public sentiment; they are also creating it. In our January 2021 survey, completed months before the announcement of the childcare policy in the April 2021 budget, our respondents were asked to choose the *top three* priorities worthy of additional public funding from among 13 possibilities. Figure 4.5 shows the percentage of respondents who chose each area as one of their top three spending priorities.

Less than 20 per cent selected childcare support as one of their top three, and less than 10 per cent picked early childhood education. They had other things on their mind, and to be fair the April 2021 budget had other things in it. What is impressive about the childcare initiative is not its embrace by the public, but its endorsement by the economic elite itself. For an economist we interviewed, it is a political assessment with an economic payoff: "Government says we're going to invest in early childhood education. I think their heart is in long-term productivity ... both in terms of women's participation in the labour force and in terms of childhood development" [Economist 21].

Many of the economic elite made similar observations. Childcare and early childhood education are not just matters of social justice; they are also matters of economic prosperity. Whether they are likely to produce much lift in growth is an important (and understudied) question. Quebec's miraculous public finance turnaround is often singled out as evidence for the positive labour market effects of publicly funded childcare, but it is not clear that these kinds of policies are capable of reversing other stronger, demographic trends, such as population aging. It is more likely that a tightening labour market will force up wages and affect how the national economic surplus is divided. In other words, labour market policies like public childcare assistance can facilitate beneficial transitions, but it is easy to exaggerate their likely effect on levels of economic growth, especially in the short term.

Conclusion

When compared with other OECD countries, Canada's level of income inequality is close to the median, but it shares with others a rapid rise in inequality at the upper-income levels. As important as the pandemic is for other aspects of fiscal policy, it is not tied directly to changes in the income distribution. A seemingly inexorable increase in the earnings of those at the top of the income pyramid predates the pandemic. It also seems to have paralysed decisionmakers. Crises might provoke reconsideration of fundamentals, but the problem of inequality is particularly stubborn. Serious efforts to clamp down on tax avoidance and to create globally harmonized tax regimes have only just begun. Whether they will reverse the current trend is difficult to predict, but inequality certainly has grabbed the attention of Canada's economic elite, and not just for social justice reasons. The effects of inequality on growth are largely unknown, but the risks are profound. For example, it seems clear that growing inequality in wealth reduces intergenerational mobility, which in turn creates social and political risks. How much economic inequality we can tolerate depends on a combination of moral intuition and prudential calculation.

Controlling inequality requires interventions at both the top and lower ends of the income distribution. As for top-income earners, few among the economic elite we sampled thought a wealth tax should be considered, both because of its political sensitivity and because of the practical problems of implementation. Recent research suggests that increasing the effective income tax rate on capital gains is a better alternative than a wealth tax. However, just like any tax on capital, an increase in the capital gains tax would be subject to the threats of capital outflow or an increase in tax avoidance.

As for lower-income earners, the pandemic has stirred interest in bold new universal programs for several reasons, such as ease of application and absence of stigma, but a Universal Basic Income program is unlikely to gain much traction because of its costs and the implicit requirement to dismantle existing targeted programs. A basic income program also invokes a clash of ideologies and moral judgments about the deservedness of help and meaningfulness of work. Until Canadians are ready to have an open dialogue on these issues, we do not anticipate a universal income assistance program. Much more likely is a stealth approach in which the need for revenues, not just the need for equity, stirs governments to reform the current tax system.

The pandemic has also sensitized decisionmakers to the supply side of the economy, especially the need for physical and human capital investment. Providing a mix of taxes and spending that reduces inequalities by addressing supply-side deficiencies is the new post-pandemic task. Most of our interviewees applauded the child tax benefit and national childcare program launched by the federal government. These initiatives were perceived to fill the gaps in our current social welfare system, encourage labour participation, and likely generate economic payoffs in the longer term. They are part of a larger shift in the social architecture of Canada's welfare state, a shift highly attuned to the number one concern of the economic elite: economic growth.

Against a background of stagnation and a fraught post-pandemic economic recovery, how much economic inequality to tolerate is both a political and an economic problem. But first, there is the matter of revenues. Massive borrowing during the pandemic years has left federal and provincial governments with mountains of debt. Coming to terms with the debt burden will be key to how inequalities can be addressed. Debts and deficits are the subject of our next chapter.

5 Dealing with the Debt

Public borrowing and public indebtedness have a long history. For over a thousand years, monarchs and states have borrowed, initially to fund wars or to deal with natural disasters, but then to finance mercantile ventures, create infrastructure, and, more recently, to ensure financial stability. Lenders normally could be found because governments, even rudimentary or insecure ones, could levy taxes (albeit at some political risk), and so be counted on to repay their debts (Levi, 1988). As lending became increasingly global and sophisticated, bankers secured their loans by organizing secondary markets for government bonds. Parliaments and legislative bodies did their best to monitor the sovereign's debt obligations, not always successfully. Defaults were not uncommon, but they did not discourage the development of financial markets on which economic growth has come to depend.

For all the apparent symbiosis between lenders and borrowers, and the prosperity that sovereign (or government) borrowing has made possible, public indebtedness has never escaped criticism, sometimes severe. Part of the general opprobrium that attaches to debt comes from the moral intuition that indebtedness is the product of poor judgment, poor management, or simply carelessness with one's assets. The Protestant ethic emphasizes diligence, discipline, and frugality (fiscal self-restraint). Accordingly, it is often said that governments, like citizens, should "live within their means," "pay as they go," and avoid burdening others with the consequences of their spending choices. The "others" in this case are the members of future generations, who, it is argued, eventually will be taxed to pay for current decisions. Of course, not all borrowing is long term – governments also run deficits to avoid imposing distortionary taxes during economic downturns. Incurring debt to allow for tax smoothing – spreading the tax burden into the future to allow for equal marginal tax rates – is presumed to be more efficient than imposing a lump-sum tax for a short-term exigency (Barro, 1979).

Justifying long-term borrowing is more complicated. For many economists, government borrowing implies fewer resource opportunities for private investment, and therefore a lower level of economic growth than might otherwise have been achieved (Reinhart & Rogoff, 2010). Increased government debt has also been linked to inflation, following the monetarist logic that an increased supply of money beyond the available supply of goods and services will prompt an increase in prices (Fischer & Easterly, 1990). Experience suggests, however, that not all borrowing produces these negative consequences. Much depends on the scale of indebtedness and the types of projects for which borrowing is deemed worthwhile. After all, while future generations might be forced to pay deferred taxes, they also would acquire the assets these public investments generate. In many cases, the return from investments financed by public borrowing is much greater than their cost. But assuming that both benefits and costs are part of the calculation, a complicated form of generational accounting is necessary to determine which types of long-term borrowing are justifiable in terms of efficiency and generational equity (Boadway, 2004).

It is doubtful that governments anywhere engage in this kind of accounting exercise. Rather than debate the wisdom of whether to raise taxes to pay for current spending or raise funds on capital markets, the governments of advanced economies have shown a strong preference for the latter strategy. Governments might be expected to reduce debt levels eagerly, given the looming costs associated with an aging population and lower fertility rates. But across the OECD, the opposite has occurred: for at least four decades, government debt has grown as a proportion of GDP (Yared, 2019). There are some exceptions – Finland, for example – but between 1960 and 2011 most European democracies ran a budgetary deficit more than half the time. Some countries – Italy and Portugal – were in deficit every year during that 51-year period (Wyplosz, 2013).

These deficits accumulate. If "debt overhang" is defined as a situation in which gross federal debt has reached the level of 90 per cent of GDP, 22 advanced economies had reached that mark by 2010 (Reinhart et al., 2012). In these countries, debt accumulated over many years, but debt levels increased substantially following adverse economic events such as wars and financial crises. A pandemic clearly qualifies as an adverse event. Even if it is a one-time shock to the economy, the conventional view is that its effects will linger on and acquire a "self-propelling character" (Reinhart et al., 2012, p. 70).

In Canada, the federal government ran budgetary deficits 81 per cent of the time between 1960 and 2021. The last budgetary surplus was in fiscal year 2007/8 (Department of Finance Canada, 2021e). Canada's most recent sovereign debt challenge occurred between 1992 and 1999, when real bond rates reached 9 per cent and the federal government imposed significant austerity measures. In 2022, Canada was back in heavy debt territory. Of course, in the midst of the pandemic hardly anyone was advocating balanced budgets or severe austerity. But now what? Have governments in Canada painted themselves into a corner, or is there a way to cope with the debt that does not extinguish the prospects of economic growth or inflict an unconscionable burden on future generations?

In this chapter we discuss the scale of the post-pandemic debt and deficit problem in Canada and the responses to it among members of our economic elite. We found differences of opinion on the severity of the challenge and on the likelihood of keeping interest rates low enough to meet debt-servicing obligations comfortably. We also discuss the role of the Bank of Canada and its unprecedented excursion into purchasing government debt. As for the future, the operative question is, what options do governments have if they choose (or are forced) to manage debt levels actively? Of particular interest is how seriously the economic elite treats the idea that fiscal rules can produce the results that proponents are expecting (or hoping for). In this chapter, we consider the theoretical possibilities and their practical limitations.

Debt Dimensions

Defining and measuring public debt is one of the first steps in assessing the current state and sustainability of government finances. Measures of debt vary in terms of coverage, instruments, and valuation (Bloch & Fall, 2015). Some economists insist on distinguishing between explicit debt, on which we focus here, and implicit debt – the claims that citizens expect to make on the state's pension, health care, and social insurance systems (von Weizsäcker & Krämer, 2021, pp. 163–92). Explicit debt measures include gross debt, net debt, and the accumulated deficit. Gross debt is the broadest view of debt, and includes total liabilities and interest-bearing debt – for example, loans and debts to finance past deficits and pension plans. Net debt is equal to gross debt minus financial assets. It is a measure of the government's solvency – that is, its ability to meet its obligations – and as such is a measure to which international institutions and credit-rating agencies accord particular attention. Finally, and consistent with Public Sector Accounting

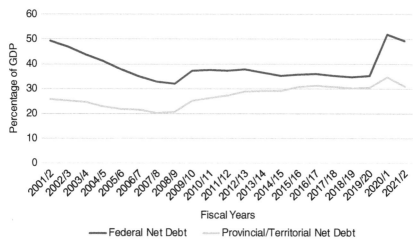

Figure 5.1. Federal and Provincial Net Debt as a Percentage of GDP, Fiscal Years 2001/2 to 2021/2

Note: Net debt as reported on a public accounts basis.

Sources: Department of Finance Canada (2022c, Tables 5.1 and 31); Statistics Canada (2022d). Contains information licensed under the Open Government Licence – Canada.

Standards, the federal government uses accumulated deficits as the measure of public debt in its official documents (Carmichael et al., 2020; PBO, 2020a). The accumulated deficit is equal to net debt minus non-financial assets.

Before the COVID-19 pandemic, the federal government had significant fiscal room – its net debt situation was deemed manageable. Following fiscal consolidation – that is, the deliberate reduction of spending commitments – in the mid-1990s, the share of federal net debt relative to national GDP steadily declined until 2008 (Figure 5.1). After the 2008 financial crisis and before the 2020 pandemic, the federal net-debt-to-GDP ratio stabilized at around 35 per cent. In 2015 the newly elected Liberal government implemented several spending programs that produced modest, but growing, budget deficits every year from 2016 to 2019. Nevertheless, as Figure 5.2 shows, Canada's ratio of total government net debt to GDP has been among the lowest of the advanced economies since 2004 (IMF, 2021e).

When the pandemic hit in March 2020, the federal government took the lead in offering the massive fiscal response we described in Chapter 3, aimed at helping businesses and individuals survive the worst of what ended up as a prolonged ordeal. The federal government

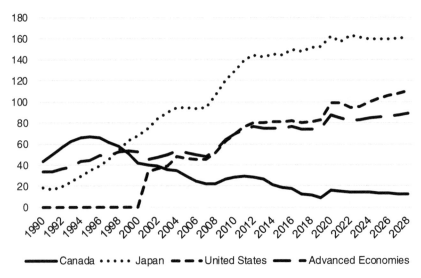

Figure 5.2. General Government Net Debt as a Percentage of GDP, Canada and Selected Economies, 1990–2027 (Projected)
Notes: General government includes all government units of central, state, provincial, regional, and local government, and social security funds. In the case of Canada, that includes federal, provincial, territorial, and local governments, and the Canada/Quebec Pension Plan.
Sources: Data from IMF (2021d, 2021e).

largely shouldered the cost of the programs, while the provinces made their own contributions. Roughly speaking, in fiscal year 2020/1, the federal portion of the pandemic effort was about 81 per cent; the provincial/territorial portion 19 per cent (Department of Finance Canada, 2021d, p. 40).

This growth in government spending produced a shock to the federal government's budget balance. Both skyrocketing expenditures and forgone tax revenues meant that the annual budgetary deficit jumped to 3.6 per cent of GDP in fiscal year 2021/2 (Department of Finance Canada, 2022b), up from 1.7 per cent in 2019/20 (Department of Finance Canada, 2021a). As for the federal net debt, as Table 5.1 shows, in the aftermath of the pandemic accumulated borrowing obligations raised the debt-to-GDP ratio from 35.14 per cent in 2019/20 to 49.34 per cent in 2021/2, an increase of 40 per cent.

Perhaps predictably, the size of the deficit and the new debt projections set off alarm bells among business-oriented think tanks. The Conference Board of Canada, for example, urged policymakers

Table 5.1. Federal and Provincial Net Debt as a Percentage of National GDP, Fiscal Years 2008/9, 2009/10, 2019/20–2021/2

Net Debt	2008/9	2009/10	2019/20	2020/1	2021/2
Federal	31.95	37.39	35.14	52.04	49.34
Provincial/territorial*	20.68	25.09	30.56	34.72	31.04

* Net Debt as reported in provincial/territorial public accounts.
Sources: Department of Finance Canada (2022c); Statistics Canada (2022d). Contains information licensed under the Open Government Licence – Canada.

to meet the post-COVID-19 era by "first stabilizing and then reducing the ratio of aggregate public debt to GDP to enable the country to get through the next crisis or recession when it comes" (Conference Board of Canada, 2021, p. 3). The C.D. Howe Institute's Fiscal and Tax Working Group echoed these concerns. Observing that the combined debt of the provinces and the federal government was likely to exceed 100 per cent of GDP within ten years, it cautioned against adding more unfunded liabilities. As it is, the Group worried, these governments had already spent almost $250 billion, or 12 per cent of GDP, on COVID-19 recovery programs (Robson & Dahi, 2021).

The respondents to our online survey, administered at the same time these cautionary notes were being sounded, agreed that the new debt level was worthy of concern. We asked them to agree or disagree with the following statement: "The federal government's debt level after COVID-19 is a more serious problem than most people recognize." Over 60 per cent agreed or strongly agreed. A Nanos survey, conducted in May 2021, reflected a similar level of disquiet (Curry, 2021a).

In addition, the provinces have their own debt profiles. Without a sovereign currency or their own central bank, the provinces are obliged to pay particularly close attention to their debt numbers or be forced to pay a risk premium on their loans. Provincial net debt-to-GDP steadily increased from 25 per cent in 2009 to 35 per cent in 2020, as shown in Figure 5.1. The accumulation of provincial debt is not a recent phenomenon. Canadian provinces are among the few subnational entities that can borrow on international markets, and according to a snapshot of 59 countries at the end of 2013, subnational government debt in Canada accounted for 57 per cent of public debt and stood at 61 per cent of GDP (OECD & UCLG, 2016). In Canada the fiscal picture is a combination of federal and provincial budgetary challenges, a subject we explore in Chapter 6.

As much as some economists sought to turn our attention to debts and deficits, it was difficult to obtain much of an audience for the topic while the pandemic raged. Part of the reason was the reassuring messaging from the federal government. In her 2021 budget, the Minister of Finance, Chrystia Freeland, reiterated the argument that Canada's debt situation – referring to the accumulated deficit or federal debt – is both manageable and well within the range of that of other OECD countries:

> We can afford this ambitious budget because the investments we propose today are responsible and sustainable ... This budget shows a declining debt-to-GDP ratio and a declining deficit, with the debt-to-GDP ratio falling to 49.2 per cent by 2025-2026 and the deficit falling to 1.1 per cent of GDP. These are important markers. They show that the extraordinary spending we have undertaken to support Canadians through this crisis, and to stimulate a rapid recovery in jobs, is temporary and finite. And our proposed long-term investments will permanently boost Canada's economic capacity. (Department of Finance Canada, 2021b)

The Parliamentary Budget Office (PBO) provided a similarly reassuring assessment. Its 6 November 2020 fiscal sustainability report projected that the federal government's net debt-to-GDP ratio would decline over the next several decades (PBO, 2020b). There was, it seemed, even room to reduce taxes or increase program spending without imperilling a debt-to-GDP ratio of less than 30 per cent. In 2022 the PBO projected another improvement in the federal government's fiscal room thanks to a rosier outlook for medium-term revenues and more congenial demographic trends (PBO, 2022c). Of course, taking comfort in these analyses means accepting some assumptions – chiefly that the future will resemble the past and that current trajectories can or will be sustained. Some members of the economic elite we interviewed were not having it: "If in the last five years, you spend a lot of money because things are going well, you're going to go broke in their [PBO's] exercise; and if you happen to have applied some austerity, maybe for the first time in your entire history, but you applied it for the last five years, you're gold forever! It's a useless exercise. Just a mindless exercise." [Economist 4]

Mindless or not, official messaging, combined with reassuring assessments from international organizations such as the IMF, provided an alternative narrative to the one offered by deficit hawks. In its Staff Report for the 2021 Article IV Consultation with Canada, the IMF stated:

> The substantial increase in the overall deficit will contribute to a significant increase in overall gross debt, but net debt remains relatively low. The wide general government deficit in 2020 will push overall gross debt

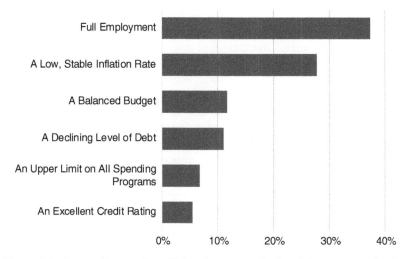

Figure 5.3. Survey Respondents' Most Important Budget Management Goals
Source: Adapted from Atkinson and Mou (2021).

to over 115 per cent of GDP (an increase of almost 30 per centage points). However, while risks have risen, Canada still does not have substantial fiscal vulnerabilities (Annex III), partly due to its strong pre crisis fiscal position and its sizable asset position. Overall, net public debt is expected to remain low – at 48 per cent of GDP – relative to other G7 countries. (IMF, 2021b, p. 13)

Another reason for suspending panic was the expectation that governments would quickly unwind their subsidy programs, making them one-time expenditures rather than ongoing commitments. This was the PBO's assumption, on the basis of which its numbers appear manageable. Canada ended its wage subsidy (CEWS) and rent subsidy (CERS) programs on 23 October 2021.

In keeping with the stress on overall economic management, the Canadians we surveyed were quite content with postponing our collective reckoning with public debt. In our January 2021 online survey, we asked respondents to rank five potential goals of budget management according to their relative importance. Figure 5.3 summarizes the level of support for each of these goals.

As Figure 5.3 shows, our survey respondents were distinctly cool towards prioritizing declining debt levels and balanced budgets as the most appropriate immediate targets. Both trailed traditional economic

policy objectives – namely, full employment and a low and stable inflation rate. The share of respondents who supported full employment as
the government budget management goal (37 per cent) is more than the
sum of the votes for all the fiscal health indicators, including a balanced
budget, a declining debt-to-GDP ratio, a limit on spending programs, and
an excellent credit rating. More than 25 per cent of respondents regarded
a low, stable inflation rate as the preferred government budget management goal. An upper limit on spending programs and an excellent credit
rating emerged as the least popular priorities, even though the latter is a
(not unreasonable) preoccupation of finance ministers across the country.

Note that assessing the relative importance of debts and deficits in the
middle of a pandemic provides only limited insight into public perceptions of their long-term importance. Research in Canada and beyond
indicates that there are limits to the willingness of voters to tolerate deficits (Jacques & Bélanger, 2022). Those limits were tested in the 1990s,
when deficits grew and Canada suffered a credit-rating downgrade. The
period of fiscal consolidation that began with the 1993 federal election
received very little pushback from a fiscally nervous electorate (Haffert,
2019; Lewis, 2003). As the pandemic unfolded, case counts soared, hospitals sagged under the stress, and protesters interrupted trade routes,
there were many things on the minds of decisionmakers other than how
to manage debt. But when minds do turn to debt management, what
do we find? Consensus on when and how to reduce debt levels or an
ambivalence towards the whole idea of debt reduction?

The Debt Threat

It might be a gross oversimplification, but let's assume, for the sake of
argument, that there are two distinct perspectives on the debt threat. The
first, more orthodox view, is that the accumulation of government debt
deprives the rest of the economy of needed capital formation. As long
as governments are in the capital market, they draw capital away from
private investment. Government borrowing, in short, "crowds out" the
accumulation of new capital and foreign assets. Government borrowing is not always a cost to the economy as a whole, but the presumption
is that, as borrowing grows, the costs show up in higher interest rates
and slower economic growth rates (Johnson, 2004). A prominent economist among our interviewees summed up the position:

> There is no licence to spend and incur debt infinitely. We should remain
> concerned by the impact of more public debt on private financial mar-
> kets (keeping in mind that real market-based activities account for three

quarters of the economy). When the economy is near full employment, more spending or less taxes financed by more public debt leads to higher interest rates on all types of debt (not the least reason being that the central bank will raise its policy interest rate as a bulwark against incipient inflation). This will crowd out of private investment. We should also not allow the debt to snowball and put the entire public sector in danger of bankruptcy. [Economist 6]

Confronting the downside of excess debt, the sound-finance school argues that the most reasonable response is to reduce government spending and allow market forces to allocate scarce resources. Debt, in this view, has its uses, mostly to smooth the effects of the business cycle, invest in future productive capacity, and provide the banking community with safe assets. But as a means of financing present-day consumption, debt is understood to be an indefensible means of redistributing resources from future taxpayers to the present.

From this sound-finance perspective, the real problem is that politicians are subject to a deficit bias. Incumbent governments that face well-organized constituent groups are assumed to be particularly vulnerable to the pressure to indulge their spending demands (Debrun et al., 2008). But the deficit bias is fundamentally a behavioural condition. Politicians pile up debt, according to the standard theory, because they are myopic, managing short-term pressures rather than long-term consequences. And should they be tempted to exert some self-discipline, politicians face the problem of time inconsistency, the tendency to commit to a long-term plan but then reverse course when a more agreeable short-term path appears (Keech, 2013). Among other unfortunate by-products is the state's larger than necessary fiscal footprint.

Because the biggest problem for sound-finance supporters is fiscal policy's tendency to bend to political forces, it is critical that the central bank retain independence from political pressure. This pressure normally comes in the form of entreaties (real or imagined) to keep interest rates low. Low interest rates encourage borrowing and (ideally) investment, and keep the government's own interest-rate payments low enough to head off debt accumulation. But if interest rates are to be a major tool in the fight against inflation, as they are in the world of sound finance, then they cannot be held at low levels simply to make life easier for governments. Governments need to find other ways of dealing with their deficits.

The second position on debts and deficits comes originally from the functional-finance school of thought. Associated with the work of a devout Keynesian, Abba Lerner, the idea is to focus political and economic attention on the performance of the economy as a whole and to ensure that government spending induces neither inflation nor unemployment. The size of the deficit at any given point in time is not a strong indicator of economic health. Lerner (1943, p. 42) summed up the position: "There is no reason to suppose that the spending and taxing policy that maintains full employment and prevents inflation must necessarily balance the budget over a decade any more than during a year or at the end of each fortnight." In fact, a fixation on deficit reduction and budget balancing is a frequent prelude to recession, as government surpluses mean deficits for the non-government sector.

This avowedly Keynesian perspective turns on the assumption that fiscal policy has a significant role to play in stimulating economic growth, particularly when monetary policy options have been exhausted. For neo-Keynesians, as long as the social rate of return from government spending is greater than the real interest rate, there is a very strong case for running fiscal deficits to maintain output at potential (Blanchard & Summers, 2017). It is true that, under some circumstances, government spending will "crowd out" private investment, and Canadians have been experiencing an investment shortfall, described by some as secular stagnation (see Chapter 3). For neo-Keynesians, the state's job under these conditions is to sustain aggregate demand, and if this means added public debt, so be it. They argue that the fear that more debt will burden future generations is unfounded when the economy is dynamically inefficient – that is, when it is in the grips of secular stagnation. Under these conditions the responsible option is to use public debt to bring consumption forward; otherwise interest rates would have to fall even further, perhaps into negative territory, something that would not be helpful to future generations (von Weizsäcker & Krämer, 2021, p. 11).

The advocates of modern monetary theory (MMT) offer an even more positive view of debt and deficits (Kelton, 2020). MMT scholars insist that countries such as Canada that issue fiat currency – currency issued by the state and untied to any other asset, such as gold – need never fear default as long their borrowing is confined to that currency (Fullwiler, 2016). Having a fiat currency means that government spending is no longer revenue constrained and governments will always be capable of repaying their debts because they control interest rates. Governments, in the MMT world, buy and sell debt chiefly to affect interest rates, not to finance their spending (Sharpe, 2013). Control over interest rates is also the key to dealing with inflation, the one risk that MMT supporters agree could be a by-product of too much government spending. But fiscal policy should also be a tool in the inflation fight. Specifically, taxes could be increased and a new spending/taxing equilibrium established.

The debt level at which this equilibrium would be established is of minor importance from this perspective.

These summary descriptions cannot capture the nuances of these arguments or the disagreements among proponents within each tradition. They do, however, provide the broad outlines of the current debate. It is worth emphasizing that, although the differences are obvious, there are points of agreement. Importantly, no one offered any serious resistance to the federal government's spending regime in fiscal year 2020/1. As we pointed out in Chapter 3, our interviewees were almost unanimous in praising the speed of the federal government's fiscal response and generally unconcerned with the acknowledged flaws in program design. All agreed on the need to spend. No one advocated increasing taxes or balancing budgets. In the colourful language of Stephen Poloz, the former Bank of Canada governor, "Picture the pandemic creating a giant deflationary crater in the middle of the economy ... Basically, we must fill [the crater] with water – liquidity – so that we can row our boat across it" (quoted in Parkinson, 2020). The alternative is a serious recession where, to extend the metaphor, we walk down to the bottom of the crater, walk across it for some indeterminate period, and then crawl up the other side. In 2020, no one was interested in doing that.

Similarly, the Bank of Canada's unprecedented purchasing of government debt was also treated as a necessary and welcome intervention to reassure capital markets that businesses and workers would be able to meet their bills. This was not the first time in recent years that central banks had reached the limits of conventional monetary policy, but this time short-term liquidity measures were followed by a program of quantitative easing (QE) – that is, large-scale purchases of long-term assets. With interest rates near their lower bound and therefore much less useful as a policy instrument, the turn to QE was intended to raise the price of the asset classes purchased – government bonds, mortgage-backed securities, and corporate debt – and encourage the acquisition of other assets, thereby easing overall financial conditions (Bank of Canada, 2015).

Evidence accumulated following the Great Financial Crisis suggests that QE did in fact provide significant financial easing during that period, lowering interest rates on a variety of asset classes (Santor & Suchanek, 2016). Scepticism about the wisdom of QE persists, but much of the attention quickly shifted to how central banks could unwind their purchases once the crisis was over (Martin & Milas, 2012). In the case of the pandemic, the Bank of Canada announced on 27 October 2021 that it would cease purchases of new government bonds. By that time, the Bank had accumulated $501.4 billion worth of assets, roughly 25 per cent of the country's GDP.

The absence of serious (or really any) disagreement among members of the economic elite we spoke with about the wisdom of the Bank's approach is a reflection of the idea that monetary policy had come to the rescue of fiscal policy. Or, perhaps less dramatically, monetary policy made it possible for governments to provide stimulus to the economy without worrying that capital markets would not support their efforts. The pandemic was a rare moment in which monetary policy and fiscal policy were both operative and in sync. The risk, however, is that increasing the money supply, which is what QE does, combined with increased cash transfers in the hands of businesses and individuals, which is what fiscal policy does, will hasten the return of inflation (Cross, 2021). In the early months of 2021, only a few of our interviewees saw inflation as a major problem. But a former minister of finance could see the writing on the wall: "We will have a V-shaped recovery, which will mean pressures on inflation. Why does that matter in terms of government spending? If inflation is higher, interest rates are higher, so all of these projections just made four months ago by the federal government might be completely out of whack already because future inflation means a higher cost of borrowing" [Politician 3].

As if on cue, by the fall of 2021 inflation began to drift upwards. Initially described by central bankers as a "transitory problem" – one associated principally with supply chain hold-ups – by the spring of 2022, it was clear that price increases were going to be more persistent than originally thought. At this point any consensus on the most appropriate fiscal and monetary response began to break down. Inflation sceptics warned that raising interest rates would create more problems than it would solve. Inflation, they argued, was the result of supply constraints, not excessive demand. As a result, raising interest rates and suppressing demand would have the effect of slowing the economy down and increasing unemployment without solving problems in the real economy (Hildebrand, 2022).

Those focused on the threat of ongoing inflation argued, on the other hand, that demand-generated inflation eventually would become important given accumulated household savings and government over-stimulation of the economy. Business-oriented think tanks continued to lobby for spending restraint, but the federal government's November 2021 Fiscal and Economic Update included over $55 billion in new projected program spending (beyond election commitments), with additional fiscal room provided by a recovering economy. In its own Fiscal and Economic Update for Parliamentarians, submitted in January 2022, the Parliamentary Budget Office observed that the federal government had indicated it would end its stimulus spending in 2021, but that "references to fiscal guardrails and winding down stimulus spending were dropped altogether" and that the rationale for spending had shifted away from COVID-19 (PBO, 2022a, p. 11).

It is fair to say that, as governments began to loosen COVID-19 restrictions and confront the prospect of persistent inflation, the debt threat was still not high on anyone's list of priorities. From the federal government, the message was "relax, we've got this." Reiterating its earlier position that Canada had a "low debt advantage" and excellent credit ratings, the federal government's November 2021 economic update showed the deficit-to-GDP ratio tracking to be below 1 per cent and the debt-to-GDP ratio, depending on different growth scenarios, to be below 48 per cent beginning in fiscal year 2023/4. The same reassuring message accompanied the 2023 budget, by which time the anticipated debt-to-GDP ratio had ticked up to 43.5 per cent and the deficit had risen to $43 billion. But not to worry: the deficit would decline every year over the forecast period, and the debt-to-GDP ratio would continue to decline from 2024/5 onward (Department of Finance Canada, 2023).

These reassuring projections are critical for future budgetary frameworks. They suggest that previous strategies for dealing with accumulated debt, particularly austerity measures, can be avoided. While some members of our economic elite predicted that austerity eventually would be needed, no one welcomed it. A senior public servant saw the problem mostly in terms of timing: "We will, as we have in the past, just delay the difficult decisions until there is genuinely a crisis and then we will in fact be forced into austerity. This is my greatest fear. I also think there is a strong risk in that. We seem to have this habit of waiting till the exact wrong moments to undertake cut exercises" [Bureaucrat 8]. But if the deficit is handled properly, and not aggravated by too much new program spending, then the worst problems of debt management could be avoided. Here is a defence of that position: "I don't think you necessarily need to have austerity but what governments will need to do is wind down the temporary supports for its programs. So, all the programs that were meant to be temporary, they'll have to be temporary. Or taxes will have to rise. So, I don't see austerity as a necessary thing going forward but it might also not be bad to use the post-pandemic world, the exiting from the pandemic, to look carefully at government programs and have a clean-up" [Economist 7].

The reason for the endorsement of program reviews and the rejection of outright austerity lies in the post 2008–9 experience. With higher levels of government debt following the financial crisis, finance departments were encouraged to reduce spending on the grounds that it would free up funds for private investment and send positive signals to hesitant investors (Alesina & Passalacqua, 2016). Austerity is a form of "voluntary deflation," to use a phrase from Mark Blyth (2013, p. 2), in which the economy adjusts downward by the withdrawal of public spending. For austerity enthusiasts, a reduction in government spending is equivalent to a deficit reduction (Skidelsky, 2018, p. 245). But after 2009, a reduction in spending slowed growth and delayed recovery, especially in the eurozone. Among economic elites across advanced economies, a consensus developed around two conclusions following the Great Financial Crisis: first, the fiscal rescue packages had been too small and, second, the shift to austerity to address government deficits was exactly the wrong move. Emerging from the pandemic, neither of these lessons was lost on the economic elite in Canada.

The Liberal government, which was a builder of this consensus as well as being part of it, made it clear that post-pandemic there would be no blanket adoption of austerity. Instead, the government would take advantage of the shift in economic thinking away from a focus on debt reduction as a stand-alone goal towards a concern for economic growth and interest rates. Specifically, as long as economic growth (g) outstrips interest rates (r), then debt levels can slowly come down without the messy matter of actually reducing government spending or raising taxes.

The idea that governments can afford to take on debt without creating a drag on the economy is a direct challenge to the sound-money position and is difficult to defend during an era of high interest rates. But before the pandemic, interest rates in Canada and elsewhere had been low for decades, and low rates changed the debt calculus. Challenging the view that government debts are too high and must be urgently reduced, Olivier Blanchard used his presidency of the American Economic Association to argue, on the contrary, that, in the United States, low interest rates combined with high growth rates had largely removed government debt as a drag on the economy. As long as $r < g$, the intertemporal budget constraint that governments (like households and firms) are assumed to face is suspended at least temporarily, and we have "debt without drama" (Reinhart et al., 2012). As Blanchard put it, "If the future is like the past, the probability that the U.S. government can do a debt rollover, that is issue debt and achieve a decreasing debt to GDP ratio without ever having to raise taxes later, is high" (Blanchard, 2019, p. 1198).

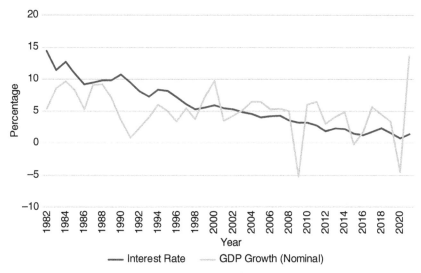

Figure 5.4. Changes in GDP Growth Rate and Interest Rate, Canada, 1981–2021
Sources: Authors' calculations; data from Bank of Canada (n.d.); Statistics Canada
(2022d). Contains information licensed under the Open Government Licence – Canada.

Until the pandemic, Canada's situation was not dissimilar. Figure 5.4 shows the federal government's benchmark long-term bond yield rate and nominal GDP growth rate. In the four decades from 1981 to 2021, both the interest rate and nominal GDP growth rate declined, albeit with greater fluctuation in the growth rate. As we outlined earlier in our discussion of secular stagnation, lower interest rates suggest an unbalanced capital market, one marked by excessive saving combined with weak incentives to make substantial capital investments. Although central banks can influence short-term interest rates, long-term interest rates reflect demand and supply in the capital market and the underlying dynamics of an economy. Based on the observed trends, the Canadian economy, like others, is vulnerable to lackluster capital formation and slow economic growth.

The Department of Finance Canada, without explicitly endorsing Blanchard's position on public debt, focused heavily on the economic growth dynamic as critical to the speed with which the country returns to pre-pandemic debt levels. Assuming interest rates would rise, the November 2021 update nonetheless portrayed the country's debt profile in reassuring terms. Even under unfavourable rate increases, the federal government's public debt charges were set to grow only modestly, in part because much of the current debt is financed at low rates and because an increase in interest rates generates additional revenue from government interest-bearing assets.

This rather benign vision – fiscal responsibility without too much fiscal discipline – does not mean that functional finance proponents have convinced everyone that deficits are entirely manageable. No matter how appealing the functional finance perspective might be to certain academic economists, it has little traction among members of Canada's economic elite. For one thing, the entire argument sounds counterintuitive. As one finance minister put it, "I'm not trained in it, so I need to be persuaded that if something sounds too good to be true it could still be true. You know, I mean modern monetary theory is social credit,[1] 1930s" [Politician 10]. Again, no one thought that massive government borrowing to meet the pandemic shock was a mistake. But with few exceptions, our interviewees were eager to discuss the aftermath. Now the question was not just how to get the economy back on track, but how to get also government back on track – back, that is, to a world in which debt is reduced and economic growth is the watchword.

A focus on economic growth is certainly consistent with the view that the true guideposts of macroeconomic policy should be employment and inflation, either one of which threatens investment and productivity. But since the past is not a reliable guide to the future, sound-finance advocates favour government restraint as well as economic growth. Specifically, governments should run primary surpluses where possible – that is, revenues should exceed expenditures, net of debt-servicing costs. This might not be possible every year, and too much of an emphasis on achieving this goal over the short term can create its own bedlam, but taxing and spending should be in some type of equilibrium independent of countercyclical measures needed to smooth the business cycle. And while inflation is also a familiar means of reducing debt, no one among those we interviewed was interested in deliberately eroding the purchasing power of the dollar as a means of securing a more favourable budgetary picture.

---

1 *Social credit* was both a monetary theory and a political movement aimed at increasing the purchasing power of consumers by providing them the financial means to bridge the gap between the prices of goods and the wages of those who make them. Major C.H. Douglas, social credit's principal theorist, held unorthodox views about the source of value in an economy, but his contention that consumers deserved income sufficient to benefit from their production ushered in attempts to wrest the credit system away from bankers and others who he believed were responsible for economic sabotage.

In fact, it is fear of inflation that persuaded most of our economic elite to adopt a cautious position on deficit financing over the long term. In the spring of 2021, when most of our interviews took place, inflation was not on the horizon, but it was clearly on the minds of our interviewees. Given the sound-finance dictum to keep the money supply in line with the size of the economy, the massive QE initiative, while appreciated for its short-term benefits, put many members of the economic elite on edge. Although all our interviewees were prepared to accept the need to "print money" to deal with a crisis, they deemed it imperative to return to normality as soon as possible. Claiming that history teaches that reckless spending is a route to disaster, several of our respondents openly worried about excessive stimulus, with one expressing concern this way: "It is unfortunate when we lose our memory of history. Economists do look back, but politicians don't. They really don't understand some of the things that Canada has been through and some of the challenges we've had in the past and things that happened to us" [Bureaucrat 25].

For most members of the economic elite, the root of the problem is politicians' bias towards deficit financing, although interviewees did not use this precise phrase: "What MMT believes is that fiscal authorities can deal with inflation when it comes by either increasing taxes, lowering government spending, or whatever. I can't even imagine a scenario where in an election year, if there's inflation, some politician is going to say, 'Yeah, we're going to increase taxes this year to deal with inflation,' and get re-elected. I just don't see that scenario" [Economist 8]. This argument is, in a nutshell, the rationale for preserving central bank independence and insisting on a single mandate for the Bank of Canada: price stability. Keeping monetary policy out of the hands of politicians and setting inflation targets to increase policy credibility is a formula that sound-money advocates universally endorse. It seems to have worked well for central banks in advanced economies, and there is no appetite among the members of the economic elite we interviewed to abandon this formula. That includes politicians who were quite content to allow the Bank the political room to manoeuvre.

With inflation on the rise in the fall of 2021, the federal government and the Bank of Canada renewed the Bank's five-year mandate with a continued commitment to stable price levels achieved by "flexible inflation targeting." The idea of flexibility is important, not only because a range of 1–3 per cent allows the Bank to deal with financial system vulnerabilities, especially shocks of various kinds, but also to achieve "the level of maximum employment needed to sustainably achieve the inflation target" (Bank of Canada, 2021, p. 3). The mention of employment levels in a statement of monetary policy objectives makes sound-money supporters nervous (Ragan, 2021), but it would be surprising if monetary policy were to be made without any concern for employment, even if it is impossible to know exactly what "maximum sustainable employment" actually means. The mandate's language is interpreted more accurately as a recognition that monetary policy on its own cannot ensure stability in the macroeconomy (Skidelsky, 2018, p. 358). Only a combination of fiscal and monetary policy can do that.

Guardrails, Anchors, and Rules

Strenuous efforts to keep monetary policy away from the push and pull of politics have been largely successful in advanced economies. Central banks have built a moat around their operations by claiming expertise in the craft of monetary policy and by popularizing the idea of a neutral rate of interest – one that promotes neither inflation nor deflation. The embrace of inflation targets in the 1990s helped to seal the argument that stability is best achieved by trusting central bankers to make credible commitments. Inflation targeting has been a key policy instrument, and although targets are subject to some flexibility when it comes to actually meeting them, the logic of having a target has become more or less unassailable even if no one pretends that there is anything magical about 2 per cent.

Doing the same for fiscal policy – establishing clear targets – is a more challenging prospect. Fiscal policy is deeply intertwined with politics because it involves a more obvious redistribution of resources across generations, individuals, and regions (Alesina & Passalacqua, 2016). Tax policy, industrial subsidies, welfare programs, health insurance, and pension plans are all subject to the political process. Some policies are demonstrably better than others in terms of public welfare, but there is a large area of politically inspired disputation that is resistant to the imposition of theoretically derived rules. Exercising judgment about what measures are politically attractive, or at least survivable, is often more important to decisionmakers than adhering to contestable commandments.

Debt is similarly a matter of political judgment or, as critics might have it, political expediency. If nothing else, the accumulation of debt by OECD countries undermines the idea that there are well-defined natural limits to what credit markets will tolerate. Since the 1960s, debt costs and debt levels have been decoupled, making it harder to predict the long-term consequences of debt accumulation (Mitchener & Trebesch, 2023, pp. 575–6). Debt limits undoubtedly exist, but they appear to be highly contingent (see Japan), and there is no agreed-upon ideal debt-to-GDP ratio, for example, despite efforts to suggest that perhaps 90 per cent represents an empirically established danger zone (Reinhart et al., 2012). In fact, credit-rating agencies assess the creditworthiness of a government against a range of criteria that includes economic growth potential, political stability, quality of governance, prudence in financial management practices, and, of course, debt and deficit projections. Although credit-rating agencies downgraded many provincial governments in the 1990s, they appear more relaxed in the 2020s, even though the debt-to-GDP ratios of provincial governments are generally higher.

Lack of clarity on what fiscal sustainability actually consists of makes rule creation a challenge. The classic definition of a fiscal rule is "a permanent constraint on fiscal policy, expressed in terms of a summary indicator of fiscal performance" (Kopits & Symansky, 1998). This definition has the unfortunate tendency to mix two distinct ideas – constraint and performance – and creates some confusion over what is a rule, an anchor, and a guardrail. Rules emphasize constraint; the assumption is that they will produce the desired fiscal performance. But regardless of their immediate impact (or performance), the logic of rules is that they are not to be adjusted, regardless of changing circumstances. They are, as the definition suggests, permanent, and one way of making them permanent is to locate them in the constitution, the preferred solution for some rule enthusiasts (Buchanan, 1997).

In 1990, only five countries – Germany, Indonesia, Japan, Luxembourg, and the United States – had fiscal rules in place. By early 2012, the number of countries covered by national and supranational rules had increased to 76 (Schaechter et al., 2012, p. 10). Some of these rules (the minority) are constitutionally mandated; most take the form of statutory requirements. Most are aimed at limiting deficits (balanced-budget rules, for example) or putting a cap on debt, but some feature limits on spending and on taxation. The popularity of rules has waxed and, occasionally, waned, but more and more countries are adopting rules of some kind. Recent fiscal shocks have illustrated their limits, although in principle it is possible to design "rules" that can accommodate, or even anticipate, the unexpected.

Why would politicians seek relief from an affliction – "deficit bias" – that seems so politically attractive? Having someone else – in this case, future politicians – take responsibility for the risks you are piling up is the very essence of moral hazard. There are two plausible reasons politicians might resist temptation and voluntarily seek restraint instead. First, voters do not always appreciate fiscal largesse. In the face of an economic crisis the voting public frequently exhibits a strong preference for austerity as opposed to spending (Bansak et al., 2021). And because crises are usually understood as widely shared events (other countries are suffering too), governments that choose austerity are often relieved of electoral punishment (Arias & Stasavage, 2019; Talving, 2017). In Canada, a tolerance for deficits in the 1970s and 1980s gave way to a demand for visible measures of fiscal discipline when voters became debt conscious (Geist, 1997; Jacques & Bélanger, 2022).

The second reason for doubting that politicians routinely choose deficits is that they listen to their advisors, most of whom are schooled in the strictures of sound finance and believe either that there is a natural limit to borrowing or that the state is an inferior investor compared to private capital operating in financial markets. The economic elite does not welcome austerity, but among our interviewees we found no support for the idea that deficits could be ignored over the long term. Hence the attraction of fiscal rules.

Of course, rules can be rather rigid instruments. In the early days of the pandemic, the term "anchor" began to be employed. Unlike a rule, an anchor is a psychological tool intended to influence expectations or, more precisely, to signal a commitment. If our expectations about inflation can be anchored at 2 per cent, then perhaps our expectations about the size of our debt could similarly be anchored, although exactly which metric would be best and which setting would produce the desired performance have never been a settled matter. The absence of consensus on measures and targets means that, as Leeper (2010) put it, "public discourse about monetary policy is far more sophisticated and helpful to private decisionmakers than are discussions of fiscal policy." The apparent lack of rigour and precision in setting fiscal anchors can even invite ridicule. One of our interviewees, for example, observed that "anchors are what you use when you don't want to go anywhere" [Bureaucrat 4]. But others thought the term conveyed a desire to avoid drift, an imperceptibly slow journey over a fiscal waterfall (to extend the metaphor). Its vagueness aside, the term "anchor" was the one we chose to employ in our interviews, and most of those we spoke with thought anchors were a good idea. They differed only on what constitutes the most appropriate ones.

At some point the Trudeau government began using the term "guardrails," rather than either anchors or rules, at least in its public pronouncements. This term is even less clear than the others. It suggests that governments believe there are limits to borrowing, but are not entirely sure what these are. Like some of those we interviewed, ministers of finance in recent Liberal governments appear to have preferred an array of possible indicators – a dashboard of signals – rather than a single requirement. This preference is a response to growing dissatisfaction with rules as too rigid and insensitive to changing circumstances. We asked our interviewees to consider different possible fiscal anchors (or rules) and reflect on their usefulness. Let us review the three possibilities that drew the heaviest commentary.

A Balanced Budget (Rule)

In Canada the 1990s was the decade of balanced-budget legislation, if only in the provinces. Beginning with a focus on spending limits, fiscal consolidation legislation shifted to balanced-budget requirements by the mid-1990s. By 2000 eight of ten provinces had adopted balanced-budget legislation, albeit with different levels of stringency and accountability. By 2013, as all of these governments experienced the Great Financial Crisis, several either abandoned, postponed, or diluted their original requirements (Atkinson et al., 2016).

To some degree, the original critics of balanced-budget legislation were vindicated by the transition from warm embrace to cool distancing. They had argued that legislated requirements were bound to be procyclical in their effects, requiring governments to reduce spending during recessions (or simply when revenues declined) at the very point when they should be injecting resources into the economy. Annually balanced budgets undermined the possibility of tax smoothing and prevented governments from addressing the effects of a downturn in the economy.

The argument for flexible rules (or rule suspension if need be) had a receptive audience among politicians in most provinces. So, most balanced-budget legislation in Canada and elsewhere was adjusted to provide additional flexibility, typically requiring budgets to be balanced over the business cycle rather than annually. This more nuanced interpretation of the balanced-budget rule is not a trivial concession. Provincial governments since the 1970s had rhetorically championed "structural fundamentalism," even if they only occasionally conformed to its requirements (Doern et al., 2013). The move to cyclical stabilization, albeit with balanced-budget requirements attached, was a recognition that unrelieved austerity was not feasible on either political or economic grounds.

Other criticisms of balanced-budget requirements focused on their political motives and sinister effects. The charge of suspect motives is rooted in the idea that fiscal rules such as balanced-budget laws typically are introduced by governments that know they can satisfy their requirements. In that event, rules are superfluous (Bird & Tassonyi, 2003) and little more than window dressing or virtue signalling. If that were the case, then little could be expected of them. But the track record of balanced-budget rules is not that dismal. Public accounts records show that, in the provinces, the likelihood of balancing the budget without a fiscal rule was very low. That likelihood improved substantially once balanced-budget legislation was in place, especially during normal economic periods. During periods of recession or recovery, budgets were balanced far less often, but more often than in provinces without any legislative requirements (Mou et al., 2018). In short, balanced-budget laws are no silver bullet, but in Canada at least they have not been a complete failure.

The pandemic, on the other hand, has shown that there are some shocks that even the most fiscally strong jurisdiction cannot withstand. Although countries with balanced-budget rules exceeded the prescribed limits about half the time before the pandemic, IMF reports show that about 90 per cent of countries with fiscal rules had deficits larger than permitted in 2020. Most of these countries employed one or more strategies to avoid the full effects of rules: temporarily suspend them, activate escape clauses, or modify them so that compliance was possible (Gbohoui & Medas, 2020).

Before the pandemic, five Canadian provinces had some type of fiscal rule that either set a deficit reduction target (Manitoba) or prohibited forecast or realized deficits (British Columbia, Ontario, and Quebec). British Columbia and Manitoba amended their balanced-budget requirements during the pandemic. The amendments allowed British Columbia to forecast deficits for fiscal years 2021/2, 2022/3, and 2023/4. In the case of Manitoba, the amendments allowed the government to exclude pandemic expenditures in determining the deficit for 2021/2. Quebec, which has balanced the budget since 2015/16, temporarily suspended its balanced-budget legislation and expects to return to balance by 2027/8 (Brossard, 2021).

Among the economic elite we interviewed, support for balanced-budget legislation was distinctly muted. Several of our interviewees mentioned the inflexibility of rules, and some simply objected to the idea that governments should be constrained artificially: "All these rules come from the idea that most of the expenditures by the government are unproductive ... I mean, to me, many of the things that governments do are productive, just as productive as what businesses do" [Economist 10]. Still other interviewees endorsed rules, but were indifferent about balancing budgets: "If it was 1 per cent of GDP in deficit, in perpetuity, that's fine because debt-to-GDP will go down. A balanced budget is a way to get there faster. Some make the argument that it's easier to commit to a 0; it is a nice round number. That's fine, I don't care. As an economist, I care about the sustainability of the public finances and to me that's stable debt-to-GDP" [Economist 13]. What a balanced-budget commitment might deliver inside government is a higher degree of bureaucratic compliance: "We've actually, internally, found a debt cap to be very useful to rein in departments. It's a lot easier for us, more importantly for our minister, to say 'no' when there are debt caps" [Bureaucrat 5]. That argument, as persuasive as it might be for sound-finance politicians, was not enough to persuade those who preferred the idea of a flexible debt limit.

Debt Limits (Anchor)

A low and declining debt-to-GDP ratio was by far the preference of the economic elite we questioned on the topic. This kind of fiscal rule is best described as an anchor because it does not prescribe a particular outcome, simply an upper debt limit. Governments that are at or approaching the limit are required to begin retiring debt to avoid adverse credit repercussions. Whereas a balanced-budget requirement stipulates a specific outcome, a debt limit allows for more fiscal leeway, assuming the limit is deemed adequate to ensure solvency. The reality, however, is that most countries that use debt limits as fiscal rules also employ balanced-budget requirements. Of the countries that exceeded their debt limits with the advent of pandemic spending, the largest deviations were among advanced economies, and these deviations are expected to last for some time. In Canada's case, where at the federal level no debt limit as such exists, the IMF persistently has asked for a "medium-term fiscal anchor" – one that would strengthen the credibility of the fiscal framework (IMF, 2021b).

A focus on debt accumulation, rather than on annual deficits, is arguably a more practical approach to debt given the track record of balanced-budget adherence. Besides, a focus on debt levels is a clear concession to the idea that debt has its uses. The real question is how much debt is sustainable. Just picking a number, a level of debt per capita, is not exactly a scientific proposition. In April 1936, when Alberta defaulted on its debt obligations, its debt-to-GDP ratio was much lower than it is for many provinces post-pandemic. The lesson: what is tolerable in some circumstances is not tolerable in others, and circumstances change. In particular, the development of capital markets and the presence of strong central banks willing to purchase government paper have allowed for much more government borrowing without setting off fiscal alarm bells. But if tolerable debt levels are a function of complex and particular circumstances, including who holds the debt, then choosing a specific ceiling beyond which debt cannot be permitted to rise is unlikely to be a precise science. It is as much a matter of bargaining and belief as it is of accurate insolvency prediction.

Whatever the terms of the bargain, lenders need some assurance of stability. "What would be my, not preferred, but my realistic anchor is not a declining debt-to-GDP ratio, but a stable debt-to-GDP ratio over a long horizon. Something like the PBO's fiscal gap measure ... That anchor has problems, lots of problems on its own, but it's probably your best practical anchor" [Bureaucrat 4]. As this observation implies, if the maintenance of a debt level is portrayed as an anchor, no immediate spending reduction is required, and for many of our interviewees, keeping the debt-to-GDP ratio stable and within familiar bounds was a sensible strategy even if debt levels are subject to political bargaining.

Debt-Servicing Costs (Guardrail)

One way to avoid a potentially fruitless debate about how much debt is tolerable is to ask how much it costs to service the debt we have or expect to have. Debt-servicing costs are best thought of as a guardrail because, when they increase, there are immediate budgetary implications. For senior public servants who worked in finance departments during the 1990s, the memory of high debt costs is vivid.

By the mid-1990s, 35 per cent of federal government spending was devoted to servicing the debt. Economic growth in that period was relatively strong and inflation had (at last) abated, but interest rates on long-term government bonds, which had fallen from the highs of fiscal year 1981/2, remained at over 8 per cent in 1994/5. These rates, combined with relatively high levels of debt, were draining public funds away from socially productive types of expenditure. For those charged with creating budgets, it was a nightmare. Someone who lived through the period described it this way: "When government gets into trouble, political trouble as much as economic trouble, is when the amount of services delivered for a dollar of taxes gets down to a very low number. We got down to sixty-seven cents in the mid-nineties" [Economist 3].

Early in the pandemic David Dodge, former governor of the Bank of Canada, argued that the federal government should move from a focus on debt-to-GDP ratios to one on debt-servicing costs as a proportion of the expenditure budget (the ratio of interest costs to revenue). With interest rates still relatively low, Dodge concluded that, "at this stage in our fiscal path, a debt servicing/revenue formula based on prudent growth and interest rate assumptions provides a better anchor for fiscal sustainability than the debt/GDP ratio alone" (Dodge, 2020). The cost of borrowing was clearly on the minds of members of the Department of Finance Canada in 2021 as they put together their November update. Observing that public debt charges in 2021 were at "historically low levels" and that debt charges were actually declining despite extraordinary COVID-19 spending, the minister of finance projected only a modest increase in debt charges, even with an increase in interest rates (Department of Finance Canada, 2021d, p. 39).

By the 2023 federal budget the picture had begun to change. Public debt charges were expected to rise annually for the next several years, reaching $50.3 billion in fiscal year 2027/8, up from $24.5 billion in 2021/2. According to the minister, even this rather dramatic increase did not warrant panic, since, as the budget once again claimed, public debt charges remain at "historically low levels" (Department of Finance Canada, 2023, p. 22). All right, but the question becomes: what level of debt-servicing costs is tolerable? By historical standards, the cost of debt coming out of the pandemic was exceptionally low, but that bargain-basement status depended almost entirely on low interest rates, and these began to increase steadily as post-pandemic inflation mounted. If debt-servicing costs are to be a guide to debt management, and the ratio of interest costs to revenue begins to rise, at some point governments can be expected to curtail expenditures or raise taxes. What is that point? No one knows for sure, but Dodge and Dion (2023), suggest 10 per cent as a reasonable anchor/guardrail. By their calculations, the federal government's "plausible but optimistic" 2022 budget projections would keep that ratio just below 10 per cent for the foreseeable future. But new debt-servicing projections had already breached that mark by 2023.

A debt-servicing ratio, even one cautious about economic growth, can be a precarious guardrail. If it encourages government to make long-term commitments on the grounds that they are relatively inexpensive today, the result might be programmatic spending that eventually will need to be rolled back when circumstances change for the worse. Dangers aside, an interest-cost-to-revenue ratio was a much more attractive fiscal rule to our interviewees than placing limits on particular spending programs. Many of these programs – Employment Insurance, for example – are not eligible for limits on coverage or rates without changes to the legislation itself. Besides, withdrawing support for existing programs, whatever their budgetary status, is fraught with political difficulties, as many of our interviewees emphasized. The political imperatives of maintaining programs on which people have come to rely can stretch budgets the moment economies confront unexpected setbacks. Then what?

Debt Options: Good, Bad, and Ugly

The debt option that creates the most heartburn for sound-money advocates is to keep on borrowing, rather than to raise taxes or curb spending. As long as credit markets accept your debt – and in Canada that seems likely for at least the foreseeable future – then governments could simply follow the functional-finance dictum to stop obsessing about deficits. Functional-finance advocates and their fellow travellers, modern monetary theorists, caution against an overinvestment in deficit management lest we lose sight of the reason for taxing and spending in the first place – namely, to stabilize the economy on a growth trajectory, ensure high rates of employment, and guard against excessive inflation.

Most of the economic elite we spoke with were much more concerned with the dangers of debt than are functional-finance theorists. They worried that governments will take on so much debt that they cannot manage a fiscal shock like a pandemic. Perhaps, given the experience of 2020–1, these fears are overblown. But that comfortable conclusion is challenged by a history of global financial instability and two recent shocks that have left behind unprecedented levels of government debt and made experienced analysts exceedingly nervous. Here is how Dodge and Dion (2023, p. 24) summarize the post-pandemic situation: "there is a significant risk that both the debt ratio and the interest cost ratios exceed comfortable levels over the remainder of this decade, both because economic conditions will turn out to be more difficult than assumed in the [Fall Economic Statement] 2022 and because the spending budgeted will turn out to be insufficient to achieve the policy goals promised."

Governments have choices in managing their debt, but at least some of these choices would be anathema to Canada's economic elite. If debt sustainability is defined as stable – that is, a non-increasing debt-to-GDP ratio over an extended time – four variables are in play: the initial debt-to-GDP ratio, the average real interest rate on the debt, the rate of growth of real (inflation-adjusted) GDP, and the size of the primary budget balance. Based on these considerations, there are four main options to stabilize sovereign government debt (Eichengreen et al., 2021; Goodhart & Pradhan, 2020, pp. 174–8).

First, governments can run primary surpluses, in which case revenues minus non-interest expenditures yields a positive balance. Governments that run primary deficits would have to undertake fiscal consolidation by reducing spending and/or increasing taxes. Deficits would still be permitted to allow for debt servicing, but program spending is reined in and taxes levied in the event that new projects are deemed sufficiently worthy. Fiscal consolidation has been a commonly used policy instrument for governments in a tight fiscal situation. Britain, France, and the United States all ran primary surpluses for decades. Alternatively, as long as g > r, governments can run a primary deficit without causing the debt-to-GDP ratio to rise, although adjustments to spending or revenues still might be necessary.

In Canada, when both federal and provincial governments went through a series of fiscal consolidations in the 1990s, they subsequently ran surpluses. Even during normal economic times, governments sometimes choose to pursue fiscal consolidation to reduce the risk premium on debts and bolster the confidence of investors. The problem is that generating primary surpluses via spending cuts requires austerity, which means service reductions. Imposed too harshly, this kind of policy can create severe political backlash, as the Greek experience following the Great Financial Crisis illustrated. But it is possible to put together a package of spending cuts that voters find acceptable. Research shows that pension reductions, for example, provoke much more voter resistance than cuts to defence spending, while corporate tax increases and reductions to public sector employment appear to have only modest effects either way (Bansak et al., 2021, pp. 498–9). There are times when austerity might be warranted, but it is not a cure-all for every highly leveraged government, and it is politically dangerous if managed poorly.

The second option is to invest consciously in a growth agenda. Economic growth is a natural vehicle to reduce the debt-to-GDP ratio because economic growth reduces debt as a proportion of GDP and increases GDP itself. Economic growth, however, comes with its own constraints. Subsidies or direct expenditures to expand private demand could contribute to an increase in interest rates and therefore the cost of servicing government debt. We can be reasonably assured that, at some point, the nominal interest rate will catch up with the nominal growth rate (Eichengreen et al., 2021, p. 221). Supply-side-driven economic growth – that is, increasing the productive capacity of an economy – requires long-term investments in human capital, infrastructure, and research and development. It can also involve an overhaul of trade policy and a reconsideration of competition policy. These are all worthwhile, but, as we pointed out in Chapter 3, they are long-term projects, there are no guarantees, and the political challenges are substantial. More important, countries like Canada face a demographic reckoning: declines in the active labour force will put downward pressure on real economic growth as the proportion of dependents in the economy increases (Goodhart & Pradhan, 2020). There are no quick fixes.

The third option involves the creation of unanticipated inflation, which would reduce the present value of government debt. A surprise inflation is like a tax on the holders of long-term government bonds: the real value of government bonds decreases. If the nominal growth rate – that is, the growth rate inclusive of inflation – remains higher than the nominal interest rate, then a sizable reduction in debt effectively will be engineered. This strategy is hardly unknown, but it flies directly in the face of orthodox public finance, in which price stability is highly valued and certainly not to be sacrificed to bail out profligate governments. For the whole economy, the risk is that government-manipulated inflation will distort prices, trigger increases in the interest rates on both government bonds and private debt, and discourage lenders from holding long-term government debt. Central banks would resist this strategy, drawing them into political conflict with elected governments. Again, the political price for this option would be high, and none of our interviewees endorsed it – although some clearly recognized the temptation.

The least attractive option – at least from the sound-finance perspective – is to default on the debt. For a country such as Canada, with its own currency, that prospect seems remote. Our standard of living would have to deteriorate significantly before such an option were contemplated, and it would deteriorate even further if it were chosen. Long before actual default occurred, a restructuring of the debt, under the supervision of the IMF, for example, likely would have taken place. Default, or preventative restructuring, might seem like a farfetched scenario, but other G20 countries have had recourse to this "solution" (Mitchener & Trebesch, 2023), and the IMF no longer treats debt restructuring in these countries as a perilous option (Cottarelli, 2017, pp. 95–7). In Canada, the federal government was obliged to confront the prospect in the early 1990s, when Canada's worsening fiscal position prompted credit-rating agencies to issue warnings. Although it is a safe assumption that the federal government at the moment is more or less immune to defaulting on its loans – at least to the extent of non-payment – the provinces are in a different position, as we discuss in Chapter 6. Default, in other words, is not out of the question, but it is a political poison pill.

Conclusion

Canada's fiscal policy response to the pandemic, widely praised in 2020, came under close scrutiny and some harsh criticism as the crisis wound down. The torrent of money creation, in the form of emergency spending programs and direct transfers to households, rescued the economy from collapse and produced the fastest economic rebound on record.

It also contributed to inflationary pressures, produced a severe stock market correction, and left the federal government with an unprecedented level of public debt. Overall debt levels (local, provincial, territorial, and the federal governments together) now exceed 130 per cent of GDP (OECD, n.d.-a). On their own, these figures are not a reason for panic. The pandemic has not had a huge impact on fiscal sustainability: aggregate provincial debt has not changed significantly and federal debt is up, but from a low base. The real challenge will come from the fiscal pressure of future demands, especially for improved health care.

As an instrument of demand management, fiscal policy can offer some relief to volatility, but is prone to mistakes of excess austerity or excess stimulus. Put more precisely, the politicians, bureaucrats, and academic advisors who make the spending, taxing, and borrowing decisions that constitute fiscal policy are unable to estimate accurately the myriad interactions that create the modern market economy or to anticipate events such as wars and famines that destabilize economies and play havoc with predictions. The estimation of debt sustainability is made particularly difficult by uncertain rates of return on capital (Blanchard & Das, 2017).

This chapter outlined two positions on how debt should factor into fiscal policy calculations. The sound-finance position warns against excessive spending both for its inflationary impact and its long-term drag on productivity. Arguing that debts eventually must be repaid (or at least be capable of repayment), sound-finance proponents aim to keep debt costs to a level that does not distort market allocations or render the state unable to respond to the next fiscal crisis. The limits of government spending might be technically unknowable, but that does not mean they do not exist. Eventually a new equilibrium must be found, credit credibility reinforced, and private sector investment unleashed.

Functional-finance theorists claim that this is the wrong way to think about the economy in general, and debt in particular. Rather than placing debt and deficits at, or near, the centre of fiscal policy, they argue that sound fiscal policy must focus on employment and inflation. Debt levels are not, on their own, inflationary, and have contributed relatively little to the post-pandemic increase in costs. These increases are real, and should be addressed with policies that redistribute income to those most negatively affected, but obsession about debt levels is counterproductive to this goal.

Obsession might be unwise, but no responsible fiscal policy can fail to take into account the current unprecedented level of public debt. Can this debt be managed? That depends on what "managed" means. Choosing a manageable level of sovereign debt is an increasingly difficult task. If there is a magic level of debt-to-GDP at which creditors suddenly lose faith and economies begin to implode, it is not clear what that level is. Much depends on the identity of the creditors (domestic or international), the currency in which debts are denominated, the interest rates that apply to different tranches of debt, rates of return on capital, and, of course, real and anticipated growth rates. What does seem clear is that larger debts are riskier than smaller ones, and this applies particularly to the provinces. That is why most members of the economic elite, if given the choice, would prefer declining levels of debt, rather than simply stabilizing debt at what might be too high a level. But very few wanted to lower government spending in order to close fiscal gaps, and enthusiasm for tax increases was equally muted. It would be much better to allow robust economic growth to do the work.

Unfortunately, strong growth, as we argued in Chapter 3, cannot simply be summoned up, and it is not currently anticipated. Critics argue that, although Canadian governments have managed to get through the pandemic, they have no discernible plans for improving growth prospects. Yet fiscal policy's most potent contribution is on the supply side. In other words, spending needs to be productive, not just stimulative. To balance the pandemic's heavy focus on macroeconomic stabilization will require an equal focus on people-centred policies to enhance innovation and spread prosperity. This does not mean simply accepting existing budget commitments or ignoring program effectiveness. As we will show in Chapter 7, there is strong support for program reviews to determine whether current spending is actually contributing to economic priorities – specifically, enhanced productivity – or whether spending is fuelling consumption and little more.

6 Holding the Federation Together

Federal constitutions, Canada's included, are peculiar political arrangements. They have two contradictory aims. One is to maintain the independence and distinctiveness of the country's constituent units. The other is to forge a nation out of diverse parts and to limit local (or parochial) interests in favour of a unified response to internal and external challenges (Diamond, 1973). These contradictory impulses invite the conclusion that federal systems are inherently unstable: they will either evolve towards complete consolidation or break apart as states or provinces insist on complete autonomy (Riker, 1964). But federalism, it turns out, does not have to be a transitory state. Most federal constitutions have survived for impressive lengths of time. Being simultaneously centralized and decentralized can work, but not easily and not all the time.

Federations are resilient because they create the political conditions for peaceful coexistence. These conditions – the specifics of the federal bargain – change with the times. Original divisions of powers need to be modified, and central institutions have to accommodate changing economic and social conditions in the regions. Canada has gone through extended periods in which the federal and provincial governments operate more or less exclusively within their own jurisdictional areas (classical federalism), periods of federal initiatives (unilateral federalism), and periods of extended cooperation (cooperative and even collaborative federalism). The task has always been the same: deliver good public policy while keeping the country together.

In Canada's case, the political project – keeping the country together – has always come first. The economic project – efficient markets and economic growth – has been modified where necessary to serve political ends. Voters and the politicians they elect cannot be permitted to become so disenchanted with the market-friendly policies of either the federal or provincial governments that they are willing to dissolve the federal bargain. As a result, economic policy is crafted with the federal dimension in mind, adding complexity to both policy and governance in Canada.

And yet a strong case has been made that federalism, far from being a burden, is actually a boon to economic policymaking. Federalism does not make governing easier, but it might make governments more responsive. A creative distribution of fiscal and monetary tools, along with appropriate responsibilities, can foster entrepreneurship in search of a locally optimal policy mix. The idea is that subnational governments will compete for the favour of voters and craft economic policy that responds to their preferences. And as long as capital and labour remain mobile, competition will favour jurisdictions that invest in economic growth and restrain rent seeking – the opportunistic pursuit of personal benefits from state-sponsored programs.

Things do not always work out this way. Regional resource and demographic disparities place some subnational governments at a persistent disadvantage. Many of the problems that cry out for collective action are not confined to a single jurisdiction: spillover effects are substantial. The presumption that spending responsibilities and fiscal resources are well matched is more hope than reality. Central governments often have far more fiscal capacity than do their subnational counterparts; in Canada, some provinces have access to revenues that are unavailable to others. The need to shore up a monetary union, persuade capital markets that investment is relatively safe, and provide a minimum standard of public services for all citizens has drawn the federal government into areas that are, strictly speaking, provincial responsibilities. The result of these complications is a fiscally messy landscape with budgetary decisions taken in different places, at different times, often in pursuit of different objectives. Political authorities have generally muddled through, albeit with occasional episodes of rancour and on two occasions formal efforts to dissolve the union itself.

If survival is the ultimate political test, Canada has survived. Has Canada done more than that? Specifically, has federalism encouraged sound policy with sufficient fiscal discipline, or does federalism introduce a risk factor that is not present in unitary governments? Has federalism contributed to a "big government" problem or has it actually achieved efficiencies and ameliorated inequalities that would be much worse without it? Or perhaps the effects of federalism are more modest than many observers will admit and federal arrangements are basically neutral in their effects.

In this chapter, we outline three criteria for evaluating the performance of fiscal federalism institutions – efficiency, equity, and accountability – and provide a preliminary assessment. We then turn to how the federation's fiscal framework coped with the arrival of the pandemic. The pandemic provides an opportunity to evaluate ongoing challenges: how to measure and address fiscal imbalances, how to cope with fiscal vulnerabilities (especially in the provinces), and how to build a risk-sharing approach to economic growth. Here, the tension between what is deemed sound public policy and what is politically feasible is most acute.

Evaluating Fiscal Federalism Institutions

The term "fiscal federalism" refers to the financial arrangements adopted to allow a multilevel political system to operate sustainably. The assignment of responsibilities to different levels is the crucial starting point, followed by an allocation of the taxing capacity needed to resource those responsibilities. Original designs typically give way to adjustments reflecting new roles for the state and new sources of revenue. No part of the federal bargain is subject to more change, accompanied by controversy and contention, than these fiscal arrangements.

Let us assume for the moment that the allocation of responsibilities and revenues has achieved a tolerable equilibrium. The central and subnational governments might wish for different arrangements, but they cannot agree on changes and are not willing to dissolve the federal bargain in their absence. In this situation, one that has prevailed throughout most of recent Canadian history, what costs and benefits of federalism can be expected? The standard economic criteria used to evaluate fiscal federalism are *efficiency* (do these arrangements create optimal policy outcomes at lowest cost?) and *equity* (do they provide for outcomes that create minimal distinctions in personal well-being based on province of residency?). To these we add *accountability* (do fiscal federal arrangements allow citizens insight into which level of government is responsible for the supply of which public goods?).

A review of these criteria helps us appreciate how difficult it is to operate a federal system. But remember, Canada chose a federal system primarily for political reasons – the co-presence of English- and French-speaking populations – not just to enhance economic efficiency. Values such as efficiency, equity and accountability are *a posteriori* considerations that often become entangled with political arguments for changes to the terms of Canadian Confederation. A federal system that cannot achieve some measure of efficiency, equity, and accountability is open to complaints and resentments that can culminate in political arguments for dissolution. And while details of the fiscal federalist terms are being renegotiated constantly, it is a rare circumstance in which all three of these values can be maximized at once.

Efficiency

The efficiency criterion begins with the (safe) assumption that there is a scarcity of resources to achieve a desired outcome. Given scarcity, efficiency requires that the most outputs be obtained with the fewest inputs. Of course, outputs are not outcomes: there is no point in efficiently providing outputs that no one wants. For this reason, the idea of efficiency typically is stretched to imply that the outcomes achieved need to be those that are also the most valued. In fiscal federalism terms, this means an assignment of responsibilities and resources between the national and subnational governments that yields the outcomes that people want at the lowest possible cost.

Those who defend it on efficiency grounds insist that federalism – as long as it is well designed – is superior to centralization in delivering more of what people want at a cost they are willing to bear. Centralized governments make extractive and allocative decisions relying on the preferences of a single set of rulers tasked with devising policies that apply to everyone, regardless of local conditions or circumstances. Under these conditions, critics argue, there is likely to be a suboptimal provision of public goods in some parts of the country – suboptimal to the degree that local tastes and preferences diverge from national ones. In short, defenders of federalism argue that it is better than centralization at preference matching. Subnational governments not only can better tailor their provision of public goods and services to the preference of the local population (the wide-efficiency criterion); in theory, they should also be able to deliver services and allocate transfers more efficiently in the narrow, less waste, sense of the term (Tiebout, 1956). So, if the central government does *not* have a cost advantage compared with subnational governments, decentralizing taxing power and expenditure decisions to local governments generates welfare gains (Oates, 1972).

The efficiency argument for federalism does not end there. Where labour and capital are mobile, subnational governments are expected to compete for investment and workers by adopting agreeable taxation and spending policies. Some defenders of federalism claim this kind of competition keeps governments responsive to constituents, attentive to what is happening in other jurisdictions, and less likely to engage in rent seeking (Weingast, 1995). As a result, federalism is said to be "market preserving" – in other words, it protects the interests of citizens as consumers. The claim is also made that federal systems allow for experimentation and innovation, with medicare in Saskatchewan often cited as a case in point (Gray, 1991). But to achieve the apparent advantages of federalism, a market-preserving federation must exhibit certain key features, among them a clear delineation of responsibilities (with subnational autonomy in economic regulation), a common market to ensure mobility of capital and labour, and a hard budget constraint at the subnational level (Weingast, 2009). Canada is not a classic case of market preservation. Responsibilities overlap, interprovincial trade barriers are serious, and budget constraints are not imposed or enforced by national institutions.

Even if the Canadian federation conformed entirely to the market-preserving model and could deliver some of the efficiencies that proponents anticipate, high levels of decentralization can produce other outcomes (Weaver, 2020). For one, provinces with significant economic autonomy could engage in a taxing and spending competition that resembles a "race to the bottom," with provinces lowering regulations and reducing taxes in a competitive effort to attract mobile resources, particularly capital investment. This kind of bidding war might delight proponents of market-preserving federalism, but imperil provincial revenues. And then there are other dynamics, including emulation and cooperation, which, in at least some policy areas, might reduce competition altogether (Harrison, 2006). Where both federal and provincial governments seek to expand their policy reach, a harmonization of standards through mutual recognition of equivalence is one potential result. The imposition of standards by the national government is another. Deliberate harmonization of standards offends the principles of market preservation, but these principles are seldom honoured in reality anyway (Wallner & Boychuk, 2014).

Of more concern for fiscal policy in a decentralized federal system is the possibility of a patchwork taxation regime combined with the absence of a hard budget constraint – such as a legally enforceable balanced-budget rule – at the provincial level. The former problem has been largely avoided in Canada by Tax Collection Agreements that authorize the federal government to collect income taxes on behalf of provinces and territories in exchange for agreeing to the federal government's definition of a common tax base (Brown, 2020). Allowing the central government to collect tax revenue from sources that are mobile, unevenly distributed, and difficult to administer is the more efficient option (Boadway, 2005), even though some provinces have opted out and harmonization of consumption taxes has not progressed very far.

A more pressing problem is the absence of any agreement regarding debt and deficit levels. Without a hard budget constraint, provinces might be tempted to lower their guard in fiscal policy on the assumption that the federal government will bail them out in the event of debt defaults (Oates, 2008). If provinces acted on this assumption, the efficiency argument for federalism would be weaker, since risk insurance normally reduces the incentive to monitor debts or invest in rainy-day funds. The fact that provinces pay close attention to their debts might have more to do with the low tolerance levels of provincial electorates than the efficiency effects of federalism.

Equity

Equality as a public value is central to the theory of modern liberalism. Liberal citizens approach the state with a set of rights and privileges and expect to be treated equally – that is, without prejudice. Equity is a closely related concept that resides at the heart of the modern welfare state. Equity as a principle permits the state to regulate market transactions and redistribute income to achieve a measure of distributive justice. From minimum-wage legislation to public healthcare services, the modern state has endorsed the values of both equality and equity.

In Canada, where constitutional responsibility for health, social welfare, education, and labour law rests mainly with the provinces, federalism creates a complication. The revenue sources available to the federal government have allowed it to enter the health and social assistance areas using the federal spending power, but a mismatch between revenues and expenditure responsibilities remains. To achieve a measure of equity among citizens, federal and provincial governments first need to balance their revenues and responsibilities. This requirement is referred to as *vertical equity*. The second requirement is for *horizontal equity*, an equitable amount of fiscal capacity (revenues) across the provinces. Equity is not just a matter of what justice for individuals requires; it is also a matter of what governments need. Put another way, without some measure of equity among governments in a federal system, it is difficult to provide for equity among citizens. The history of fiscal federalism in Canada is the story of endless quarrels about exactly what equity demands.

What seems clear is that central governments are the most efficient at collecting taxes from mobile, unevenly distributed sources (Boadway, 2005). The relatively unconstrained taxing authority enjoyed by the federal government has enabled it to redistribute income to Canadians regardless of provincial residence. Individuals pay the federal income tax, federal consumption tax, payroll taxes, and other taxes, and they receive from the federal government public pensions, Employment

Insurance, child benefits, and public goods in the form of defence and infrastructure. Ability to pay is almost never a criterion for access to these benefits (Heath, 2020, p. 154). A great degree of income redistribution occurs through these channels, rather than through intergovernmental fiscal arrangements.

By the same token, provincial governments draw on many of the same tax sources and operate their own health, education, and welfare programs. Social citizenship is therefore a product of what both levels of government provide, which implies the need for a division of revenue sources sufficient to allow both the federal and provincial governments to discharge their responsibilities. Is there an equitable division of revenues between the federal and provincial orders of government (vertical equity)? There is no easy answer to the question, but under the current distribution of revenues and responsibilities, it is the provinces, taken together, that face the steepest fiscal challenge when it comes to balancing budgets consistently.

Horizontal equity is an equally fraught topic. In a federal structure, there are bound to be relatively rich subunits and relatively poor ones. Giving the provinces legal access to adequate revenue sources is part of the answer, and in Canada there are no longer serious restrictions on the taxes that provinces can impose. The real source of inequality is the different tax bases on which the provinces are able to draw. Canada's highly fragmented economy means that some provinces have much richer revenue sources than others simply because their residents are wealthier or because they have access to resource revenues that other provinces do not. This reality has led federal governments since 1957 to provide additional revenues to provinces with a lower-than-average fiscal capacity to ensure that they are capable of delivering "comparable services at comparable rates of taxation" (Brown, 2020, p. 259). To institutionalize this commitment, the principle of equalization was added to the Constitution in 1982, reinforcing the need for seemingly interminable discussions and arguments about how to calculate the level to which provinces should be equalized.

For many years, economists accepted the dictum that a search for equity inevitably would compromise the search for efficiency. Put another way, there is bound to be a trade-off between the two, as redistribution often undermines efficiency (Okun, 1975). In the case of Canadian federalism, for example, efforts to create more equitable outcomes for citizens regardless of provincial or territorial residence might discourage them from leaving places with fewer prospects and heading to places that can make better use of their talents. Provinces on the receiving end of equalization payments might be discouraged from developing alternative revenue sources. Why bother, if transfers will make up the difference?

These are *possible* outcomes of federal arrangements, but evidence for them is meagre. Provincial governments do not relish being dependent on Ottawa, as evidenced by the wide variety of schemes, not all of them sound, that have been embarked upon to lure business and develop own-source revenues. The fact that transfers continue to be required is not a sign of federalism's failure. As Osberg (1995) pointed out some time ago, countries with higher levels of equality tend to grow faster than those without. The redistribution of benefits across jurisdictional lines does not inevitably produce a weaker national economy. The opposite is more likely.

Accountability

Like efficiency and equity, accountability is a political-economic criterion. When social actors have to answer for their actions, there are anticipated economic payoffs in the form of less rent seeking and more attention to the public goods that voters want. The advent of environmental, social, and governance reporting requirements, intended to link economic growth with accountability for social progress, is a case in point.

In the past 30 years, political accountability has most frequently been modelled as a relationship between a principal and an agent who acts on the principal's behalf. Understood this way, accountability requires the agent to answer for its actions, including accepting penalties for failing adequately to protect and advance the principal's interests. In these conventional treatments of accountability, the major problem is asymmetric knowledge. The electorate, for example, might be sovereign, but politicians have privileged information that permits them to dissemble, mislead, and rent seek. To these problems one must add simple incompetence and negligence. Given that agents can be unreliable in these senses, securing accountability requires a clear delineation of responsibilities, adequate and reliable information about performance, and the ability to penalize those who conspicuously fail to deliver what is expected of them.

Federalism confounds these problems. As long as two orders of government are supplying public goods entirely independent of each other, the accountability problem reverts to the singular problem of holding each government accountable for its particular responsibilities. The moment equity or efficiency requires (or recommends) collaboration, or even coordination, it becomes difficult to sort out who is responsible for what. The oft-observed tendency of politicians (and their advisors) to blame others for deficiencies in public policy outcomes is made significantly worse by the opportunity to lay responsibility at the feet of another government. In the case of fiscal policy, deficiencies in provincial healthcare delivery are frequently laid at the feet of the federal government, which, allegedly, has failed to provide adequate resources. Alternatively, blame for housing shortages can be attributed to provincial regulatory recalcitrance as opposed to interest rates and lending practices.

The difficulty of attributing responsibility in federal systems is part of a broader problem that public-choice theorists describe as fiscal illusion. As long as governments have multiple revenue sources, spending can occur without taxpayers' being aware of the costs to them. The fear is that government will become too large as politicians seek to capitalize on the naivete of voters by excessive short-term spending. Federal systems contribute to fiscal illusion to the degree that they hide from voters the true scale of budget commitments, especially those that go to debt servicing. In Canada, as we have seen, both levels of government run deficits. And although the federal government transfers funds to the provinces, the scale of provincial indebtedness is obscured by this dependence.

When transfers are used to increase the size of fiscal commitments, rather than reduce exposure to debt, the sense of getting something for nothing, or something paid for by others, is enhanced. Some fear the result will be a "flypaper effect" in which subnational governments that receive unconditional grants spend more than they would have if revenues had been raised locally. In other words, the grant sticks where it lands – in the hands of receiving governments (Béland et al., 2017). Under these conditions, voters lose the incentive or the ability to hold politicians to account. Rodden (2019, p. 92) summarizes the situation: "Voters face strong incentives to monitor service provision when they understand their role in paying the bill, and may be willing to tolerate much higher levels of inefficiency and rent seeking if intergovernmental transfers foster the perception that other people's money is being wasted."

Federalism can, in theory, protect voters from fiscal illusions and exact a measure of fiscal discipline, but only if each order of government remains within its constitutionally described boundaries. In 2006 the government of Stephen Harper took office with a promise to inaugurate an era of "open federalism" in which governments would be disentangled from each other, fiscal balance would be restored, taxes reduced, and accountability enhanced (Harmes, 2007). Commitment to market-preserving federalism might aggravate issues of equity, but in theory, efficiency and accountability would be improved and transfers made unconditional. Mr. Harper did not invent the idea: the Rowell-Sirois Commission came to a similar conclusion in 1940, and at least one of Mr. Harper's predecessors, Pierre-Elliott Trudeau, was, initially at least, a champion of "classical federalism."

That a blurring of responsibilities and authority has emerged in Canadian federalism is a testament to the power of efficiency and equity values in the federation. Leaders at both the provincial and federal levels have found it advantageous to enter into detailed agreements, negotiated by political executives, that combine the fiscal resources of the national government with the administrative capacity of the provinces (Schertzer et al., 2016). The result has been, in the words of Donald Savoie (2019, p. 120), "a potpourri of federal-provincial agreements, federal-provincial policies, federal-provincial measures, federal-provincial initiatives and federal-provincial regulations." Parliament and provincial legislatures have been largely left out of the negotiations, with the result that accountability is sacrificed in two ways: voters have difficulty attaching responsibility for programs to an identifiable set of decisionmakers, and legislative bodies struggle to hold their executives to account for multiparty agreements.

Observers often feel exasperated at the interminable tensions that linger beneath the surface of fiscal relations in Canada and occasionally break out into open hostility. But is there any wonder? Fiscal federalism in Canada (and elsewhere, no doubt) is subject to a trilemma. One or two of these desirable qualities might be obtained, but securing efficiency, equity, and accountability at once is a daunting, probably impossible, task. When equity and efficiency are both secured, the result is a very messy set of arrangements that make accountability exceedingly hard to achieve. A combination of accountability and efficiency takes us back to the model of market preservation with its insistence on extensive economic authority at the provincial level. This formula has not worked in Canada, where equity considerations demand a strong measure of centrally orchestrated redistribution. A combination of equity and accountability would require one order of government – in Canada, the federal government, where substantial financial capacity resides – either to appropriate programs traditionally delivered by the provinces or to require stringent national standards that could compromise local preferences. This model offends many of the normative tenets of federalism, but it is the one that is typically employed in emergencies, and it is the one that surfaced in the face of the pandemic.

The Pandemic: Addressing a Fiscal Emergency

The Constitution Act, 1867 (Canada, 1867), does not mention pandemics, much less identify which government might be responsible for managing them. National emergencies, on the other hand, were understood to be the job of the federal government under the residual authority of "peace, order, and good government." Of course, provinces can declare emergencies as well, and during the pandemic several did, but these announcements did not give rise to jurisdictional disputes. Disputes arose, as might be expected, but they involved the wisdom of public health regulations, the supply of vaccines, and the appropriate response to protests. There was no dispute over which order of government would lead the fiscal response. This response was going to require massive fiscal capacity and a monetary authority capable of supplying liquidity to panicking markets. Only the federal government could supply the needed fiscal capacity. It was the most efficient player by a significant margin, and the quality of its fiscal response could not be laid at the feet of others. Accountability would not, in theory, be a problem.

The federal response was unequivocal: "Financial considerations should not and will not be an obstacle to hospitals and health systems making the necessary preparations" (Prime Minister of Canada, 2020a). As we described in Chapter 1, the Bank of Canada began to cut interest rates early in March 2020, and the Department of Finance Canada rolled out large employment-support programs beginning with adjustments to Employment Insurance eligibility. The major federal fiscal support for individuals came on 25 March, when the initial emergency-support programs were replaced by the CERB. By then the federal government had already announced changes to Employment Insurance to support business employment and, on 13 March, the $10 billion Business Credit Availability Program.

Because the federal government took on most of the burden of pandemic relief, the provinces had fiscal room to implement their own programs. They responded by postponing interest payments, deferring tax deadlines, or cancelling scheduled tax increases (Gosselin et al., 2020). Provinces also announced their own income-support programs – in some cases to provide wage premiums, in others to help fill gaps in the timing of federal supports, or, in the case of student debt relief, to harmonize with the federal government's initiatives. British Columbia had the largest increase (48.7 per cent) in social protection spending during 2020, mainly through the BC Recovery Benefit and the BC Emergency Benefit for Workers. A series of targeted measures followed, most of them launched at the federal level without much consultation with the provinces. Complaints also followed. When it became clear that for some employees collecting the CERB was going to be more lucrative than working, provincial governments argued that the program was exacerbating worker shortages (Gallant, 2021). To retain and attract workers, including essential workers, they had to offer additional top-up benefits. The federal government's offer of income assistance to students and seniors was similarly criticized. Because these programs did not replace lost income, they created work disincentives and so stifled provincial efforts to reopen their economies (Gosselin et al., 2020).

These flash points aside, at the outset of the pandemic the provinces generally supported the fiscal leadership of the federal government. The response of both orders of government was broadly complementary and, in some cases, coordinated. The public, including residents of Alberta and Saskatchewan (Wesley et al., 2020), were generally satisfied. In other words, federalism did not get in the way of an effective crisis response, although the combined actions of federal and provincial governments might have provided more support, and perhaps more stimulus, than was strictly necessary (Lester, 2020).

What is indisputable is that the federal government bore the largest portion of the cost. Many of the programs launched at the outset of the pandemic involved deferments, and so the overall cost is difficult to estimate, but the direct costs of business and individual support show the scale of the federal commitment. In 2020, spending by all levels of government in Canada increased by 33.4 per cent (Statistics Canada, 2021j). The largest spending category was for social-protection programs, which increased by $106.5 billion, mainly due to the CERB and the Canada Recovery Benefit. In the same vein, the Canada Student Grant was responsible for a 25 per cent increase in education spending by the federal government. As Table 6.1 shows, the federal portion (82 per cent) of the country's economic response during the pandemic was more than four times that of provincial and territorial governments (18 per cent) (Department of Finance Canada, 2021b, p. 79).

With federal funding support in place, provincial and territorial governments closed schools and shut down nonessential businesses. Both before and after federal employment-support programs were announced, provincial governments offered bridge benefits to individuals who did not qualify for the federal programs or were waiting for federal benefits. Since the federal government has unmatched taxation capacity, while provincial governments have jurisdiction over health and education (and presumably have a better understanding of the needs of the local population), the division of work between the two

Table 6.1. Percentage of Federal and Provincial/Territorial Shares of the Economic Response during the Pandemic, as of 9 April 2021

Economic Response	Federal	Provincial/territorial
Direct measures	81.7	18.3
Tax and payment deferrals	73.0	27.0
Credit support	96.9	3.1
Total	82.1	17.9

Source: Department of Finance Canada (2021b).

levels of governments was logical and effective (even if some specific actions were not).

Although the provinces and territories initially were overshadowed by the federal government's fiscal firepower during the pandemic, their regulatory authority was soon on full display in the months that followed. In deciding to close and open schools, impose and suspend masking requirements, and schedule vaccine eligibilities, the provinces were in a strong position to express the will of local electorates. Some managed the task better than others, but no government escaped criticism from affected constituencies. Blame avoidance was on full display whenever the federal government ventured into the realm of mask mandates or travel restrictions.

Compared with these tensions, and occasional clashes, the fiscal situation was remarkably peaceful. All governments benefited from a public relatively passive about increasing debts and deficits. For most people, providing income support dwarfed other priorities (Atkinson & Mou, 2021). Still, academic observers worried that, as the pandemic receded and budgets were presented across the country, the scale of the fiscal challenge would come into focus. Expenditures would increase, especially in the health care arena, and revenues would decline, especially in resource-dependent provinces (Tombe, 2020). Increases in debt would require "future tax increases and expenditure cuts, as interest payments slowly eat into program expenditures" (Hanniman, 2020b, p. 280).

As if to confirm these predictions, during the height of the pandemic Newfoundland and Labrador made it clear that it lacked the capacity to fund a pandemic support program. On 20 March 2020, the premier of that province asked the federal government for urgent financial help when the province could not borrow to finance the operation of government because bond and short-term funding markets had frozen. The Bank of Canada's liquidity supports stabilized markets, and the federal government subsequently provided loan assurances and a proposal to financially restructure hydroelectric generation and transmission projects on the Lower Churchill Falls (Prime Minister of Canada, 2021). With other provinces also confronting fiscal stress because of the pandemic, the time seemed ripe to revisit transfer programs and put provincial finances on a firmer footing (Béland et al., 2020).

In spring 2021, members of the economic elite, especially those at the provincial level, were certainly willing to entertain the possibility of a new fiscal deal. As one provincial public servant put it, "federal-provincial fiscal arrangements are just a total mess. There needs to be a root-and-branch reform" [Bureaucrat 30]. The biggest complaint, however, was not the lack of federal generosity or the worry that without reform the provinces would soon be insolvent; it was the complications of equalization and the unreliability of revenues from transfers. Being beholden to the federal government and having to wait on federal budgets was more troubling for the provinces than the overall state of their finances.

As it transpired, post-pandemic provincial finances were not in the dire straits that many had imagined. At least not for the immediate future. The provinces emerged from the pandemic's highest spending period with much smaller deficits than had been predicted. Expenditures had increased, but rapid economic recovery and surprise inflation meant that revenues increased as well. Part of the revenue boost came in the form of a direct transfer from the federal government under the "Safe Restart" agreements signed with the provinces and territories in late 2020. These agreements provided a transfer to the provinces of $19 billion to address COVID-19 financial stressors, including vulnerable populations, personal protective equipment, contact tracing, and paid sick leave. The other major source of financial relief was increased provincial tax revenues generated by taxes paid on federal programs such as CERB and subsidies to business. As a result, provincial income tax revenues actually increased in 2020/1 by almost $6 billion over the previous fiscal year (Tombe, 2021b).

The fears of provincial distress were at least temporarily in abeyance, but a sustainable federal-provincial fiscal bargain was no closer to being realized. Since the Great Financial Crisis, the provincial and territorial net debt-to-GDP ratio had increased from 25.1 per cent in 2009 to approximately 31 per cent in 2021. The fiscal sustainability problem lies as much with particular provinces as with the provinces as a group. Some are on a relatively solid fiscal footing while others are under continual fiscal stress. Figure 6.1 shows the net-debt-to-GDP ratio of each province from 1981 to 2021. In a dire warning offered in November 2020 as the pandemic gained momentum, the Parliamentary Budget Office

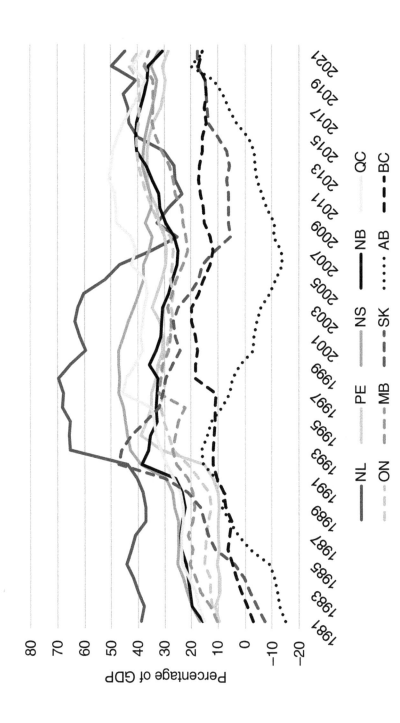

Figure 6.1. Provincial Net Debt as a Percentage of Provincial GDP, 1981–2021
Notes: Net debt level of provinces (millions of dollars) on a public accounts basis; provincial GDP is expenditure based (millions of current dollars).
Sources: Data from Department of Finance Canada (2022c); Statistics Canada (2022d). Contains information licensed under the Open Government Licence – Canada.

predicted that the debt-to-GDP ratio of the provinces and territories as a group would grow in the next decades while the federal ratio would decline (PBO, 2020b). More ominously, the report concluded that only three provinces – Ontario, Quebec, and Nova Scotia – were on a fiscally sustainable path; the other provinces and territories faced fiscal gaps of varying degrees. A more recent assessment by the PBO maintained that the fiscal situation of the provinces and territories is not sustainable over the long term, except for Quebec, Alberta, Saskatchewan, and Nova Scotia (PBO, 2022b).

Tombe (2020, p. 1107), whose conclusions parallel those of the PBO, calculates that over a 70-year horizon and without changes to tax regimes or transfers, provincial expenditures will outstrip increases in revenues by about 3 per cent. Nearly 60 per cent of the gap will arise from increases in health care costs, while 40 per cent will be traceable to slower growth. Alberta and Newfoundland are at greatest risk, although for very different reasons.

The pandemic was a reminder that, although fiscal shocks require unfamiliar, even risky, responses, these responses will not solve the problem of financial instability in a fiscal union. Stability, as we have discussed, is difficult to achieve, so in federal systems risk-reduction and risk-sharing strategies typically are employed to reduce the spillover effects of generalized and asymmetric economic shocks. Risk sharing implies a pooling of risk such that individual subnational governments are not forced into debt default in the face of significant economic downturns or increased calls on government services. Risk reduction requires fiscal discipline, the imposing of rules that require governments to abstain from excessive spending (or in some cases insufficient taxing) that would imperil the credit worthiness of other governments. The federal government needs to maintain enough budget discipline to preserve its capacity to assist provinces, while the provinces are expected to adhere to fiscal rules so that bailouts are not required. Canada has more experience with risk sharing than with risk reduction, but we begin with the latter because economic shocks such as pandemics and their aftermath remind us that the demands of resilience and sustainability require a consideration of unfamiliar policy responses.

Risk Reduction

The European Union pioneered the adoption of fiscal rules to reduce the risks associated with a monetary union composed of "core" and "periphery" countries. Countries that join the EU have to meet the conditions in the Maastricht Treaty: a strict limit on annual budget deficits of 3 per cent of GDP and a limit on the accumulated debt-to-GDP ratio of 60 per cent. The treaty also has a "no-bailout clause" that prohibits the EU or a member state from directly purchasing government debt (Eichengreen & von Hagen, 1995). Most member countries have, at one point or another, run afoul of these rules and been subject to an Excessive Debt Procedure – advice followed by monitoring – but very little has been done to enforce the rules. Much more effort has been expended changing them to accommodate exceptional circumstances or changing economic conditions. As these rules faltered, EU countries began looking more intensely at risk-sharing strategies, the most extreme of which would entail the creation of a fiscal union with a central government possessing significant taxing and spending powers (Bilbiie et al., 2021).

In Canada, the federal government has declined to follow a risk-reduction approach, at least not one that entails adopting fiscal rules for itself or imposing rules on the provinces. Provincial debt and deficit situations are monitored, of course, but the Constitution provides no legislative basis for direct intervention, even though loss of faith in the creditworthiness of a province could have a deleterious effect on the credit of all Canadian governments. Attempts to advise and assist provinces have been indirect. Before Alberta defaulted in 1936, the federal government and the Bank of Canada sought to offer loans and debt restructuring, mostly to avoid downgrades in the Dominion's credit rating and that of neighbouring provinces (Ascah, 1999). William Aberhart's Social Credit government declined this assistance, laid blame for the impending financial collapse at the feet of the "money power," and proceeded to legislate reductions in repayment rates and schedules. The federal government resisted the temptation to penalize the province, beyond isolating it as an "aberrant debtor," and sought, instead, to calm financial markets (Ascah, 1999, p. 80). This highly unusual confrontation has not been repeated, but Saskatchewan did flirt with insolvency in the 1990s, and both it and Newfoundland and Labrador have required cash infusions from Ottawa to tide them over and allow the country to retain a reputation for fiscal trustworthiness.

The problem of fiscal soundness within the Canadian federation would be far less worrisome if provincial debts were not so substantial and/or if federal transfers were larger and more reliable. As it is, the provinces have more outstanding debt than any other subnational governments in wealthy federations (Hanniman, 2018, p. 57). In 2019, the provinces (plus municipalities) were responsible for 58.6 per cent of the country's total outstanding debt, while the federal government was responsible for 36.5 per cent. In Spain, subnational debt was only 21 per cent of the total in 2019; in Germany, the states were responsible for 34.1 per cent (OECD, 2021a).

Why are provincial debts so high? Most explanations begin with the open-ended character of provincial spending responsibilities, especially health care, combined with highly variable revenue sources (Hanniman, 2020a, p. 1). In general, small, less diversified economies, especially those that are resource dependent, are subject to revenue shocks, both positive and negative. Health care spending, on the other hand, is relentless and brooks few limits. This observation brings us to the other frequently cited source of provincial financial problems: the apparent inadequacy of federal transfers. Although federal officials contest this explanation for provincial fiscal stress, many of our provincial interviewees mentioned the size and stability of fiscal transfers.

Then there is the question of provincial taxation. David Macdonald (2022, p. 18) makes the point that the provinces differ in their "fiscal effort" – that is, the amount of revenue they raise from their own sources relative to the size of their economies. Quebec, whose net debt-to-GDP ratio has been falling since 2013, relies on own-source revenue more than any other province. Ontario, on the other hand, has the highest debt-to-GDP ratio among the provinces, but one of the lowest levels of own-source revenues. Provincial deficits, in this interpretation, are a function not of increased spending but of lower than necessary levels of taxation. From the Department of Finance Canada in Ottawa the point is made this way: "If Alberta had Quebec's tax system, they would have a forty-billion-dollar surplus. Are we going to cry for them? They're being stubborn, but it's their choice, right?" [Bureaucrat 18].

Whether deficits are the product of exogenous forces or internal policy choices, provinces can maintain a relatively high level of public debt because no federally imposed fiscal rules stand in their way. As we outlined in Chapter 5, most of the provinces have experimented with fiscal rules since the 1990s, and most of these rules call for balanced budgets within a given time frame. But these rules were not adopted to curry favour with the federal government; they were meant to signal to voters that provincial governments would be prudent stewards of provincial finances. Credit-rating agencies welcomed these rules as well, but it is not clear they had much effect on the rates the provinces paid on their loans. Credit-rating officials expressed some of the same scepticism found among finance journalists: "Some provinces still have balanced-budget legislation but it never seems to hold up; it's always given a pass in times of stress. What value does it really have?" [Economist 20].

Of much more value is the overall management of provincial debt. For example, by lengthening the average term of their debt stock, provinces increase credit agencies' comfort with interest costs ten years out. When debt financed at high interest rates is rolled over at lower rates, fiscal room appears without any fiscal effort. According to Macdonald (2022, p. 21), in 2022 "nine out of 10 provinces are paying less interest, as a proportion of GDP, than they were after the last recession." This happy situation is the product of lower interest rates overall, and the rollover of debt on more agreeable terms.

Of course, low interest rates are not guaranteed, and post-COVID-19 they were on the rise. The point, however, is that any reassurance provided by fiscal rules at the provincial level is one (probably small) part of a larger picture of sustainability. Another part is the speed with which spending can be unwound in the event that a rapid reduction is required. Here the federal government has a distinct advantage, as the pandemic illustrated. As one provincial deputy observed: "The federal government has an easier job; their programs are more time limited. If you look at the wage subsidy, the rent subsidy, the EI program and before that CERB, those come to an end sometime, probably over the next twelve-to-eighteen months. Not quite the case for provinces" [Bureaucrat 20]. The fiscal room obtained by winding up temporary programs leaves the federal government with the opportunity to strike out in new directions, such as childcare and long-term care, issues that the pandemic brought to the fore. For the provinces, the option of beginning and then ending programs is much more limited.

What the provinces can do is borrow at relatively low interest rates – not as low as the rates charged the federal government, but much better than they would be without the safe haven of a national government with a hard money currency. Problems arise with economic reversals, such as a combination of high interest rates and low growth rates. Then, debt has to be repriced and the spread between federal and provincial borrowing begins to matter. Even floating provincial bonds can be difficult. Credit-rating agencies are naturally attentive to changes in fiscal fortunes, but Moody's, for example, assigns all provinces a very high probability of bailout from the federal government.

For political reasons if nothing else, the presumption that the federal government will bail out a province that cannot meet its obligations is almost certainly correct. Hanniman (2020a) argues that the relative dependence of provinces on federal transfers has little, if any, effect on bailout probabilities. In our online survey of more than 500 Canadians (Figure 6.2), half agreed or strongly agreed that, "even if provinces make poor decisions, the federal government should never allow a province to declare bankruptcy." The substantial number in the "I don't know" column suggests that this is a prospect many had not contemplated.

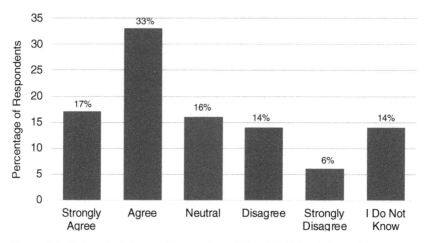

Figure 6.2. Public Opinion on Economic and Fiscal Policies: "Even if provinces make poor decisions, the federal government should never allow a province to declare bankruptcy."
Source: Atkinson and Mou (2021).

The danger is that this implied guarantee, plus the safe haven of the Canadian dollar, will encourage provinces to assume an inadvisable level of risk. Fiscal shocks or not, provinces continue to borrow, and credit markets continue to accept their business. In 2022, the credit ratings for the provinces varied from Aaa for British Columbia to A1 for Newfoundland and Labrador, while the post-pandemic federal rating sat at Aaa (Moody's Investor Service, 2022). Note that none of the provincial officials we interviewed expressed any interest in borrowing beyond the need to smooth the business cycle and invest in capital projects. In fact, the flurry of fiscal rules provinces embarked upon in the 1990s suggests a willingness to accept fiscal discipline as long as it is imposed by the provincial governments themselves. But very few people, credit agencies included, take these rules seriously; they rely, instead, on the federal government to come to the rescue in the event of a fiscal collapse. In the meantime, what the provinces seek from the federal government is more risk sharing, ideally in the form of permanent fiscal transfers to reduce the effects of a fiscal shock.

Risk Sharing

If national governments in federal states are unwilling to impose risk-reduction rules on subnational ones, they need to find ways to share risk that do not involve bailing one out every time a fiscal crisis occurs. Risk sharing involves providing permanent programs that pool resources so that some, or all, constituent units do not become fiscally stressed in trying to meet citizens' demands. Some risk sharing involves transfers across individuals and regions with the intention of permanently narrowing the vertical fiscal imbalance. Some risk sharing is aimed explicitly at providing collective insurance against asymmetric shocks. In practice, most transfers programs do both.

In the early twentieth century, very few risk-sharing mechanisms existed; when the Great Depression hit, some provinces were completely overwhelmed. The initial response from the Dominion government took the form of loans and grants-in-aid, but these were stop-gaps, not solutions. In federal systems, two orders of government must reach some form of agreement, or modus vivendi, on how the risks of financing the modern state (especially its welfare components) are to be shared among them, rather than being shouldered exclusively by subnational units. Risk sharing can be accomplished in two ways: 1) centralize fiscal policy by adopting mutual insurance systems such as an unemployment insurance, health insurance, and universal pension plans to supply common income supports and services; and/or 2) adopt a system of fiscal transfers from the centre to the subnational units to stabilize their revenues, establish service standards, and permit local tailoring of programs. Political necessity dictates that Canada employ both of these strategies.

Centralization

Governments in market economies have sought to reduce the risks borne by individual citizens as they confront the challenges of raising children, earning a living, safeguarding their health, and providing for their old age. The modern welfare state is built around programs that have been in place for over a century to help avoid the catastrophic consequences of failure to navigate these risks successfully. Governments differ substantially in their attitudes towards risk sharing, the generosity of their contributions, the appropriate recipients, and the design of their programs (Esping-Andersen, 1990). These differences aside, a hallmark of the welfare state is a willingness to provide a "social safety net" for citizens.

In Canada most of that social safety net is provided directly and indirectly by the federal government. From the Great Depression onward, the history of income security in Canada has been that of massive centralization (Banting, 1982). The logic is explicitly one of risk sharing.

As the Rowell-Sirois Commission pointed out in 1940, business needs a level playing field for fear that the costs of social security will create competitive (dis)advantages. As long as there are no restrictions on mobility, factors of production will migrate to the jurisdictions that impose the least tax burden or that provide the most public goods. To generate the harmony required to sustain a political union, all else being equal, federal governments are well placed to provide for more redistribution than are provincial governments (Usher, 1980). Add to that the federal government's unimpeded access to all tax fields, and you have the conditions for central provision.

Of course, the provinces have had a lot to say about the intrusive character of the federal spending power. Even as they willingly surrendered authority over Employment Insurance to the federal government, in other areas, such as pensions, negotiations proved to be highly contentious. Not only did Quebec insist on its own plan, all provinces had different ideas about the scale of benefits that should be provided by the Canada Pension Plan and the level of contributions that should be required of employers and employees. As long as national programs had to be negotiated with the provinces, the fear was that the federal government would grow to reflect the ambitions of provincial politicians. Rather than too little government – the likely outcome of exclusive provincial jurisdiction – the fear was that cooperative federalism would mean too much government, or at least too much overlap and confusion (Cairns, 1979).

Despite the federal government's commitment to fiscal retrenchment in the 1990s and again in the early 2000s, it has maintained a consistent preference for direct federal provision, adopting a "social investment" approach to social spending (Boychuk, 2013). Support for dependent children is a good example. From tax deductions for children, through Family Allowances and child tax credits, the modern welfare state has privileged children on efficiency grounds – namely, that spending on children produces positive externalities, and without support parents might not be able to make the necessary investments (Milligan, 2016). At the federal level, the pattern over time has been a significant consolidation and expansion of benefits and increased targeting to income. The provinces operate complementary programs, and most rely on the Canada Revenue Agency for implementation, while employing different eligibility criteria. There is nothing to stop the provinces from using their taxes for different purposes, since the Canada Child Benefit would still be available, but, in the spirit of competitive federalism, no province has shown any interest in abandoning this jurisdiction.

The same pattern of federal leadership is evident in the childcare area, and for many of the same reasons. In 2004, Paul Martin's Liberal government proclaimed the need for "a truly national system of early learning and childcare" (Parliament of Canada, 2004), and followed up with federal-provincial agreements that the Stephen Harper Conservative government subsequently cancelled (Boychuk, 2013, p. 253). It was not until 2021 that a fully fledged program became part of the federal government's fiscal commitment. The program was modelled after Quebec's daycare program – an example of the policy spillover effect of federalism. Unlike the Canada Child Benefit, the childcare program is built around a shared-cost formula familiar to students of fiscal federalism. Provincial reaction initially was tepid, but eventually all the provinces signed on, for the same reason they typically agree to other federal cost-sharing initiatives: to obtain a share of the tax revenues required to fund the programs.

As a risk-sharing feature of fiscal federalism, central provision is made possible only by the exercise of federal spending power – the constitutional doctrine that asserts the federal government's right to spend or lend funds for any purpose it chooses, including attaching conditions where it has no direct legislative authority (Banting, 2005; Hogg, 2001). Long-standing objections to the use of the spending power – that it contradicts the *Constitution Act, 1867* (Canada, 1867), and so rests on dubious legal grounds (see, for example, Kellock & LeRoy, 2007) or that it offends the principles of classical federalism (Telford, 2003) – have been largely ignored or discounted by the courts. The federal government's legitimacy, like that of any government, depends on giving the democratic electorate what it wants, at least some of the time. And because, for fiscal or other reasons, the provinces have been unable or unwilling to shoulder the fiscal risks associated with major social programs, the federal government has chosen to engage in both risk sharing and, simultaneously, nation building. Not even Quebec, the province that has offered the most resistance to the use of the spending power, objects to its existence. What the provinces traditionally have asked for is some kind of limitation on its exercise (Telford, 2003, p. 44).

Interviews with provincial finance officials make it clear that the point is not to debate the legality of the spending power but to establish its sustainability. The provision of national programs has been accepted as inevitable, but the provision of the revenues to maintain them is a constant source of tension. Rather than object to the proffering of financial incentives, something over which they have no control, provincial politicians and public servants instead insist that the federal government refrain from dumping the financial risks onto them. Most federal systems accomplish the sustainability task by transferring significant revenue from the national to subnational governments. In Canada the result is often open conflict and doubts that any form of federalism that depends on intergovernmental transfers can deliver efficiency, equity, or accountability.

Specific-Purpose Transfers

As we have pointed out, scepticism about the wisdom of transfers revolves around the concept of fiscal illusion. By separating the source of funds from their ultimate use, transfers allegedly increase the overall size of government, promote rent seeking, and reduce accountability. The evidence is mixed: not all transfer-dependent federations exhibit these pathologies, although transfer dependency generally contributes to poorer macroeconomic outcomes (Rodden & Wibbels, 2002). From the perspective of decisionmakers, transfers create other kinds of headaches that have little to do with state expansion or political predation. Perhaps the biggest problem, for members of the Canadian economic elite, is not knowing if transfers will continue or if the conditions for receiving them will be adjusted unilaterally. From our interviews, here is a particularly forceful expression of these concerns: "We need to get the feds to stop doing the bait and switch that they tend to engage in, which is, they take the flavour of the month, prescription drugs or long-term care facilities, and they say, 'Here's a bag of money for the provinces if you agree to do this programming.' But there's no long-term guarantee that that money is going to be available, and the feds are really quite shameless. Five years down the road, they just kind of walk away from that, but have the public hooked on that program and the provinces are left completely holding the bag" [Bureaucrat 30].

This position on fiscal risk is expressed most pointedly in the health care arena, where provincial officials make constant reference to the federal government's declining share of the cost: "I don't think people understand that the federal government only pays between twenty and twenty-five per cent of health care costs. I just don't think people know that, because there's a health minister in Ottawa, so clearly, they must pay their share, but they don't" [Politician 17].

Health care is the largest single expenditure for provinces and territories, comprising between 30 and 50 per cent of their annual budgets. For provincial politicians, nothing is more important: "The fiscal imbalance, in fact, is the CHT [Canada Health Transfer] question. I think we should have a goal in terms of percentage ... It is now roughly at twenty-three per cent, depending on how you count ... The objective we had set in talking with the feds was to put it back around thirty-five per cent" [Politician 5].

This fixation on the federal government's cash transfer ignores the income-tax points transferred to the provinces under the *Established Programs Financing Act* (Canada 1977). The original 50/50 split for health care was amended at that time so that half of the federal government's contribution would take the form of a tax-point transfer rather than cash. Although provincial officials (politicians and bureaucrats) claim (to a person) that the federal contribution has shrunk to less than 25 per cent, and in March 2021 insisted that it be raised to 35 per cent, the federal government continues to maintain that its commitment has not diminished in proportionate terms (McIntosh, 2021, 2022). As it is, the Canada Health Transfer (CHT) is the largest federal transfer, totaling $43 billion in fiscal year 2021/2. Over the nine fiscal years from 2012/13 to 2021/3, the total CHT grew by nearly 51 per cent, while the total Canada Social Transfer (CST) grew by only 30 per cent.

Still, there is sympathy for the provincial position, not necessarily on historical grounds, but on grounds of financial stability. From the heights of the Ottawa economic establishment, this observation from our interviews sums up a broad consensus: "Obviously, the provinces need more money for the medical system. They're going to get more money, but they're going to have to ensure that they agree to all the parameters and national standards. That's how you bail out the provinces. You don't give them money to pay their debt; you just give them more money to cover their most expensive expenses" [Economist 17]. Public finance economists are generally on board: "I'm willing to say that my concern is that there's a long-run fiscal imbalance and that the distribution of tax powers in this country now probably favours spending too much on federal constitutional priorities and too little on provincial constitution priorities" [Economist 21]. Most Canadians agree. Surveys find a substantial majority favours increased federal transfers to help the provinces cope (Breton & Parkin, 2022). If increasing transfers is such a good idea, you might wonder why it took so long to secure an agreement. As we explained in Chapter 5, it is not because the federal government has a greater need for the revenues: the PBO (among others) has pronounced the federal fiscal future relatively healthy compared to that of the provinces. The real problem is to agree on the most appropriate formula and to establish what, if any, conditions should apply.

When, in 2015, a majority Liberal government came to power in Ottawa, one of the first items of business was the negotiation of a new health care accord. Deliberations on an increase in transfers broke down, but bilateral agreements provided the provinces that signed on with $11.5 billion targeted to improving home and community care, mental health, and addiction services (Canada, 2022). As a condition of receiving this additional federal funding, recipients all agreed to report on 12 common performance indicators, including improvements in wait times. The idea behind specific-purpose transfers was to incentivize innovation, increase efficiency, and improve health outcomes. As part of the rationale, the then health minister, Jane Philpott, pointed out that, although the provinces had enjoyed 12 years of substantial increases in transfers, health outcomes, including wait times, had seen few meaningful improvements (Tasker, 2016).

These kinds of conditional transfers annoy provinces, but they address the elusive issue of accountability and the political imperative of credit taking. The federal government has made it clear that new funding needs to be responsive to centrally defined priorities where some political credit can be mustered. At the federal level, the idea of simply increasing cash payments is met with the familiar argument that feeding provincial coffers is equivalent to giving the provinces a free ride: "The provinces have their own taxation power, like the federal government … We cannot just give them money because the idea was to cover fifty per cent of spending. That instantly led the provinces to spend more because it's going to be partly covered" [Bureaucrat 16]. But so far, the accountability mechanism for special funding on mental health and home care is limited to reporting requirements (Mou, 2021). There has been no funding scale-back or penalty for provinces or territories that fail to improve health outcomes. Accountability, in other words, is more a matter of input (credit for dollars spent) than of outcomes (improvements in health care performance).

If spiking health costs are a function of organization, negotiation, and medical practice, it is not irrational to insist that new monies address the cost-curve problem. Or, if that is too much to ask, then transfers could be spent on agreed-upon national priorities. In November 2022, federal and provincial health ministers met at Vancouver to negotiate just such a deal. Federal officials were prepared to increase health funding via the CHT, but insisted on attaching two conditions: establishing a nation-wide database to track health outcomes based on common indicators, and creating a national health human resources plan (DeRosa, 2022). At the time, premiers instructed their health ministers not to accept any conditions, and talks broke down. They resumed in January 2023, and by February a long-term funding arrangement had been negotiated in which the federal government agreed to provide $46.2 billion in new spending in exchange for provincially determined targets around access to primary care and specialized services. Specific agreements with each of the provinces are intended to preserve an element of local prioritization while ensuring better compilation and sharing of electronic health information.

Arguably, a formula that recognizes differences in provincial costs would also add an element of rationality to the debate (Marchildon & Mou, 2014). The Atlantic provinces have pointed to a future in which many of their residents will be older than the national average and therefore more dependent on the health care system. Our interviewees appreciated the logic: "Newfoundland per capita health care will be different than Alberta or somewhere that doesn't have some of those geographic challenges. All that needs to be reflected" [Bureaucrat 11]. So perhaps some kind of demographic adjustment would be reasonable: "They probably should put in some type of aging component to the health transfer because some of the provinces are aging at a faster rate. I think that would be a reasonable tweak" [Economist 2]. An age-adjusted allocation of CHT might be more generally accepted and widely understood than adjustments to equalization (MacNevin, 2004; Marchildon & Mou, 2014).

These sorts of shifts to recognize fiscal risks are a possibility, but it is hard to be optimistic. For one thing, there is no agreement on what drives costs. Even interviewees from the Atlantic provinces conceded that costs are not driven exclusively by demographics: "I don't believe that we can conclude that the Maritimes are fiscally sustainable or not, for the following reason: the big driver of health care spending is not demographics, it's the wage escalation that results from competition among various jurisdictions for scarce health resources" [Economist 19]. Still, for critics of fiscal federalism who argue that transfers promote waste and incentivize risk taking, attaching conditions represents a constructive response, albeit one that works best when the parties to the transaction agree on the basic goals. The finance officials we interviewed were on board. As one federal politician commented, "the government of Canada can certainly show leadership and take the initiative, but they have to recognize from day one, it's not going to work if it's a unilateral approach" [Politician 9]. Provincial officials, who can be counted on to resist unilateralism, agree: "It's better, if we have national priorities, that the premiers agree on it and the provinces either have the tax room in order to fund it from the local tax base or that there is an envelope program [that] doesn't require us to enter into multiple small agreements" [Bureaucrat 26].

Signs of harmony in the form of long-term funding agreements should not be interpreted as indicative of a new dawn in federal-provincial relations. As Banting (2005, p. 136) reminds us, "[t]he shared-cost model places greater emphasis on inter-governmental negotiation and agreement, but retains the potential for unilateral action." Unilateralism would need to be justified, but it is worth noting that most of our survey respondents were comfortable with the idea that transfers should come with conditions. We asked if they agreed or disagreed with this statement: "Financial support from the federal government to the provinces should have no strings attached. That is, support should not require the provinces to do certain things." Only about a third of our respondents (34 per cent) agreed. Special-purpose transfers need to have a purpose, ideally one that is agreeable to both the federal and provincial governments.

Equalization

Most Canadians are aware that richer provinces, those with higher per capita incomes, provide financial support to those whose residents are less well off. Many, perhaps most, are unaware that equalization is a federal program. The federal government collects taxes across the country and provides a portion of those revenues to provinces that are defined as "have not." Hardly anyone understands the formula that calculates the size and allocation of these "equalization payments" (but see Tombe, 2021a), which has changed numerous times over the years. But one part of equalization is widely understood: it is a controversial redistributive program. Shifting tax revenue from some parts of the country to other parts, and doing so over an extended period, is bound to provoke grumbling, even anger.

As a federal program involving the transfer of funds to provincial governments, equalization began in the 1950s, but the collection of revenue in one part of the country and the spending of revenue in another has been a controversial feature of Canadian politics since before Confederation (Béland et al., 2017). Political leaders in Canada West – George Brown, for example – were convinced that tax monies collected there were being lavished on projects to benefit the residents of Canada East (Heaman, 2017). The sense of fiscal grievance did not stop there. Every part of the country seemed to believe it was inadequately compensated for the taxes it had given up to join Confederation. The first complaints came from the Maritime provinces, whose political leaders petitioned for "better terms." And they got them, albeit in modest amounts that kept them in a state of dependency on federal patronage. Manitoba, Alberta, and Saskatchewan were all deprived of the revenues from public lands and natural resources on entry into Confederation, and had to fight for decades to achieve equity with other provinces. As Heaman (2017, p. 459) observes, "[v]iewed through a fiscal lens, the early history of Confederation reveals a pattern of systemic consolidation and centralization of power."

The structure of fiscal federalism has changed fundamentally since the era of clientelism and federal patronage. Legislated programs of support long ago replaced political discretion as the source of federal support for provincial governments, although special arrangements continue to be negotiated. None of these programs is more controversial, or fundamental to nation building, than equalization. The federal government began to make equalization payments to the provinces in 1957, partially to accommodate Quebec and make secession less appealing to Quebecers (Béland & Lecours, 2014). The formula for equalization is designed to address horizontal fiscal imbalances that emerged with the modern welfare state. These were not the only payments that were launched in this period – subsidies for hospital insurance began at the same time – but they were unique in being entirely unconditional. Authorized under federal legislation, the payments followed a formula based on the ability of each province to raise revenues. Initially all provinces except Ontario received payments, but as the formula changed to include revenues from natural resources, Alberta and British Columbia joined the ranks of the "have" provinces: their citizens contributed to the program, but their governments until recently had not been recipients.

In contemporary Canada, virtually all members of the economic elite support the concept of equalization. They have little choice. With the passage of the *Constitution Act, 1982* (Canada, 1982), the principle of equalization became an entrenched part of the country's constitutional framework. The commitment to provincial equity was made clear in section 36 (2): "Parliament and the government of Canada are committed to the principle of making equalization payments to ensure that provincial governments have sufficient revenues to provide reasonably comparable levels of public services at reasonably comparable levels of taxation." Equalization tracks the economic fortunes of the provinces and offers a mutual insurance program to account for changes in fiscal capacity. The rationale was nicely summarized by one of our interviewees: "A challenge here in Canada has been a very asymmetric economy across provinces, where some provinces will be booming while others are not ... An important thing the federal government can do is to smooth over those regional shocks a bit more easily than any provincial government can do" [Economist 13].

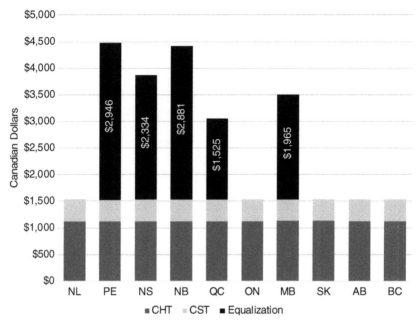

Figure 6.3. Canada Health Transfer, Canada Social Transfer, and Equalization
Payments per Capita, by Province, Fiscal Year 2021/2
Notes: CHT = Canada Health Transfer; CST = Canada Social Transfer.
Sources: Department of Finance Canada (2022d); Statistics Canada (2021f). Contains
information licensed under the Open Government Licence – Canada.

Discontent with the formula grew in the early 2000s to the point that
various commissions were created to review the terms and suggest
reforms. The thorny issue of natural resource inclusion was settled in
2007 in favour of counting 50 per cent of those revenues while using a
ten-province base for the calculation of average revenues. At the moment, the program equalizes the less wealthy provinces' fiscal capacity
to the national average of revenues produced by an array of provincial
taxes. The current formula includes caps on the total amount available, but allows for increases based on growth of the economy. It also
contains rules establishing the time frame for calculation (currently a
three-year weighted moving average) and rules to prevent perverse
outcomes, such as situations in which a recipient province would be
better off in per capita terms than a non-recipient province (Tombe,
2021a). As Figure 6.3 shows, equalization payments are not the largest
federal transfer, but they are the most explicit expression of risk sharing.

Generations of economists and politicians have debated the merits of existing and potential formulas for calculating equalization. Politically, the most vexing problem is that certain provinces are perpetual contributors, in the sense that their residents' taxes pay for equalization, while other provinces are persistent recipients. Their citizens also contribute, of course, but they receive more than they give. The program unambiguously establishes a commitment to equity at the level of individual service provision, but it does so at the expense of inequity at the level of provincial finances. Windfall revenues from natural resources complicate and occasionally destabilize the formula, but certain realities persist. Quebec, for example, has never been a net contributor to equalization; Alberta has not been a recipient since fiscal year 1964/5 (Staples, 2018). Newfoundland and Labrador, along with Saskatchewan, have oscillated between have and have-not status based on oil prices. One of our interviewees explained some of these oscillations this way: "In places like Alberta, Saskatchewan, and Newfoundland, with a drop in the price of oil things have changed fairly dramatically. And it was also not anticipated that provinces like Ontario would be on the receiving end, which has happened fairly recently" [Economist 5].

Discontent persists, and has been fostered in one or another province for political purposes. In 2021, the Kenney government in Alberta went to the trouble of orchestrating a referendum on equalization, ostensibly to gauge the extent of public discontent with a federal program that only a handful of people understand. The referendum's main appeal for provincial politicians was as a bargaining chip in negotiations with the federal government on issues such as environmental regulation (Jacques et al., 2021). This pattern of persistent complaint, gamesmanship, and periodic reform obscures an important fact: equalization has created an expectation that Canadians will take care of one another on the assumption that economic fortune will always be unevenly distributed. Some provinces have little need for the insurance that equalization provides, while others could not survive as recognizable entities without it. Mary Janigan (2020, p. 4) captures the program's importance to national, solidaristic, risk sharing: "Equalization is the improbable glue that holds the nation together. It does not inspire fierce patriotism like a flag or a pledge of allegiance. It is not flashy. Money whisks between governments with a digital flicker. But those transfers create an east-west bond that is stronger than trade ties or cultural differences. Poorer governments know that when times are tough, Ottawa will contribute to their bottom lines."

Clearly, the equity values of federalism are well served by a program that, by definition, is intended to provide equal services to Canadians.

But equalization is not the only program that has differential regional effects. To appreciate the extent of regional impact, consider the amounts the federal government spends in each province (all major transfer programs included) and the amount raised. As James McAllister (2018) points out, the federal government relies on taxpayers in Ontario, British Columbia, Alberta, and Quebec for about 90 per cent of corporate and personal income taxes. In a "normal" year, such as 2019, these provinces received less in federal spending than their residents contributed in taxes, as Table 6.2 shows. Quebec is the outlier here. In that year, the federal government returned more to Quebec residents than it collected. By 2020, a distinctly unusual year, pandemic spending meant that all provinces received more in federal spending than they contributed in federal taxes. Debt made up the difference. The point is that regional redistribution is a characteristic of all these programs, with a persistent tendency to draw heavily on the residents of particular provinces for the regular benefit of those who live in others.

The efficiency goals of equalization are more challenging, not just because equalization might discourage economic adjustment to improve own-source revenues – although there is little evidence that provinces lack ambition – but also because equalization is a ponderous means of coping with short-term economic slowdowns. Its phase-in features are intended explicitly to allow for a smooth stabilization of provincial budgets rather than a rapid adjustment for fiscal emergencies. In the latter case, the Fiscal Stabilization Program allows provinces to apply for relief in the event that revenues experience a precipitous decline for economic reasons, not because of a reduction in provincial taxes. In 2020 the federal government agreed to increase substantially the per capita funding associated with the program (from $60 to $169.82) and to index it to changes in nominal GDP per capita in subsequent years.

Like equalization, the presence of a federally funded program designed to insure provinces against substantial downturns is a key feature of the risk-sharing strategy that characterizes Canadian federalism. Unlike equalization, fiscal stabilization is intended to address a fiscal shock, not to support ongoing programming. And while none of the members of the economic elite we interviewed objected to the program, a centrally resourced fiscal stabilization fund is vulnerable to the argument that it discourages provinces from creating their own substantial rainy-day funds. In US states, where no credible bailout policy exists, rainy-day funds are in widespread use. In Canada, the fact that increases to the Fiscal Stabilization Program were in train as the pandemic began suggests that the federal government is prepared to share

Table 6.2. Federal Revenues and Expenditures, by Province, 2019, $ Billions

Province	Federal Revenues	Federal Expenditures	Difference
British Columbia	59.8	48.5	11.3
Alberta	58.2	37.7	20.5
Saskatchewan	12.9	13.2	−0.4
Manitoba	13.2	17.8	−4.6
Ontario	174.7	152.1	22.6
Quebec	61.2	80.3	−19.0
New Brunswick	6.9	12.6	−5.6
Prince Edward Island	1.4	2.9	−1.5
Nova Scotia	8.9	16.8	−7.9
Newfoundland and Labrador	6.0	7.3	−1.2

Note: Includes disbursements to and from the Canada/Quebec Pension Plan.
Source: Statistics Canada (2021h). Contains information licensed under the Open Government Licence – Canada.

the risks of fiscal shocks, even if these are made worse by the mismanagement of provincial debt.

As for accountability, public finance economists generally would prefer to avoid or reduce the amount of risk sharing by transferring revenue sources from central to subnational governments. A more complete matching of revenues to responsibilities would allow voters a better line of sight into the costs and benefits of tax changes and spending priorities, at least in theory. A transfer of all corporate taxes to the federal level, for example, combined with a transfer of all goods and services tax revenues to the provinces, would improve both efficiency and accountability (see Stevenson, 2006). A transfer of tax points to support health care spending, along with the elimination of bloc grants, would have a similar effect (Coyne, 2023). On the other hand, moves of this magnitude would introduce an element of uncertainty in the short term that would be resisted by any province that depends on the federal spending power – in other words, most provinces. Risk sharing, combined with incremental adjustments to complicated formulas and special packages when needed, continue to be the politically preferred option among policy elites.

Conclusion

It can be stated with some confidence that, in Canada, federalism did not make the pandemic's fiscal pain worse than it would otherwise have been. Although certain corporations and some individuals might have profited unfairly from hastily assembled programs, no province benefited unconscionably, and none suffered beyond the self-inflicted wounds of ill-advised regulations. The provinces and territories emerged from their earliest fiscal shocks with better-than-anticipated revenues and budgetary balances that, over the short term, were sustainable. The programs that had been continuously adjusted over decades proved remarkably able to even out and reduce the impact of a rapid and substantial economic slowdown.

Our interviewees were generally reluctant to demand anything other than sensible adjustments to existing programs. They did express frustration with fiscal arrangements, and some clearly would prefer a complete rethink, but this perspective was not widely shared. Federal officials would like the provinces to tax their residents to provide additional public services; provincial officials would appreciate federal programs that did not require constant renegotiation or were subject to unilateral withdrawal. But for the most part, the emphasis was on flexibility: "What I've observed in all my thirty-one years of federal-provincial relations is that the federalism that we have in Canada – you can make it work; it's very flexible. So flexible, I think it kind of breeds more conflict than needs be ... The provinces will always want more money from the federal government, the federal government will always want to intrude in areas of provincial jurisdiction. We'll be testing in the courts endlessly – who's got supremacy over what issues. But you know, fundamentally, I think it's quite workable" [Bureaucrat 19].

Flexibility is at a premium because, as we suggested at the outset of this chapter, it is not possible to devise programs that simultaneously maximize equity, efficiency, and accountability. The claims made for the efficiency-inducing qualities of federalism rely on the unrealistic assumption that provincial governments will endorse market outcomes, no matter the impact on provincial residents. The reality is that provincial governments are mainly protectionist. Although no tariffs are imposed on internal trade, the common market in Canada is distorted by subnational governments' protectionist regulations and the federal government's regional development programs (Berdahl, 2012). Flexibility has often meant a lack of coordination on rules and regulations across jurisdictions, disputes over transprovincial projects such as pipelines, and federal interventions aimed at steering resources to specific regions for reasons related only tangentially to efficiency. Flexibility has also led to uncertainty about future transfers, fostering tensions in intergovernmental relations.

Where efficiency and equity are pursued together, it is largely because of the risk-sharing commitments made at Confederation and subsequently entrenched in the Constitution. Federally sponsored transfer programs might be distortionary, but they are far more efficient than the alternative: waiting for provincial agreement. And although they will fail to eliminate inequities, they are preferable to tacitly permitting parts of the country to be economically hollowed out.

From the voter's perspective, accountability is often lost in the shuffle. The economic elite is well aware of the issues, and the business press covers them as well (Brown, 2020, p. 276), but it is unlikely that voters consider the process entirely transparent. When the federal government assumed leadership for the income-support programs required to address the pandemic recession, it was reasonably clear that success or failure would be assigned to Ottawa – specifically to the politicians and bureaucrats who sponsored the programs. Before long, however, the provinces became involved with their own programs, and new initiatives, such as childcare, were launched on a wave of federal-provincial negotiations. Addressing shortcomings in long-term care, to the extent that it remains a national priority, will not be accomplished by one order of government on its own. If the required negotiations produce a more equitable and efficient deployment of public resources, then it might be argued that federalism deserves the credit. But perhaps a single, national program that made no room for local or provincial priorities would be even better.

As Daniel Treisman (2007, p. 224) emphasizes, national governments are quite capable of designing programs that respond to local needs without being compelled to do so by empowered subnational governments. Capable, but not necessarily motivated. Trying to answer the counterfactual – could policies have been better designed without the high overheads of federal-provincial diplomacy? – is probably not worth the effort. It does seem certain, however, that the bureaucratic apparatus required to make fiscal federalism work is not a transparent process and does not produce transparent outcomes. Defenders of fiscal federalism, as well as seasoned practitioners, probably need to admit that it generates an efficiency-equity-accountability trilemma. Having two of these desirable qualities reflected in programming is a reasonable ambition. Having all three is a pipe dream.

7 Keeping Government Accountable

The economic elite, whose views we have been conveying, operates with a sophisticated appreciation of the economy and an expansive capacity for data collection and interpretation. Democracy requires that somehow these expert decisionmakers be made accountable to those affected by the fiscal and economic policies they fashion. These policies are inherently difficult to understand, and the stress of pandemic-induced disruptions, expansive fiscal programs, and an avalanche of misinformation hasn't helped. The task would be somewhat easier if elites could draw on a reservoir of trust, but we are living in sceptical and cynical times. It is not easy (nor should it be) to persuade the democratic public that Canada's economic elite not only possesses superior knowledge and discernment, but also acts scrupulously on behalf of the public at large.

For the vast majority of the economic elite, acting in the public interest means demonstrating competent stewardship. Stewardship requires a measure of fiscal discipline consistent with a growth agenda. Overinvestment in consumption or in unproductive assets is inconsistent with economic growth. Similarly, underinvestment in human, intellectual, or physical capital creates output gaps. Stewardship implies the removal of programs that are demonstrably wasteful. There can be a lot of disagreement about how to achieve these basic goals, but there is no disagreement that those who make policy decisions should be accountable for them. How well do the institutions of parliamentary government deliver on accountability? Very few are entirely satisfied.

Using the federal government's fiscal response to the pandemic as a focal point, this chapter examines governmental institutions of accountability, specifically Parliament, the bureaucracy, and independent agencies. Of course, there are other contributors to accountability: journalists, think tanks, and academics, for example. But as important as public commentators are, it is office holders with defined responsibilities who are legally required to hold one another accountable. We distinguish between political and formal accountability and argue that, in Canada and in other parliamentary systems, political accountability mechanisms are relatively weak and vulnerable, especially in economic emergencies. The mechanisms of formal accountability – fiscal rules, program reviews, audits, and forecasts – have become increasingly important as an accountability bulwark. But these institutions have their own legitimacy problems and their work has produced mixed results.

Being Accountable

The democratic public selects its rulers but does not rule in any substantive sense. Macroeconomic decisions are not made by referendum, and decisions to launch, continue, or curtail government programs are not made by neighbourhood committees. Budgetary consultations have become increasingly common, and efforts to gather information increasingly sophisticated, but the economic elite continues to dominate decisionmaking and there is no question about where parliamentary authority lies. The government of the day (i.e., the cabinet) is responsible for preparing an annual budget document that contains its macroeconomic targets and its spending and taxing priorities. The decision field is complex, the terrain is often unfamiliar even to the experienced, and the value conflicts are profound. So although it is not possible to avoid an economic elite with a preponderance of influence over the shape and execution of policy, elite decisionmaking does not mean internal consensus and no conflict. It does mean that technical knowledge is elevated in importance, specialized tools are deployed, and debate participants are expected to stay in their lane – that is, to discharge the responsibilities defined by the offices they occupy.

Delegation of economic decisionmaking to an elite made up of elected politicians, appointed officials, and their technical advisors can be made consistent with democratic norms only if this elite can be held accountable for its decisions. The demand for accountability has been so thoroughly subsumed within democratic discourse that it is sometimes treated as equivalent to good government writ large. But while there is a variety of good-governance practices that are congruent with accountability, the origins of the concept are in the descriptive task of accounting – taking a count of something deemed valuable and making that count known. Accountability has moved on from its accounting roots, without ever entirely leaving them, to now mean, generically, "the obligation to explain and justify conduct" (Bovens, 2007, p. 450).

All forms of accountability envisage both exposure/visibility and sanction/punishment (Borowiak, 2011). Exposure implies the transparent imparting of information and the requirement to justify action or inaction. Sanctioning implies that failure to be accountable – that is, failure to provide an adequate account – has consequences appropriate to the office holder's responsibilities.

Canada, like other modern liberal societies, employs both democratic and bureaucratic institutions to achieve accountability. *Political* accountability is a product of democratic competition for public office. Partisanship and opposition are critical elements (Philp, 2009, p. 38), and accounts are given to several different audiences: those predisposed to be supportive, those inclined to oppose, and those who ostensibly are available to be persuaded in either direction. In Canada, where coalitions are rare, a single-member-plurality electoral system means, at the federal level in particular, that the political executive is normally chosen by less than 50 per cent of the electorate. Often far less. And while majority rule is an arithmetic concept, rather far removed from the "the public interest," modest electoral support means that most federal governments in Canada begin life with a legitimacy deficit. Elected politicians with limited democratic bona fides toil to persuade a sovereign democratic public that their interests are being advanced, while their political rivals concentrate on finding fault.

Between elections the legislature bears the burden of exacting political accountability. It is in the legislature that governments are formed and where the elected executive is obliged to provide an account of its exercise of public authority. Legislative chambers originally were conceived as deliberative assemblies in which the public interest would be fashioned by reasoned debate. That romantic vision has become a fantasy. Legislatures are the scene of set-piece battles, and compromises (when they are required) are fashioned around organized interests (Rosanvallon, 2011). The concept of parliamentary privilege does give members the rights and protections they require to participate in the scrutiny of legislation and hold governments to account (Chaplin, 2020), but a majority government's legislative agenda is overwhelmingly adopted. In the case of financial legislation, the legislature's approval is required for a series of supply resolutions that authorize government spending. These are critical moments, but because failure to secure passage of supply is tantamount to rejection of the government itself, the stakes are high, but the risk of (unanticipated) failure typically is low. Ordinary citizens are tasked with distinguishing between partisan posturing and genuine critique – in other words, between signal and noise. The difference is not always obvious.

In contrast to political accountability, *formal* accountability relies on the fulfilment of legally defined roles and responsibilities in a non-partisan, non-competitive environment. Whereas political responsibility relies on the flourishing of partisan critique, formal accountability depends on the impartial performance of formal, office-defined duties. Parliamentary democracies rely on judges, public servants, and officers of the legislature to be formally, not politically, accountable. They are expected to share a non-partisan commitment to professional standards agreed to in advance. Their work is pivotal to democratic resilience because of its inherent capacity to generate trust by reassuring citizens that the competition of democratic politics is limited, controlled, and adjudicated by impartial officials (Rothstein, 2011). The offices they occupy are not meant simply to tidy up the political process; they "frame the political system and define and limit the scope of political accountability" (Philp, 2009, p. 39).

The central bureaucratic institution is the public service, whose accountability is secured principally through the convention of ministerial responsibility. Most of the work involved in framing and fashioning fiscal policy is supplied by the coterie of senior public servants who offer expert advice in exchange for permanent employment and protection from political retribution. But it is ministers who are individually and collectively accountable. Put another way, in Canada, bureaucrats are servants of the Crown, not of the electorate. Their actions are reviewable by ministers who alone are accountable to the democratic public. This hierarchical model of accountability is firmly entrenched, and is the principal manner in which accountability is rendered in the public service. In this version of accountability, there is little or nothing the democratic public needs to do to evaluate individual public servants or discover how they are performing. This task is performed by supervisors and ultimately the political executive. Public servants provide evidence and offer advice, but they are protected by a cloak of anonymity such that the uses made of evidence and advice are not their responsibility.

Of course, senior public servants are not completely anonymous. Their comings and goings are the subject of lively speculation. One year into his stint as the deputy minister of finance, insiders revealed that Michael Sabia was struggling without much success to make an impression on the fiscal policy agenda of the Justin Trudeau government (Fife & Chase, 2021). We will never know for certain, at least not in real time. The terms of the "bargain" between bureaucrats and politicians have evolved over the years (Savoie, 1999), but the fortress has not been breached. Reformers continue to propose ways of closing what are described as accountability gaps, but dissatisfaction with the system has not led to its abandonment or formal modification – ministers are still the accountable parties. And although no single person can possibly be responsible for everything that happens within a department, convention requires that the minister be accountable. This convention persists (in theory if not in practice) despite the complexity of modern governing, the participation of many players, and the all-too-regular haplessness of ministers.

Conformity to the requirements of hierarchy is the principal way public servants are held accountable, but it is not the only way. Public servants are "servants," but they are also moral agents whose scope of authority and influence is sufficiently large that in many cases their decisions are the ones that form public policy. Their zone of indifference cannot be so wide or their commitment to political neutrality so deep that they pay no attention to the public interest (Kernaghan & Langford, 2014). Senior officials serve their masters, the political executive, but they have a professional commitment to one another that is ignored by standard hierarchical models of accountability. This commitment is what Joseph Heath (2020, p. 53) calls "vocational accountability," a form of formal accountability in which peers – people who share the same or similar positions – enforce professional norms. Unlike accountability to superiors in the hierarchical setting, or to the public in the democratic setting, vocational accountability is horizontal. It depends crucially on a corpus of professional practice and a set of professional ethics. Accountants, physicians, lawyers, and professors are among those whose behaviour is subject to regular assessment by outsiders who share the same professional status.

Because academic treatments of accountability can be rather mechanical, it sometimes escapes notice that public servants are accountable to one another in this professional sense. They develop their own codes of conduct and their own standards of practice. How to behave in the presence of politicians, for example, is not simply a matter of adhering to hierarchical norms. Other values are in play: discretion, balance, caution, humility, and occasionally courage. Among these values none is more important than the commitment to act impartially. Public servants must abjure not only political projects, but also even the hint of a conflict of interest. Their professional status depends crucially on the independence of their judgment, which is subject to rigorous review by others who are similarly tasked. After all, public servants work with other public servants. What they produce they produce in concert. Poor performance reflects on everyone involved, whether it arises from poor advice or poor implementation. So public servants take pains to learn from their peers, emulate strong performance, and revise standards of practice – all without direct pressure from either their superiors or the democratic public.

The same expectation of professional standards and performance applies to formally constituted actors in the economic policy world. In a crisis such as COVID-19, where both an economic and a public health response was required, non-partisan offices acquire particular prominence as key watchdogs of public business (Gay & Winetrobe, 2008). Supreme Audit Institutions (auditors general) are called on to monitor and report on programs that authorize vast expenditures, while parliamentary budget officers are charged with the independent and transparent reporting of fiscal policy implications. These officers provide a species of accountability that derives directly from legislation establishing their economic policy roles.

Of particular importance is the Bank of Canada – more specifically, the governor of the Bank, who is said to have *"ongoing* responsibility for monetary policy, while the minister of finance has *ultimate* accountability" (Coleman, 1991, p. 720, emphasis in original). For the governor of the Bank, being responsible means acting responsibly, and the norms and practices that define responsible behaviour are established by the central banking community as much as by practising politicians. Appreciating how accountability is rendered in these environments means including "vocational" norms – ones that place stress on independence, expert knowledge, and professional standards in the exercise of discretion.

Formal accountability is an expanding feature of economic policy-making at least in part because of the weakening of political accountability. For complex reasons, including an inability to understand them, Canadians gradually have lost faith in key political institutions – particularly political parties and Parliament (Atkinson, 2011; Malloy, 2023). Criticism of individual actors has spilled over into political institutions and even democracy itself. Elections shorten time frames for politicians, and permanent campaigns have replaced debate and discussion in legislative environments. Parliament's modest and largely ineffectual role in the budgetary process is a testament to the deterioration of political accountability. Those offices organized on the basis of formal accountability are stepping into the gap.

Unfortunately, being formally accountable is not a substitute for being politically accountable. Consider central banks such as the Bank of Canada. In place of direct political accountability, central banks aim for credibility. They are said to be credible when they do what they say they will do, which often means acting consistent with a professional commitment to price stability (Blinder, 2000). Central bank independence is sometimes taken as a proxy for credibility, and central bankers are convinced it helps persuade others that they mean what they say. But the conduct of monetary policy has significant lags and is not error proof. There are also distributive effects, even with so-called neutral rates of interest. When these effects are perceived as unfair, then being credible in the "we will do what we say" sense is not a guarantee of credibility in the "we make good decisions" sense. When central banks lose decisionmaking credibility in this latter sense, the weak accountability afforded by political independence can actually undermine legitimacy.

Increased reliance on formal accountability has other downsides. There is no *a priori* assurance, for example, that the professional norms these office holders adhere to are uniformly positive for the public interest. Groupthink and excessive caution are also persistent dangers. And, of course, none of these offices is directly accountable to the democratic public. These caveats aside, on balance we should take some comfort that the offices that embody formal accountability actually exist, especially since traditional forums for political accountability, as we are about to explain, are uniformly unimpressive.

Parliament and the Budget Process

If there is one undisputed "function" of Parliament (to use somewhat dated language), it is the granting of supply. This process, which includes passage of the annual budget and support for a motion testifying to the government's competent management of the economy, is a central feature of parliamentary business. It sounds like an important forum for political accountability, but it isn't. Testimony of the economic elite in Canada is broadly consistent with external academic evaluation: Parliament's influence over budgetary matters is minimal and in decline. Crises, such as the pandemic and its fiscal response, reveal further vulnerabilities and significant accountability deficiencies.

"Normal" Budgeting

For purposes of public consumption, the presentation of an annual budget, and occasionally a budget update, is an opportunity to query the government's spending priorities and its intended tax changes. Prior to the presentation of the budget, the House of Commons Standing Committee on Finance holds prebudget consultations and subsequently makes recommendations to the minister of finance. But responsibility for creating the budget lies exclusively with the Crown, and no vote on any "money bill" takes place without its prior consent. Thus, a royal recommendation is provided by the governor general, on cabinet's request, to any spending initiative seeking Parliament's authorization. The minister presents departmental and program expenditure plans (the main estimates) before 1 March and asks for approval of the budget's general direction. The budget is tabled after that, generally before the beginning of the fiscal year on 1 April. This process was temporarily modified for fiscal years 2018/19 and 2019/20 so that, for those two years only, a set of interim estimates was tabled before the federal budget, and the main estimates were tabled afterward to include spending and tax announcements made in the budget. If government spending requirements change, supplementary estimates are submitted to Parliament for approval. What follows is a series of appropriation bills that give legislative authority to these budgetary proposals. The process culminates in June when the final appropriation bill, authorizing "full supply," passes the House of Commons and is sent to the Senate.

This complicated process has a number of serious shortcomings from an accountability perspective. First, the budget itself is produced entirely within government and is subject to the highest levels of cabinet secrecy (Campagnolo, 2021). Leaks of budget details have been considered minor catastrophes for finance ministers – although selective leaks are no longer unknown. As a result, major errors of judgment, such as the Harper Conservative government's fiscal update in November 2008 and the highly criticized Trudeau Liberal government budget of 1981, make it all the way to the floor of the House of Commons before difficulties emerge. Ministers of finance themselves have found the secrecy tradition an irritation, if not a hindrance, to good policy (MacEachen, 1982), and they have suggested opening it up for more scrutiny regardless of secrecy conventions.

Improvements have been made and consultation processes have expanded over the years. Following the Harper government's budgetary meltdown, the 2009 normal consultation process was "superseded by highly visible discussions and consultations with businesses, provincial leaders, municipalities, industry associations, social groups, and Aboriginal leaders" (Good, 2014, pp. 173–4). But consultations are managed entirely by the government itself with little or no input from opposition parties, which are left to pick over the details, a task they seldom take up with vigour in the absence of clear political advantage.

The second serious shortcoming involves the timing of spending and budgetary approvals. These are sufficiently convoluted that Members of Parliament (MPs) are often confused about what they are actually debating and voting on. The minister of finance's budget will contain items that require approval, but when the estimates are tabled, these items are often not present, in part because the timing of budget presentations is, once again, entirely in the hands of the government. In 2022, the parliamentary budget officer suggested adopting a fixed budget date to remove uncertainty about whether and if a budget would be presented and to allow Parliament adequate time to consider its contents. Without some regularity to the process, MPs find themselves unclear on what their role actually is. One of our interviewees described the lack of coordination in the following way:

> In just a couple of days after having heard the budget, they look in the ways and means for budget items and they don't find them, only to be told, "Oh no, the budget was too late for us to include that in the main estimates, so those budget items will be in supps A or B or maybe C." So, an MP looks and listens to that and says, "what the hell? What am I voting on then?" "Oh, you're voting on the status quo, don't worry your little head, it's standard so just rubber stamp it." And that's literally what they're being told in briefings. So, all that is to say, fiscal accountability when it comes to budget making, personally, I think it's close to a mess. [Economist 7]

The point about confusion is made by others: "At no point do parliamentarians really understand what they are appropriating. How it has evolved over time, what's pre-existing or what's incremental" [Bureaucrat 24]. Some of the blame might rest with MPs themselves, or at least with their preparation. One federal minister explained that there is no training in matters budgetary: "Functionally, Parliament exists to approve supply, and yet there has never, even in my time, been any training in how to read the estimates, which is complicated stuff and voluminous" [Politician 10].

MPs are ill equipped to understand the budget, let alone scrutinize it. So they don't. The estimates are sent to relevant parliamentary committees for examination, but the questioning is seldom focused on budgetary matters, and there is no requirement that committees actually approve expenditures. If committees decline to make a report on estimates to the House by 31 May, the estimates are "deemed" reported. Observers understandably see the process as largely symbolic (Malloy, 2023, pp. 211–15). Parliamentarians can, in theory, reduce or reject estimates, but there are precious few times when circumstances combine to make even minimal adjustments possible (Good, 2014, pp. 264–76).

So, whatever else happens in committee hearings – and profitable exchanges between parliamentarians and public servants do take place – "there's no real ... scrutiny of the budget or of the main estimates when they're tabled or the supplementary estimates when they're tabled" [Bureaucrat 6].

Nor do these judgments pertain to particular governments. In 1997 the Standing Committee on Procedure and House Affairs reported that MPs themselves described the process as "futile" and "a total waste of time" (quoted in Blöndal, 2001, p. 54). As a result, MPs typically avoid the estimates themselves and concentrate on what they see as political vulnerabilities, whether or not these have spending or taxing implications: "All those years, I would go with the minister for the main estimates and the minister was never once asked a question on the main estimates ... They were all political questions" [Economist 4].

A third problem involves the format of budget legislation. Increasingly the budget implementation takes the form of so-called omnibus bills that address topics well beyond the taxing and spending initiatives that are the stuff of the budget itself. Complaints about these bills are routine for opposition parties, but once in power it is hard to resist the convenience of bundling legislation into a single package (Malloy, 2023, p. 121). The result is a piece of legislation with a vast array of changes contained within its many pages, only a few of which have anything to do with the budget presented to Parliament. Andrew Coyne (2012) was only one of a number of journalists who decried Bill C-38, the Harper government's most notorious version of this practice: "The bill runs to more than 420 pages. It amends some 60 different acts, repeals half a dozen, and adds three more, including a completely rewritten Canadian Environmental Assessment Act. It ranges far beyond the traditional budget concerns of taxing and spending."

All true, but other governments in other jurisdictions have adopted the same technique (Massicotte, 2013), and the Justin Trudeau government, having decried the practice while in opposition, adopted it themselves in a 392-page omnibus bill in 2019. Hidden inside these bills are legislative changes that, under more standard practice, would have their own debate and their own votes. One of our interviewees put the issue starkly: "I think if you want Parliament to have an accountability role, then you have to get rid of budget omnibus bills and make government budget bills include only tax changes and changes in spending that you introduced in the budget" [Bureaucrat 5].

Finally, the majority of the government's spending is directed by statutory requirements that exist independent of any given budget. In Canada, according to the federal government's fiscal year 2022/3 main estimates, of $397.6 billion in authorized spending, $207.3 billion (52.1 per cent) was to come from statutory authorities and the rest, $190.3 billion (or 47.9 per cent), from allocations voted in Parliament (GC InfoBase, 2022). Of statutory spending, the largest items are the health and social transfers to the provinces, Old Age Security, and equalization payments. Together these four statutory spending items make up almost two-thirds of total proposed spending in 2022/3. The list of those receiving the remaining statutory funding is extensive and includes Crown corporations, the judiciary, and regulatory agencies. All are provided for by previously approved legislation, not by annual votes in Parliament. And not to be forgotten is spending on debt servicing. This type of statutory spending, undertaken in accord with legislation, is presented in the estimates for information, but Parliament's approval is not formally required.

The upshot of this summary assessment is that the legislative power of the purse is exceedingly weak in Canada. Put another way, the power of the executive is exceedingly strong. While constitutional theory continues to attribute considerable authority to legislatures, the reality is that, in parliamentary systems, a distinct constitutional model of public finance has developed in which the executive, not the legislature, is at the apex of financial authority (Bateman, 2020). This constitutional model is not unique to Westminster parliamentary systems, but it is thoroughly established there. Using a survey conducted by the OECD in 25 member countries, Wehner (2006) shows that the level of legislative scrutiny of financial commitments differs significantly across liberal democracies, but that Westminster systems post some of the lowest scores on an index of legislative oversight. In terms of both formal legislative authority and organizational capacity, Canada, along with Australia and the United Kingdom, is in the lowest quartile of countries considered, while New Zealand's parliament is on the borderline. The index constructed to estimate legislative authority is scaled from 1 to 100: Canada's score was 26.4; compare that with Sweden at 65.3, Germany at 52.8, and Argentina at 50.

Within parliamentary systems variations exist, of course, and some legislatures have adopted rules that provide for more time, more resources, and more authority in the hands of MPs. But the original design of Westminster systems, in which no money is appropriated without the consent of the Crown, and the organization of financial accounting is in the hands of the executive, means that escape from the logic of expansive executive authority is virtually impossible. Subnational governments in parliamentary systems, having inherited the same constitutional formulas, provide for a similarly hamstrung legislative branch (Bateman, 2020). Our provincial interviewees tended to be more generous in their assessments of legislative authority than were their federal government counterparts, but the differences are a matter of degree, not kind.

What everyone can agree on is that constraint on ministerial excess or indifference is supplied mostly by the prospect of attending the legislature to discuss and defend decisions. These restraining effects were summed up nicely by a senior provincial deputy minister: "It's true you don't have much to show for it, but the fact that the government knows they have to go through the [budgetary] process does have a powerful disciplining effect. It really does stop government from doing stupid stuff" [Bureaucrat 30]. Interviewees also pointed to Question Period, the public accounts committees, and the confidence convention as sources of legislative power, but these are blunt instruments and perhaps best seen as experiences that ministers must endure rather than sources of budgetary insight or opportunities for genuine scrutiny.

Political accountability requires that the executive attend open forums in which they must confront their critics. Emergency situations, such as a pandemic, pose special problems in this regard. Parliamentary systems share a commitment to regular, public confrontation between the executive and members of both the governing party and an institutionalized opposition. Pandemics and similar emergencies threaten the regular interrogation of the executive by disrupting the rhythm of legislative sessions. If interrogation can be avoided or delayed past the point of relevance, the institutional edifice of accountability is undermined. When legislatures do not meet, or meet with fewer members present, the energy these confrontations are supposed to generate is dissipated. As the pandemic experience shows, public health emergencies are opportunities for governments to modify this fundamental requirement.

The Pandemic Process

During periods of economic crisis, when rapid response is essential, it is reasonable to expect the normal budget process to be superseded to some degree and extraordinary steps taken. The suspension of normal operations is often tolerated until such time as an account of the extraordinary measures can be made. These measures typically take the form of overspending – that is, spending beyond the limits of what had been previously approved. In the United Kingdom, for example, the financial crisis of 2008 prompted a major bailout for the Royal Bank of Scotland, a move that required the treasury department to spend far beyond the legal limit imposed by Parliament (Bateman, 2020, p. 144).

During the pandemic, the major departure from standard budgeting involved the authorization of significant new spending and a massive and rapid increase in government debt. As we have already explained, members of the economic elite generally applauded executive action. But what about the parliamentary accountability process?

As expected, Canada's political accountability weakened during the pandemic largely because Parliament was adjourned in March 2020, shortly after the pandemic began, and did not reconvene until September of that year. In the meantime, the House of Commons was recalled on several occasions to pass emergency legislation, but attendance was restricted to 10 per cent of the membership and debate was severely truncated. In virtually all provincial legislatures, similar attendance restrictions were enforced to comply with physical-distancing requirements, and legislative assembly meetings were similarly brief (Rayment & VandenBeukel, 2020). With very few of the normal procedures employed, legislatures across Canada placed the need for expeditious action ahead of thorough examination.

It is common for Westminster systems to provide for emergency measures that can be employed without the direct authorization of Parliament. In the face of the pandemic, Australia and New Zealand, for example, used existing legislation to access emergency spending authority. The United Kingdom and Canada, on the other hand, passed new legislation to expand executive power. In Canada's case, the government amended the *Financial Administration Act* to allow for extraordinary payments using special warrants that enable governments to make financial commitments when the legislature is not sitting (Canada, 2020a). Of course, the House of Commons was sitting, but these were deemed to be extraordinary times.

To underline that fact and to ensure that the government could spend beyond what special warrants permit, Parliament also passed Bill C-13, the *Public Health Events of National Concern Payments Act*, to allow the government to pay out of the Consolidated Revenue Fund "all money required to do anything in relation to that public health event of national concern" (Canada, 2020b, section 2 [1]). This piece of legislation, which passed with extraordinary rapidity, represented a large blank cheque. Although the government eventually must account for its use of this blank cheque, MPs are unable to insist on a vote requesting cancellation of an emergency public health declaration, and the Senate has no mechanism to review spending decisions (Thomas, 2020a).

The vulnerability of Parliament to executive overreach was illustrated most vividly in the debate over Bill C-13. The original draft of the bill would have given the government spending powers without parliamentary approval until 31 December 2021, over 18 months after passage (Curry & Fife, 2020). In response to a united opposition outcry, this date was amended to 30 September 2020. A similar effort by the UK government to secure extended authority was also rejected by the opposition, but this was accomplished on the floor of the House of Commons, where members also succeeded in securing successive six-month reviews of the emergency legislation. In Canada, Parliament did receive an assessment of the programs launched under emergency legislation, but not until March 2021, a year after the pandemic legislation had been approved (OAG, 2021c). In contrast, New Zealand's government provided an economic and fiscal update in May 2020, presented a budget on time, and offered weekly briefings on the economic legislation and interim monthly financial statements (Treasury New Zealand, 2020). Comparisons with other Westminster systems suggest that, for these reasons and others related to the opportunity for oversight, Canada's accountability performance was among the weakest (Lozano et al., 2021; Thomas, 2020b).

A final observation involves the temptations that arise when vast amounts of money are suddenly injected into the government's program delivery process with very little administrative preparation. Among the new initiatives created in Canada to target economically vulnerable populations, the Canada Student Service Grant stood out as a program with implementation challenges. According to the minister responsible, bureaucrats had recommended administration by a third party because of the "scale and scope" of the program. WE Charity, the designated program delivery agency, was selected without a competitive process and despite the fact that family members of both the prime minister and the minister of finance at the time had worked with the organization. Worse, neither politician had recused themselves when the decision was made to select WE Charity.

In this case, accountability was served in two ways. First, the opposition queried and criticized the contract to the point that it was eventually withdrawn; second, the prime minister and the minister of finance were investigated (not for the first time) by the federal ethics commissioner for a possible breach of the *Conflict of Interest Act* (Canada, 2006a). The investigation subsequently cleared Mr. Trudeau of any wrong doing, but not Minister of Finance Bill Morneau, whose relationship to the WE Charity principals was described as a friendship too close to remove the possibility of personal gain. In this case, political and formal accountability pulled in the same direction.

The pandemic budget process in Canada put an already problematic accountability system under intense pressure. In the face of an emergency, the federal government suspended or amended standard operating procedures and invented a process that was barely recognizable from the perspective of parliamentary scrutiny. It should not be surprising that the speed with which vast sums of money were committed and the distance at which Parliament's oversight machinery operated encouraged experiments in public administration. These experiments included the delegation of program delivery to an untested, but politically connected, organization. The grants-for-students program never got off the ground, but most spending programs survive parliamentary approval and persist long after that. Is there a robust means of assessing whether they continue to serve their original purpose and/or the public interest?

Bureaucrats, Budgets, and Program Reviews

Accountability in government is about more than fastidiously following the rules – although following the rules is generally a good idea. Good process is not enough to ensure good outcomes, and since the advent of New Public Management,[1] with its commitment to introduce private sector techniques into government, it is outcomes that increasingly matter for accountability purposes (Perrin, 2015). One means of obtaining accountability is to task those most familiar with the operation of programs with their periodic evaluation. By the 1980s, the federal government was making these expectations clear: program managers were expected to "periodically produce credible, timely, useful and objective findings on programs appropriate for resource allocation, program improvement and accountability" (Treasury Board, 1981, p. 3).

This commonsense expectation has given rise to a large coterie of professional program evaluators and an academic subdiscipline devoted to best practices. It has also generated expectations that program evaluation cannot reasonably meet. Specifically, the idea that the evaluation of specific programs can contribute to more rational expenditure management decisions is resisted by most professional evaluators.

---

1 *New Public Management* is an umbrella term used to denote a wide array of innovations in the public sector based on managerial techniques pioneered in private business. Inspired by the idea that citizens should be seen as customers, New Public Management places emphasis on organizational responsiveness to clear, measurable objectives. Incentive techniques such a pay-for-performance, organizational concepts such as management-by-objectives, and financial practices such as public-private partnerships are examples that epitomize the movement.

Programs can be modified based on evidence and funds transferred among programs based on results, but "the targets of study from a program focus to a budget focus do not line up" (Shepherd, 2018, p. 348). Ensuring that funds are being spent well is a program evaluation issue, and managers can be reasonably expected to collect data and monitor results. Ensuring that funds are being spent wisely is a different question. The wise expenditure of funds involves global goals and trade-offs among them, and accountability for the results of that process is much more difficult to achieve. Put another way, strong economic performance depends on choosing wisely and executing well, but one of these cannot substitute for the other.

For decades governments in the OECD world have attempted to create a rational expenditure management system. Rational, in this case, means efficient and effective. Effectiveness involves the choice of rational ends and at bottom answering the question: Is this something government should be doing? Efficiency involves answering the question: Are we going about it in the right way? Program evaluation, its practitioners explain, is better at answering the second of these questions (Mayne, 2018). The idea that an expenditure management system can answer them at all was an early and rather persistent conceit. Such a system could ensure that pertinent information is brought to bear by the right parties at the right time, but the choice of rational policy goals is another matter. This would forever be a political question. Accountability for making the right choices and, in an expenditure management system, the right trade-offs would need to be handled through the political process. What bureaucrats can contribute is the design and management of a process that disciplines the making of choices and the evaluation of performance.

Discipline in the Canadian federal system is supplied largely by departments of finance in collaboration with treasury boards. Since the advent of the Program, Planning, Budgeting System in the 1960s, numerous changes have been made in terms of process, players, and structures. New Public Management, in particular, produced a flurry of "surreal" management reforms that overwhelmed senior public servants (Clark & Swain, 2005). Summary judgments by insiders have seldom been generous: "it is striking how little difference any of them [reforms] actually made in the end, despite the efforts of many talented people" (Kroeger, 1996, p. 462). As Geneviève Tellier (2019, p. 162) observes, there is no sign of a "true transformation" in the budgetary process as a result of these review processes.

Still, notwithstanding these organization changes, a basic idea persisted: departments of finance would act as "guardians" of the expenditure budget process by taking a total budget approach, in contrast to "spenders," who sponsored departmental programs and paid little or no attention to the macroeconomic picture (Wildavsky, 1974). David Good added to this dynamic two other sets of players: "watchdogs" (especially auditors) and "priority setters" (such as the Privy Council Office) (Good, 2014). This more complete institutional configuration was accompanied by a shifting of roles. With new budget practices around reserves, spenders often became guardians as well, generating their own savings, while at the federal level the Treasury Board became focused primarily on management issues. The finance department emerged as the principal agency responsible for framing the expenditure budget by making forecasts and establishing fiscal targets. Determining how large the fiscal dividend might be and where it should be allocated put the finance department in an increasingly powerful position (Good, 2013). Meanwhile, accountability for expenditures would be rendered by following a stringent set of guidelines supplied by the Treasury Board, implemented by the chief financial officer of each government department, and supervised by the Office of the Comptroller-General (Good, 2014, pp. 248–53).

The emphasis on compliance and robust performance measurement increased following the discovery in 2004 of major misallocations of resources in the Liberal government's sponsorship programs. The auditor general described these misallocations as "such a blatant misuse of public funds that it is shocking" (CBC News, 2004). One of the new Harper government's first steps was the introduction of C-2, the *Federal Accountability Act* (Canada, 2006b), which ran to over 200 pages, amended several existing acts, created new offices (including the Parliamentary Budget Office), and set forth an approach to accountability that emphasized blame and punishment (Sutherland, 2006). The impulse to make public servants directly accountable received further impetus even though "accountability" was never defined.

In the midst of these various efforts to create and strengthen an accountability regime inside government, economic exigencies periodically required an approach that was more macro in orientation and more conspicuously political in motivation. One of the earliest accountability shocks came in 1978, when Prime Minister Pierre Trudeau returned from a G7 meeting and announced that he had agreed to major cutbacks in government spending. These cuts were imposed in classic top-down style, with reductions in proposed spending, freezes to program spending, and across-the-board cuts to operating costs. But they did not signal a change in fiscal policy. In the face of inflation and slow growth, the federal government continued to add to its debt burden so that, by 1984, when the first Mulroney government was elected, Canada's debt and deficit situation was among the worst in the G7.

That unenviable situation prompted another attempt at comprehensive cost reduction, this time under the direction of Deputy Prime Minister Erik Nielsen, who secured the assistance of a phalanx of external consultants. This review produced a series of recommendations, including broad across-the-board cuts, reductions in transfers to the provinces, and privatization. If fully implemented, these reductions might have saved the federal government $6 billion. One estimate of the real savings achieved put the number closer to $500 million (Bourgon, 2009, p. 20).

It was not until 1993, and another new government, that the attack on public spending at the federal level would be engaged fully. All parties had promised to cut or at least to constrain the deficit in line with other G7 countries. The Chrétien Liberal government launched Program Review to accomplish the task. Across the board, cuts were out; this time, there would be a portfolio approach in which nothing was sacrosanct (Tellier, 2022). Importantly, the public service was involved fully, with deputy ministers given a conceptual framework to use in interrogating programs and committees of ministers and senior public servants vetting proposed program reductions (Bourgon, 2009). The 1995 budget set out an ambitious planned reduction in program spending, over half of it aimed at statutory expenditures, including Employment Insurance and transfers to the provinces. By 1998 the federal government had its first surplus in almost 30 years, aided, it should be acknowledged, by economic growth and changes to the tax system.

For members of Canada's economic elite, this was a galvanizing moment, recalled with a mixture of pride and amazement by those who participated in our interviews. Earlier efforts had been disappointing, and subsequent program reviews failed to duplicate the impact of the 1994–96 exercise. The secret sauce was a combination of fear and courage. The fear originated with the growing consensus outside the country that, without a dramatic response, Canada was headed for insolvency. Moody's had issued a private warning of substantial downgrade, and the *Wall Street Journal* (1995) had described Canada as an "honorary member of the Third World." The courage was supplied by a political leadership – Prime Minister Chrétien and Minister of Finance Paul Martin – willing to endorse whatever a systematic program review uncovered. That included enduring the dismay and wrath of the provinces, whose contribution to the exercise was substantial. Senior bureaucrats were mobilized as never before to engage in an exercise that resulted in cutbacks almost everywhere and in the end a smaller footprint for the public service.

The budget reductions were a major political success, but insiders doubt that the content of the Program Review exercise was the ultimate source of final decisions. Consistent with the view that expenditure budget decisions and program evaluation do not "line up," seasoned observers of the 1995 process have concluded that there is no evidence that politicians responsible for retrenchment actually used program evaluation to identify programs for elimination or expenditure reduction (Dobell & Zussman, 2018, p. 381). Program reviews build foundational knowledge, but crisis decisionmaking requires political intuition coupled with the tacit knowledge of senior program managers. It is an art, not a science. And as art, politicians are increasingly inclined to employ external assistance rather than rely on the analytical machinery assembled within government. Both the Harper government's cost-reduction exercises and Justin Trudeau's "deliverology" agenda were heavily influenced by external consultants, at least partially on the grounds that public servants are too self-interested to be trusted with the task.

Trust, then, is at the heart of deficit-spending-reduction exercises – trust, and belief that the exercise is necessary and worthwhile. When the federal government began to run surpluses after 1997, austerity was not a popular project. And when austerity was implemented following the Great Financial Crisis, it was far from a cure-all. The idea of imposing austerity for purposes of reviving the economy is no longer (if it ever was) an article of faith within the economic elite. Having lived through years of sluggish performance and slow growth, the consensus has formed that austerity, far from generating strength in the economy, has the effect of lowering the level and quality of public service without improving the prospects for economic growth. Not even finance officials are enthusiastic supporters. Consider, for example, this observation from a senior federal deputy minister: "Austerity is a 'bad thing' if you're overly aggressive, clamping down on entitlement, income support, stuff like that ... Look at the Greek example. When you start going after people's pensions just to bring the budget back into alignment, that's counterproductive. At the same time, again, program spending is going to continue to be under very tight watch" [Bureaucrat 7].

So, although enthusiasm for austerity is at a low ebb, the economic elite is overwhelmingly in favour of a close assessment of existing discretionary programs. Consider this sample of supportive comments from our interviews:

- "Look carefully at government programs and have a clean-up ... it's not necessarily austerity, it's sound management" [Economist 7];

- "I think [program reviews] are necessary, and I think they should be ongoing" [Politician 4];
- "There should always be spending reviews. You should always have regular program reviews of everything you are doing to see if they're hitting the targets that they were set up to hit" [Bureaucrat 27];
- "It will be critical emerging from COVID that governments take a look at program spending. There's a risk programs may morph and have morphed even through COVID" [Politician 15].

As if to oblige, the Justin Trudeau government announced in the 2022 budget a strategic policy review that would, it was anticipated, yield $6 billion in savings (revised upwards in the 2023 budget) while helping to achieve net zero greenhouse gas emissions. Strategic reviews make eminent sense according to our interviewees. What is not so clear is whether these kinds of reviews can or should be used to achieve fiscal targets. There is a constant tension in program review exercises between achieving savings and determining if programs are actually working (Lindquist & Shepherd, 2023). A reduction in program spending is a source of savings, but the economic elite is sceptical that reviews are the right way to impose fiscal discipline. The problem is the scale of the challenge and the absence of obvious targets that would produce genuine, sizeable savings. At the provincial level, where costs are increasing rapidly, the idea of whittling away at program spending is not an especially attractive means of achieving a balanced budget: "I don't know how you do that coming out of this pandemic. I just don't see how that's possible, there isn't enough money there. So, it's not just that I think it would be politically difficult, I actually think it could be socially destructive ultimately" [Politician 2].

All the efforts of Canadian governments to restrain spending and improve service delivery have justified reforms by invoking "accountability." From the 1979 Royal Commission on Financial Management and Accountability through the 2006 *Financial Accountability Act* to "deliverology," being accountable has become the litmus test of sincerity regarding goals. But accountability within the bureaucracy, whether among program managers or at the highest levels of the public service, is hard to achieve. In fact, it might be impossible using the instruments of program evaluation or managerial reform. What about a return to the ancient concept of a separation of powers in which different elements of government oversee one another? Specifically, can independent agencies charged with bringing evidence to bear on spending decisions make a difference in the accountability equation?

Auditors and Budget Officers

In the face of conspicuous institutional failures, such as those that seeded the Great Financial Crisis, governments have found it necessary to identify the responsible actors, apportion blame, and promise fixes, typically in the form of more accountability. US president Barack Obama identified the regulatory failure that led to financial collapse as a problem of insufficient accountability on the part of regulators. The solution was the *Dodd-Frank Act* (United States, 2010), an overhaul of the financial regulatory apparatus that included the creation of the Bureau of Consumer Financial Protection. A similar rather mechanistic approach to accountability followed the Sponsorship scandal in Canada. Attention was focused on lapses in the auditing process and on alleged gaps in the accountability system. The auditor general delved into the program's organizational shortcomings, new frameworks expanded the scope of internal audits, and a new agency, the Parliamentary Budget Office, was created to signal genuine commitment to financial oversight. In these and similar cases of misfeasance and malfeasance, the response has been to invest in new accountability mechanisms, strengthen existing ones, and employ the rhetoric of accountability as a means of restoring legitimacy to governments whose operations have gone awry (Dubnick & O'Brien, 2011).

Investment in a robust internal accountability apparatus is testament to the growing importance of formal accountabilities as a means of buttressing weaknesses at the political level. In fact, it is most often politicians who have commissioned these agencies either out of a genuine belief that they are effective or as part of an effort to shield themselves from direct political accountability. In the matter of economic policy – specifically the federal government's own programmatic efforts – two offices stand out as particularly important: that of the auditor general, responsible for post-factum assessment and the PBO, responsible for pre-factum, anticipatory assessment.

The Auditor General

Supreme Audit Institutions are the organizations responsible for conducting external, independent assessments of national governments' legal compliance with taxation and spending rules (compliance audits), financial results (financial audits), and program efficiency and effectiveness (performance, or value-for-money, audits) (Shand, 2013). These after-the-fact studies usually lack the drama of a budget, but they can produce their own surprises and they have the benefit of being far less speculative. As Elizabeth Marshall, a Conservative senator put it: "Everybody focuses on the budget and I could never understand that, even when I was the auditor general in Newfoundland ... You could put whatever you want in the budget and the estimates. It's the actual numbers that I'm focusing on" (Curry, 2021b).

The Office of the Auditor General (OAG) was established in 1878. The auditor general receives a ten-year Order-in-Council appointment and operates under the authority of the *Auditor General Act* and the *Financial Administration Act* (Canada, 1985a, 1985b). The traditional audit function requires the auditor general to provide an opinion on whether the audited financial statements fairly present the government's financial position. The OAG does this by reviewing a sample of transactions and balances and by observing generally accepted accounting principles and generally accepted auditing standards. Since 1999, the consolidated financial statements of the federal government have received an unmodified (clean) audit opinion from the auditor general (Department of Finance Canada, 2022a).

Accountability by financial reporting is by no means the end of the story. In the 1980s enthusiasm for auditing spread well beyond financial statements. In what he characterized as an "audit explosion," Michael Power (1999) observed that, beyond the traditional accounting field, we now have environmental audits, managerial audits, information technology audits, and many others, making it somewhat difficult to distinguish among audits, assessments, and evaluations. The terminological confusion grew significantly with the advent in 1977 of "value-for-money," or performance, audits. According to the International Standards of Supreme Audit Institutions, performance audits are concerned with the "economy, efficiency and effectiveness" of government programs (INTOSAI, 2021, p. 12).

Early reaction to this expanded mandate was far from positive. Sharon Sutherland (1980; 1986; 2002) argued that value-for-money is not an objective review process; it is an assessment made by unelected officials based on ill-defined standards of success and failure. Worse, it substitutes a suspect form of bureaucratic judgment for real political accountability. By insisting on the need for "measured results," this form of auditing can put in jeopardy any program that cannot supply auditable indices of success. Shand (2013, p. 825) agrees that, because performance auditing is not grounded in accounting standards, it is "subjective" and "open to debate." In fact, according to Barzelay (1996, p. 19), performance auditing is more "an evaluative activity of a particular sort whose name happens to include the word 'auditing'."

These objections, or cautions, have done little to stem the demand for audited assurances that programs are achieving their stated objectives. Because not every program can be audited, choices have to be made and the process should not be arbitrary (Taft, 2016, p. 476). Entities or sectors are selected for performance audits based on assessments of risk and knowledge of business (OAG, 2019a). At the federal level in Canada, these form the basis of a Strategic Audit Plan, which is reviewed and updated by the Performance Audit Practice Oversight Committee and the auditor general. While the auditor general occasionally has expressed interest in auditing fiscal policy, it is mostly at the provincial level that this kind of auditing has been done. For example, the Office of the Auditor General of Nova Scotia reviews the assumptions used in the government's revenue estimates and reports their results with the annual budget. In Ontario, the auditor general must review and report on the most recent multiyear fiscal plan before a general election.

Auditors and governments are not natural allies, but they experience their highest levels of tension around the most appropriate indicators of fiscal health. As auditors seek to build a detailed and nuanced appreciation of program risk, ministers and their advisors remain attached to simpler ways of communicating stewardship. As one auditor put it: "Governments prefer a very clear single-point measure; they can say yes or no, I met it or I did not ... whether it's a budget number, like a budget surplus or deficit number or a debt to GDP number, however precise or imprecise that calculation is" [Bureaucrat 17].

The accounting profession long ago embraced a much more holistic approach that some refer to as the "net worth of government." The move to accrual accounting in the 1990s is indicative of this balance-sheet approach. Whereas the cash basis of accounting records transactions "when payments are made and revenues collected, that is, when cash actually changes hands" (Tellier, 2019, p. 110), accrual accounting records transactions when the activity takes place regardless of whether money has been received or paid. Although an accrual basis of accounting has been widely used in the private sector, governments began employing it as part of the New Public Management movement of the 1980s (Buhr, 2012). Supporters argue that it provides a "more comprehensive measure of fiscal sustainability" (Khan & Mayes, 2009, p. 15), as it captures changes to assets and liabilities (for example, pension liabilities, consumption of assets) that have long-term fiscal policy implications (Blöndal, 2003; Efford, 1996).

For governments, this kind of thinking can be problematic for purposes of fiscal accountability. As long as financial statements concentrate on revenues and expenditures as recorded in the consolidated

revenue fund, it is possible to report on the annual surplus/deficit situation compared with previous years and with fiscal objectives. Once
governments are obliged to respond to summary financial statements
that capture the financial condition of government business enterprises
(GBEs), such as Crown corporations, as well as the consolidated revenue fund, the picture becomes more complete but less reflective of government decisionmaking. Because GBEs have delegated financial and
operational authority, their financial results are not a (direct) result of
government decisions, so the "bottom line" becomes murkier from a political accountability perspective. As one provincial minister observed,
"We have workers' compensation funds, we have auto insurance funds,
we have these different funds in government which are invested. So, a
change of two or three basis points can put your balanced budget into
massive deficit" [Politician 16]. (Or surplus, if the change is in a more
agreeable direction; either way, this lack of control is enough to discourage thoughts of balanced-budget legislation.) The minister continued: "I would not do balanced-budget legislation because I'll be happy
to be held accountable for things I can control and decisions that our
government made, but not for something that happens in the interest-
rate world that plunges us into deficit" [Politician 16].

The battle over how to present the public accounts is one that politicians largely have lost. The accounting profession is organized interna-
tionally, and in assessing financial statements, it has used its leverage
to insist on a set of standards that meet changing professional requirements. The government's spending estimates, on the other hand, are
still prepared on a cash basis, and discussion typically is bottom-line
oriented. Auditors find this exasperating: "They [politicians] don't use
the information that they get and they're not understanding the information that they get. I think there's way too much discussion about
balanced budgets, whereas there's a broader array of things that we
need to look at" [Bureaucrat 1].

At the provincial level one of these "things" is the ratio of own-source
revenue to government transfers. Auditors see a different risk profile
with transfers from other governments than revenue raised from your
own tax measures. They are not convinced that politicians appreciate
this kind of distinction. The financial literacy of politicians is a common
lament – "Where I see the big gap in parliamentary debate is the people doing the top end of the debate don't have enough information"
[Bureaucrat 10] – but so is the absence of a forum to discuss what auditors see as the relevant issues. The bureaucrat continued: "You can
be as transparent as you want but if you've got no forum to actually
talk about that budget, other than the media - what are you doing in

terms of accountability?" [Bureaucrat 10]. Public accounts committees are not seen as particularly effective mechanisms for the simple reason that programs seldom have clearly articulated criteria for determining success.

Despite these process deficiencies, auditors and the auditing profession enjoy an enviable status as accountability champions. Research conducted by the Public Policy Forum (2018, p. 11) concludes that, among officers of Parliament, the auditor general is widely regarded as a "model for successful agents." This positive evaluation and the overall legitimacy of the audit function derive mainly from auditors' independence and their professional credentials (Posner & Shahan, 2014; Public Policy Forum, 2018; Saint-Martin, 2004; Shand, 2013).

Independence is a function of organization, responsibilities, and budget (Fiedler, 2004). Auditors need to be free to choose audits and determine processes. And they need to have sufficient earmarked resources to accomplish their tasks. Generally, auditors in Canada have independence, but there has been consistent tension around resources, both information and financial capacity. The *Auditor General Act* makes it clear that the auditor "is entitled to free access at all convenient times to information that relates to the fulfilment of his or her responsibilities and he or she is also entitled to require and receive from members of the federal public administration any information, reports and explanations that he or she considers necessary for that purpose" (Canada, 1985a, sec. 13 [1]) It doesn't always work out that way. In 2017, the OAG found itself in a dispute over access to the information needed for audits on fossil fuel subsidies and customs duties (OAG, 2017). Access was denied in this case and again in 2017, when the Department of Finance Canada refused to provide its analyses on the administrative costs incurred by the Canada Border Services Agency for collecting and enforcing the minimum threshold for customs duties on goods imported by courier or postal services. Both instances were reported to Parliament, and the government issued a new Order-in-Council to address these complaints (Hall, 2017).

Funding for the OAG's activities is provided through the minister of finance, who is responsible for tabling the Office's departmental plan in Parliament. This funding arrangement has also been a frequent source of tension. Requests for additional funding began in 2016, and in 2018 the Office received a third of the amount requested. The then interim auditor general, Sylvain Ricard, during an opening statement to the public accounts committee in June 2019 (OAG, 2019b), argued that "the fact that government departments that we audit are involved in determining how much money is allocated to us is not consistent with our independence or our accountability only to Parliament." In July 2020, Auditor General Karen Hogan requested and received an additional $26 million in permanent funding in addition to the $91 million in budgetary authority approved for fiscal year 2020/1 (Nardi, 2020; OAG, 2021d, 2021e).

In addition to independence, formal accountability presumes professional standards, and the accounting profession is highly regulated. Like other professionals, auditors are subject to demands that arise from standards-setting bodies and from external reviews by peers (Hayne & Salterio, 2014). Technical standards, codes of professional conduct, and ethical requirements are all part of the training, and adherence to them is necessary to maintain the credentials granted by national or regional regulatory bodies. Auditors are expected to emerge from this training as professional sceptics. The Canadian Auditing Standards require auditors to "exercise professional judgment and maintain professional scepticism throughout the planning and performance of the audit" (CPA Canada, 2021). Neither Parliament nor the public decides how the auditors should perform their job. It is professional accountants and other auditors who, independently, determine what it means to do the job well (Heath, 2020; Saint-Martin, 2004; Tellier, 2019, pp. 188–9).

What we have described is a robust but far from perfect accountability mechanism. It relies heavily on professional norms and distance from political intrigue. Opportunities exist for responses to audits, but, overall, governments have avoided open combat. Government-auditor relationships are "predictable, but not necessarily comfortable" (Taft, 2016, p. 482), especially when there are disagreements with audit findings and recommendations. Contestation on specific audit findings is not unusual, but governments draw up short of debating the appropriateness of generally accepted accounting practices, at least in public. Even when auditors and politicians have opposing views on what professional standards demand, governments are in an awkward position when it comes to challenging auditors. Formal accountability trumps political accountability when the credibility and impartiality of independent agents is well established.

Parliamentary Budget Officers

Financial audits are an uncontested feature of fiscal governance. Providing timely assessments of intended or recently launched fiscal projects is a much newer innovation. Except for a few cases, such as Belgium's High Council of Finance (established in 1936) and the US Congressional Budget Office (CBO, established in 1974), most of the current independent fiscal institutions (IFIs) were established between 2010 and 2015 (OECD, 2021b). Although there are important differences across IFIs in OECD countries, they fall generally into one of two institutional models: independent parliamentary budget offices and fiscal councils.

Parliamentary budget offices assist parliaments and budget committees with independent, non-partisan analysis of the state of public finances. Fiscal councils monitor compliance with fiscal rules and determine whether corrective measures should be taken (European Central Bank, 2014, p. 96). Some of the more specific tasks that both PBOs and fiscal councils perform include preparing or endorsing the executive's macroeconomic and fiscal forecasts, costing and evaluating fiscal proposals, and undertaking long-term fiscal sustainability analysis. A smaller group of IFIs operate in connection with other independent agencies such as the audit office (e.g., Finland's Fiscal Policy Monitoring Team) or the central bank (e.g., Austria's Fiscal Advisory Council).

The Congressional Budget Office is the gold standard of independent financial institutions. Established to provide non-partisan budget information to Congress, the CBO has succeeded in persuading the public and various participants in budget formation that it is capable of making believable economic forecasts and budget projections. It has also developed methods of "scoring" different budget proposals and so injecting a non-partisan analytical perspective into fiercely ideological legislative debates. And although the CBO began life as a modest operation, by 2021 it had grown to employ 275 people and manage a budget of US$57.3 million (Congressional Budget Office, 2021). As a creature of Congress, in an extreme separation-of-powers system, its independence from the executive branch is no longer questioned. But, as the founding director explained, the CBO is required to make "sometimes precarious inferences, about taxpayer or beneficiary behaviour in new situations" (Rivlin, 2014, p. 27). The same risks apply to all IFIs given serious space in which to operate, but, in the CBO's case, legislation can languish and die if the results are unfavourable.

Canada's Parliamentary Budget Office began life under relatively propitious circumstances, but it has endured internal operational divisions and external criticism that have threatened to undermine its credibility. The PBO was the product of an election-campaign promise made by the leader of the Conservative Party, Stephen Harper, following criticism of a series of federal projects with large cost overruns, including the Canadian Firearms Registry and the Secure Channel project (Page & Yalkin, 2014). Established in 2006 as part of the *Federal Accountability Act* (Canada 2006b), like other IFIs the PBO struggled in the early years to pursue its mandate, achieve sufficient independence to be credible, and obtain the resources necessary to satisfy its various constituencies.

The mandate of the PBO is currently the least of its problems. For one thing, it is very broad. Under the *Parliament of Canada Act* (Canada, 1985c), the PBO is charged with providing research and independent analysis on the state of the nation's finances and trends in the national economy. This broad mandate undoubtedly was enhanced by the rapid deterioration of public finances following the Great Financial Crisis, but the PBO is also expected to assist Parliament with the examination of estimates and help minimize cost overruns by doing proactive cost assessments. Although not specified in legislation, proponents hoped the PBO would bring an alternative perspective to revenue projections, since the Department of Finance Canada had acquired a reputation for excessive pessimism (Levy, 2008). And then there is the matter of scepticism in financial markets. Credit-rating agencies pay very little attention to public accounts (how the money is actually spent); they focus instead on trajectories. If the PBO could supply independent assurances about long-term financial sustainability, so much the better.

During its relatively short history, the PBO has produced over 200 reports on many topics. Those with which observers are most familiar involve large sums of money and controversial costing assumptions. In the case of both the military's Afghan deployment between 2001–2 and 2010–11 and the planned F-35 fighter jet acquisition announced in 2010, the PBO's cost estimates were far higher than those the government originally delivered to Parliament (PBO, 2008; 2011). As Brooke Jeffrey (2013) has observed, the PBO's reports and projections, unlike the auditor general's, are announced as issues are being aired and debated in the public domain, not afterwards. They are, for that reason, much more politically sensitive. And while no one disputes the need for an audit of government spending, the idea of creating an agency with responsibility for checking and potentially contradicting the work of government departments, particularly the Department of Finance Canada, met with bureaucratic resistance from the outset. At the heart of the dispute over the mandate and status of the PBO is the degree to which, if at all, Canada's Constitution relies on the separation-of-powers doctrine. The first director of the PBO, Kevin Page, described Canada's commitment as "weak," observing that, as long as the executive exerts firm control over the legislature, the PBO will have no champion in either the executive or legislative branches of government (Page & Yalkin, 2014, p. 183).

During the first several years of its existence, the PBO fought for increased formal independence and sufficient resources to carry out its statutory functions. The details of this battle, which involved the speakers of the House of Commons and Senate and the parliamentary librarian, are a matter of public record. They depict an office that fit awkwardly into the existing framework of parliamentary government, attracted suspicion, and yet enjoyed widespread public support. Since then, a measure of peace has been achieved. In 2017 the parliamentary budget officer became an officer of Parliament, holding appointment "during good behaviour" rather than "during pleasure," thus ensuring security of appointment and removing an original disparity in treatment compared to other parliamentary officers.

Of course, the PBO still requires a budget, authority to hire, and access to information. All of these have been a struggle, with resistance coming from bureaucratic and political sources. The biggest challenge, however, remains the need to maintain credibility in a system where the PBO has few natural friends and many potential enemies. In the throes of the jurisdictional disputes that dominated the early work of the PBO, a former deputy minister, Michael Warren, speculated on the origins of some of the difficulties experienced by Kevin Page, the first incumbent: "His track record of economic and deficit forecasting has been outstanding. More accurate than the government, the opposition, the Bank of Canada, most private-sector economists and the media. And nobody likes to be wrong" (Warren, 2009).

This generous assessment aside, accurate forecasts are difficult, and defining what is financially sustainable is equally hard since there are a variety of sustainable levels of debt (Wren-Lewis, 2014, p. 57). Taking the current fiscal path and projecting it into the distant future can appear rather arbitrary, as one of our interviewees pointed out (with some exaggeration): "They take the most recent five-year spending trend and extrapolate it for a hundred years." [Economist 4]. Controversy will undoubtedly follow the PBO whatever it does, but controversy is unlikely to threaten its existence. The appetite for independent analysis of public finance is too great to be extinguished by methodological criticisms or assurances that the government's numbers and projections can be trusted.

As if to illustrate the point, in 2013, the government of Ontario created the Financial Accountability Office (FAO), modelled on Ottawa's PBO. This office was the product of an agreement between the Liberals and the New Democratic Party to secure the latter's support for the Liberal budget. The financial accountability officer is appointed by the Legislative Assembly for a renewable five-year term (up to a maximum of ten years in office), and the incumbent can be terminated or suspended only "for cause" by a vote of at least two-thirds of the members of the

Assembly. Similar to its older federal sibling, the FAO exists to support members of the provincial legislature with research and analysis of Ontario's economic and fiscal performance, government spending plans, and financial analysis of specific government policies (FAO, 2021).

An alternative to adding a new IFI is to expand even further the work of auditors. Rather than waiting for the dust to settle on a controversial program or project, some auditors prefer to engage ahead of disaster. As one of them put it in our interviews, "coming in after it's over and saying OK now what was the impact of all that, is going to be a little late to the game." [Bureaucrat 1]. Provincial auditors already have been recruited to do this kind of proactive work. Whether that pattern will continue or new offices created, it seems certain that, for the foreseeable future, IFIs will be an important part of fiscal governance and accountability regimes in Canada.

Conclusion

In democratic theory, the case for accountability is straightforward; delivering accountability is another matter. Definitional disputes are part of the problem, but far more important is the challenge of devising a workable fiscal governance system that can deliver a degree of accountability sufficient to legitimize elite decisionmaking. This task is made much more difficult in policy areas as broad and complex as macroeconomic policy. It is difficult to expect politicians, and other elites, to be accountable in a world of radical uncertainty where best, or simply reasonable, guesses are subject to significant error.

In Canada political accountability continues to depend on constitutional conventions associated with parliamentary democracy. These conventions concentrate authority and protect advisors, but provide only limited opportunity for public and legislative engagement with fiscal choices. In Europe coalition governments and weak finance ministries pose a different kind of accountability problem (Hallerberg et al., 2007). In both cases the mechanisms of political accountability can only deliver weak process assurances. Outcome assurances, in the form of fiscal rules or similar enforceable requirements, face serious political and economic obstacles. Politicians are reluctant to adhere to rules that undermine their own political fortunes or that force them to take responsibility for outcomes they can influence only marginally. Although they are eager to be accountable for outcomes that are agreeable, they resist taking responsibility for imposing hardships, even if these are deemed necessary by other elite players. Politicians bring a natural and healthy scepticism to projects that involve sacrifice with uncertain benefits. Calls for accountability defined in terms of fiscal discipline are a hard sell absent external threats such as credit downgrades, and even these are not guarantees of action.

In the face of these political realities, formal accountability mechanisms have come to occupy a larger role in reassuring a sceptical public and a nervous investment community. A strong Department of Finance Canada oversees the preparation of budgets without much interference from line departments (Good, 2013). Consultations take place, but norms of budget secrecy and the absence of coalition politics have cemented a centralized approach to budget making at the federal level and in the provinces. On the other hand, the very institutional features that supposedly assist strong finance regimes inhibit accountability for budgetary decisions. A weak legislature, in particular, means that budgetary decisions are made without the prospect of serious, detailed review. Budget secrecy, long criticized by finance ministers themselves, continues to thwart extensive public participation in the budget process, either before the budget is tabled or after its contents have been revealed.

Much of the work associated with ensuring that governments in Canada are answering for their decisions now falls on independent offices, particularly the auditor general and, more recently, the Parliamentary Budget Office. These mechanisms are vital to the accountability project, but fiscal policy decisions are fundamentally political. Independent fiscal watchdogs can and do alert the public to waste, blind optimism, and chicanery, but they cannot correct entirely for a budgetary process that is opaque for most of the public and weak at the political level, where accountability for political decisions matters most.

8 Canada's Fiscal Future

Pandemics are by nature episodic affairs. They have beginnings and endings, although the latter are never entirely clear. They are crises and shocks, but they are not revolutions. They bring normal social and economic behaviour to a standstill, but on their own they do not convey new beginnings. Those have to be invented, and the proponents of radical change know they have a limited opportunity before the forces of inertia and sociopolitical reality take over. This sense of immediacy was captured nicely by the founder of the World Economic Forum (WEF), Klaus Schwab, who wrote early in the pandemic that it "represents a rare but narrow window of opportunity to reflect, reimagine, and reset our world" (Sutcliffe, 2020). The so-called Great Reset initiatives hoped to catalyze these rare disruptions to our old lives and build "a healthier, more equitable, and more prosperous future."

On the health front, we saw progress. Scientists, supported by small firms and Big Pharma, developed COVID-19 vaccines. At an unprecedented speed, the vaccines passed various government regulatory hurdles and were transported to the arms of millions of people. Vaccines prevented serious illnesses and deaths, allowing many of us to resume an almost normal life. When we look back at this episode of history, we can gratefully call the vaccine rollout a victory. In one of its recent COVID-19-related reports on vaccine procurement and distribution, the Office of the Auditor General found that Public Services and Procurement Canada provided "efficient procurement support" to obtain sufficient vaccine doses for eligible Canadians (OAG, 2022a, p. 4). Although there was chaos and confusion at the beginning of the pandemic, countries have vowed to combat the next one collaboratively. In June 2021, G7 leaders signed an international treaty on pandemic prevention and preparedness centred on the leadership of the World Health Organization (G7 Health Ministers, 2021). We will see if these achievements have lasting effects.

On the economic and social front, we witnessed mixed results. Economic rescue efforts were widely and appropriately praised, but they were not going to provide the "more equitable, and more prosperous future" that the WEF anticipated. Pessimists pronounced the opposite. In April 2020, Ray Dalio, the head of the world's largest hedge fund, predicted that after the pandemic we would see a depression – a contraction of the economy lasting for years rather than months. He projected a "double-digit unemployment rate" and more than 10 per cent decline in the US economy (Huddleston, 2020). But the US economy didn't shrink, and by April 2022 the employment rate had returned to pre-pandemic levels. In Canada, unemployment rose from 5.7 per cent in February 2020 to 13.4 per cent in May 2020, but by April 2022 the unemployment rate had dropped back to 5.2 per cent. With a growing sense of relief, governments began to relax public health restrictions and resume business as usual.

Of course, things have not gone back to normal because normal has changed. Old problems have presented themselves with a new vengeance. What the pandemic has done is amplify them. Health care, already under strain, is breaking down. Inequalities are more pronounced and are taking new, disturbing forms. Debt levels, both government and household, are so high that they would have prompted the label "crisis" at just about any other time in our history. Meanwhile, and largely independent of the pandemic, international conflict has exacerbated food shortages, and climate change has sparked droughts, wildfires, and intense storms. No wonder people are asking for a reset. However, changes in politics or policy depend on timing and conditions. Some changes are feasible. More dramatic change is much less likely. Let's start with some of the things that are difficult to change.

Stubborn Realities

The pandemic is the most recent in a series of unnerving shocks, coming from within the economy (housing bubbles), from the biosphere (viruses, climate change), and from the political world (Ukraine). Increasingly, these shocks are international in scope; Canada is not an originator, but it is swept up in the larger picture. Whether these events merit a new concept – "polycrisis" – is beside the point. Taken together they threaten to overwhelm our collective capacity to respond effectively. Our current response – highly defensive, parochial, and keyed on the immediate source of distress – is unlikely to sustain us as the world changes in ever-more complex patterns.

Risk and uncertainty have increased.

Towards the end of 2021, when inflation clearly had settled in, economists debated its origins and struggled with some anomalies. Spending was back to pre-pandemic levels, but prices continued to climb. Interest rates were increasing, but employment remained strong. Paul Krugman (2021) offered this slightly unnerving assessment: "Maybe the real takeaway here should be how little we know about where we are in this strange economic episode. Economists like me who didn't expect much inflation were wrong, but economists who did predict inflation were arguably right for the wrong reasons, and nobody really knows what's coming."

In Canada, hand wringing about the state of public finances gave way to improving balance sheets as most provinces enjoyed an unexpected upswing in revenues, the product of surprise inflation, robust revenues, and agreeable changes in international commodity prices. No one predicted an upbeat revenue picture, and no one can predict how long it will last.

The world economy has developed into a complicated global network with many key drivers changing simultaneously. Extended value chains, created deliberately to capture the advantages of cheaper labour and to reduce the risk of supply disruptions, now divide production among a host of international sites. Capital is highly mobile; production is highly fragmented. As a result, changes, or crises, in one part of the world are quickly felt everywhere, Russia's war on Ukraine being the latest in a long list of examples. Even without wars or natural disasters, the world is becoming more volatile because of a cascade of changes, including an aging population, technical advances, growing risks from climate change, accumulating debts, and increasing inequality (Poloz, 2022). As they interact with one another, these developments amplify uncertainties and undermine accepted formulas for dealing with them.

As the economic environment becomes more difficult to understand – and hence riskier – governments are expected to provide clear signals, stable policies, and concrete investments. These requirements test the capacity of governments at the best of times. Monetary instruments are blunt, and as interest rates approach zero, increasingly ineffectual. When inflation is on the rise, liquidity tightening threatens to spark recessions. Fiscal policy can offer some relief, but it is prone to either too much stimulus or too much austerity. Besides, it is not well suited to handle long-term sources of deflation – including aging populations, inequality, and low demand for capital investment. The traditional answer to these problems has been somehow to grow the economy, and it is still the answer preferred by Canada's economic elite.

Slow growth will persist.

The slowdown of economic growth in the past decade has been the most important background phenomenon for economic and social policy in Canada. Between 2010 and 2019, the average annual real economic growth rate in Canada was 2.3 per cent. Although the post-pandemic reopening has boosted the economy over the short term, it will be difficult for Canada or other countries to reverse the long-term trend towards stagnation. The factors that contributed to the post–Second World War economic expansion, including a baby boom, increase in female labour participation, increase in education attainment, and technological and organizational changes, were each exhausted or reached plateaus by the mid-2000s (Lindsey & Hammond, 2020).

Spikes in commodity prices bring short-term reprieves, but the growth they offer depends on demand in shifting global markets. Not only have our exports been declining relative to the size of our economy, but our reliance on oil and gas and traditional heavy industries to generate those exports leaves Canada vulnerable in the shift to a low-carbon world. The best that can be said is that governments are aware of these transitions and the investments they require, but our track record of response is not encouraging. Compared to other OECD countries, the level of knowledge intensity in Canada's economy has been declining, reflective of our anaemic commitment to research and development (Karaguesian, 2023). In such an economic environment, what Canada realistically can hope for is a steady, albeit low, economic growth rate.

There are many reasons offered for the slowdown Canada and other OECD countries are experiencing. For proponents of the secular-stagnation hypothesis, one is certainly investors' reluctance to choose value-added enterprises over rent-seeking opportunities. Another is the idea that we might have exhausted the readily available technological fixes. We are less pessimistic than others about the opportunities for technological advance on a host of fronts, but perhaps more pessimistic about the effects of demographic change on growth. Declining fertility has many sources, but its consequences should focus our minds (Cave et al., 2021). The short-term effect is to increase the demand for labour as the number of those actively in the workforce versus those who are dependent on their efforts decreases. This shift alone will tip the political scales in favour of workers. Immigration will slow the process down, but generalized demographic decline eventually will reduce population inflow. Some will celebrate any demographic developments that provide relief from ongoing extractions of natural capital, but others worry about the conflicts a shrinking, bifurcated workforce will engender (Bricker & Ibbitson, 2019).

Conflict is already part of our political life, as the generational effects of wealth inequalities show up in reduced opportunities for younger Canadians to achieve a lifestyle that resembles the one enjoyed by their parents. A slow economic growth rate means slow growth in total incomes and tax revenues and potentially an entrenchment of inequalities. The division of income within the current generation is close to a zero-sum game. The likely winners are those who either inherit wealth or create economic value using their resources and skills; those with lower education levels or less valuable skills are vulnerable to being displaced. We have already seen that, without compensatory public policy, the losers in a slow-growth economy will express their anger through protest or the election of populist politicians.

In theory, equipped with a large share of economic resources, governments could step up to promote innovations and economic growth. However, the neoliberal economic philosophy that triumphed in the era of Margaret Thatcher and Ronald Reagan continues to influence attitudes towards the capacity of governments. To be sure, the coarseness of this brand of economic thinking is largely gone, and very few defend unbridled capitalism. But among members of the economic elite, there is widespread scepticism about government's ability to manage major economic development projects or spur innovation. As much as an earlier era of massive investments in railways and waterways continues to feed into national myth making, it is even easier to recall our recent difficulties in building pipelines and liquefied natural gas facilities or launching the Infrastructure Development Bank. Getting things built remains a big challenge.

As for the transition to a services-driven economy, Canada has failed to provide adequate broadband Internet service to remote communities, protect intellectual property, or develop a national data strategy in areas such as health care, agriculture, and energy. The list of failures is long enough to provoke academics and public servants to remind us that, in fact, there have been policy successes, even relatively recent ones (Himelfarb, 2019; Lindquist et al., 2022). And that's the frustrating part. Governments could play a constructive role in promoting innovation (Mazzucato, 2018), but finding the formula for doing so has been a journey of trial and (often) error (Munro et al., 2022).

Without a strong-growth agenda, the economic elite will look for ways of living with debt while fending off the pitfalls and consequences of fiscal mismanagement. Confidence in the elite's ability to balance growth and inflation is highly qualified. One part of this formula – inflation – can be controlled in theory, but it is vulnerable to political interference and uncontrollable global forces. The other part of the formula – economic growth – is the most problematic part of sustainability requirements. It is a good bet that politicians, bureaucrats, and their advisors will continue to concentrate most of their energies on trying to solve business-cycle problems. There are good reasons to do this, but short-term stability is not the same as sustainability. Boosting the economic growth rate requires targeted and substantial investments and a restructuring of the economy, something neither the economic elite nor most voters seem eager to embrace.

Risk aversion and status quo bias persist.

We have remarked already on how members of the economic elite, quick to applaud heroic interventions during the pandemic, nonetheless welcomed a rapid return to "policy as usual." Early calls to use the pandemic as a springboard to reconsider basic economic assumptions have gone largely unheeded. The problems of economic growth, persistent inequalities, and debt management are recognized, to be sure, but the economic elite has no appetite to attack them with anything other than conventional tools. The topic of modern monetary theory (MMT) is a case in point. Although a strong fiscal response to the pandemic was occasionally acknowledged to be consistent with MMT precepts, its core concepts were routinely dismissed. Perhaps they deserved to be, but the rapid rejection of different ideas about how the economy works when it is clearly not working as expected does not bode well for the prospect of new thinking at any point.

At least part of this preference for the familiar can be traced to the observation that negative outcomes are more readily condemned than positive outcomes are praised. For those who are at or near the centre of political decisionmaking, this asymmetry helps explain the extent to which elite members work to avoid or deflect blame. At the political centre, misjudgments about risks and vulnerabilities can be deadly to careers. Under these conditions, risk taking is uncommon but not non-existent. In the case of the pandemic, the public's positive response to lower interest rates and income supports was short lived, as persistent inflation followed welcome interventions. Yesterday's heroes were suddenly held accountable for failing to anticipate the negative side effects of a well-executed rescue.

Of course, risk aversion is not without its benefits. If negativity bias reduces the chance of egregious error by bringing a cautionary approach to innovation, those whose interests might have been jeopardized presumably will be grateful. Politicians are also grateful for the chance to delegate difficult decisions to "experts," even if the experts are subsequently ignored. Citizens might also prefer an approach to problem solving that does not rely on the intuition of politicians, which is often tuned to partisan advantage.

These behavioural tendencies are enhanced when the architecture of institutions is deliberately designed to muddy the waters about culpability. At the extreme, where no one takes responsibility for decisions, cynicism is the normal by-product. But by far the worst consequence of an overinvestment in avoiding blame is the propensity to do little or nothing in the face of clear requirements for change. Reaching for a standard operating procedure, one that generates a mediocre outcome, might comfort process fetishists, but it puts the lie to the idea that outcomes matter. If outcomes are important in fiscal policy, then bold responses are sometimes the only ones that will do. Conspicuous rewards for risk taking are seldom on display, but without them the danger is too little change – not too much.

Pandemic Effects

The short-term effects of the pandemic were highly disruptive: a collapse of supply chains, critical shortages of equipment, new demands on caregivers, remote learning for students, new patterns of work – the list goes on. It seems that almost everything we do, from how we buy groceries to how we find entertainment, was affected. The desire for all this change to be over and for things to go back to normal has been palpable and understandable. But it is likely that at least some things will not be the same. For governments, standard assumptions have been upset and debates about what lessons to draw will continue for years. Some trends, however, seem more plausible than others. Here are a few possibilities.

Governments will seek to improve resilience and self-sufficiency.

As a public health event, the pandemic revealed inadequate preparation, poor communication, immature science, and misinformation. After two years of public health restrictions, Canadians were fatigued and began resisting cooperation with any new lockdowns or mandates. Some residents lamented their loss of freedom and expressed their discontent through protests. Controlling the spread of an infectious virus and protecting individual freedom at the same time is like walking a tightrope. In Canada different governments chose different points on a trade-off curve, sparking complaints of inconsistency and confusion.

How much genuine learning will take place is anyone's guess, but it seems safe to anticipate that, in the future, more attention will be paid to how advice external to governments is channelled into decisionmaking and communication. More and better redundancy planning in the event of organizational failures would be a welcome side effect, but note that any new organizational forms will be met with resistance from some quarters regardless of the pandemic performance of existing bureaucracies. At the very least we should expect a stronger organizational response to health care crises, with an emphasis on information flows, communication protocols, stockpiles of equipment, vaccines, and monitoring tools. In addition, most countries will emerge from the global pandemic with a stronger appreciation of the virtues of self-sufficiency. The forces of protection will be given a limited boost, at least in the areas of public health products.

On the other hand, there is little chance that the pandemic will bring about the end of globalization any more than the Great Financial Crisis ended neoliberalism. International trade will continue to grow because without it the expected slowdown in economic growth will only deepen. Trading patterns, however, are likely to change as countries join de facto trading blocs based in part on shared geopolitical objectives. In certain strategic commodities such as silicon chips, governments will place more emphasis on establishing self-sufficiency or guaranteed supplies. With a huge dynamic economy at its doorstep, Canada has been willing to outsource security and rely on established, and recently renewed, trade relations to protect against economic shocks. The pandemic revealed what we already knew in principle: governments are obliged to look after the needs of their own citizens before helping others. The pandemic helped shake Canadians out of a complacency borne of geopolitical positioning. Without independent manufacturing capability, strong network alliances are needed, and even these cannot be entirely counted on when shortages occur.

Building capacity will take time, but one message of the pandemic is that speed is important. Decisionmaking needs to be rapid and well communicated. Transitions cannot drag on for years. This means shorter response times in the face of immediate danger and a much greater emphasis on rapid economic transitioning to strengthen resilience. In the case of energy risk, demands will increase to remove regulatory hurdles that postpone energy projects, such as liquefied natural gas facilities, but also to speed up the adoption of green-energy technologies. The US *Inflation Reduction Act*, passed in 2022, provides an enormous fiscal boost to clean-energy transitions (United States, 2022). It is forcing Canada to increase its own commitments rapidly on penalty of losing corporate investors and project developers. Meeting the need for rapid transition will tax governments' capacity for strategic planning and likely reignite tensions between provincial governments and Indigenous leaders. But a passive approach to disruption preparation would be much worse.

Social investment will continue to be a priority.

The pandemic taught us that, when an emergency strikes, talented and skilled people matter. In the aggregate we need a fully functioning labour market in which the talents of all are realized to the highest degree possible. Expect more investment in training and preparation for critical areas such as caregiving and primary education. Canada's track record on the former is abysmal; on the latter we risk resting on our laurels. The tragedies that occurred in long-term care facilities across the country and in overcrowded hospital emergency rooms show that our health care system is far from adequate and our human capital easily exhausted.

In the workplace, the pandemic experience fundamentally changed many workers' perspectives on work and life and accelerated changes in the labour market. According to the 2022 Microsoft Work Trend Index, 47 per cent of respondents, particularly parents and women, said they were more likely to prioritize family and personal life over work than they were before the pandemic (Microsoft WorkLab, 2022). This trend adds pressure to an already tight labour market and calls for governments to implement "people" policies. As the availability of workers continues to contract under demographic pressures, expect union organization to grow and with it a demand to rebalance returns to capital and labour.

Prompted by the pandemic, flexible work arrangements are becoming permanent features of the workplace. The transition to a low-carbon economy and a workplace dominated by artificial intelligence will generate more rapid job turnover. Our current Employment Insurance system proved inadequate in responding to large-scale labour displacement during the pandemic. The new labour market trends that feature frequent changes and flexible work arrangements mean that gaps in the

Employment Insurance system will need to be filled to address a more precarious workforce (Busby et al., 2022).

Income-relief programs to help people through crises also need to be better planned. During the pandemic, the federal government's income-support programs were extensive and responsive, but governments need to think about how to make emergency income-relief programs more efficient. Trust among governments and between governments and citizens is essential; bickering among levels of government is counterproductive (Institute on Governance & Brian Mulroney Institute of Government, 2022). Although the federal government is best positioned to implement emergency relief programs, closer consultation and coordination with other levels of government would have avoided some program distortions. Parliament and budget watchdogs also could provide stronger political and formal accountability around the emergency support programs.

Tension between monetary and fiscal policies will grow.

Finance departments and central banks are a big part of the economic policy regime, but both operate in a wider political world. Finance departments are dominated by macroeconomists concerned principally with fiscal policy and attentive to the political implications of budgetary choices. In the world of monetary policy, central bankers focus on inflation rates and rely heavily on one another for guidance and support in an environment that is wary of political interference. During the pandemic these two worlds came together to confront a crisis that threatened their credibility. Creating liquidity and supporting incomes were policies that synchronized nicely around the idea of sustaining demand in a recession. Post-recession, and facing increasing levels of inflation, the symbiosis that characterized the pandemic and much of the period before it will be put to the test.

The idea that central banks could stabilize the economy on their own had always been wishful thinking. During a crisis, central banks' ability and willingness to absorb the loan requirements of governments made them indispensable in both the Great Financial Crisis and the pandemic. But monetary policy has its limitations. The low levels of inflation that encouraged ultra-low interest rates provided stimulus, but also generated asset bubbles that benefited the economically powerful. Increasing rates of interest to combat rising inflation stranded borrowers and threatened to throw economies into recession. Central banks are ill-equipped to deliver a neutral public policy: Either borrowers or lenders are bound to be dissatisfied since there is no such thing as a monetary policy that has no distributional consequences. Central bank policies, moreover, always seem to be behind the curve, either raising interest rates too late to discourage inflation or lowering them too late to head off economic slowdowns.

As Canada's pandemic economy shifted from too little liquidity to too much, critics began agitating to rein in the Bank of Canada somehow by making it more responsive to political direction. In spring 2022, as inflation was becoming entrenched and not transitory, the incoming leader of the opposition's call to "fire" the governor of the Bank of Canada was greeted with dismay in the banking community. When central bankers enjoy policy success, they become mythical figures managing risks on behalf of everyone else without much direct oversight. When things go wrong, their independence begins to look like an affront to democracy. Then again, how much independence does the Bank actually have? The coordinated deployment of monetary policy and fiscal policy prompted by the pandemic had already challenged the image of an independent central bank (Platt, 2022). Here's the problem: when a critical part of economic policy's institutional apparatus sits outside the conventional accountability system, its status as a legitimate framer of economic policy is bound to come under intense scrutiny eventually.

The circumstances prompting post-pandemic scrutiny are the scale of inflation, the size of interest-rate increases, and government's tolerance for increased expenditures devoted to servicing the debt (Goodhart & Pradhan, 2020). For now, and because the Bank of Canada's mandate has been recently renewed, a form of modus vivendi is likely to prevail, but tensions will increase as monetary policies deliver uneven economic impacts. If housing, for example, becomes steadily out of reach for younger Canadians, political pressures will increase to do something dramatic. Ideally, coordination between finance departments and central banks is always within reach. The question is, on whose terms? Since central banks can influence economic decisionmaking only to a point, and are not independent of the political structures in which they are embedded, expect political requirements ultimately to prevail in the event of a conflict (Eich, 2022).

The debt debate will intensify.

During the pandemic, governments suspended the fiscal-frugality principle: they accumulated debts and handed out billions of dollars to individuals and businesses. Such policies would have been widely criticized as inefficient and irresponsible before the pandemic, but with the collapse in demand brought on by COVID-19 restrictions, the federal

government's easy monetary policy and generous income-relief programs were given a pass, at least for the short term. Both scholars and
policymakers relaxed their assumption that a low government debt-to-
GDP ratio is essential for maintaining low inflation. Meanwhile, modern monetary theory received a hearing in academic circles, but, as we
have discussed, made little headway among the economic elite.

The soaring inflation rate in the first half of 2022 inconveniently shat-
tered any confidence that inflation could be managed without risking
another recession. Many pointed to "loose" monetary and fiscal policies during the pandemic as the source of inflationary pressures, even
though disrupted supply chains, substantial household savings, and
the Russia-Ukraine war made their own contributions. By early 2022,
the fiscal prudence tradition was back in vogue. In Canada, groups such
as the C.D. Howe Institute claimed the federal government was using
the pandemic to justify a bigger role in the economy and that massive
spending increases for health care, pharmacare, and emissions reduction, together with the costs of pension obligations, would add billions
to an already overly large fiscal footprint (Robson & Laurin, 2022).

The debate over how to manage the debt could have reverted to its
usual form were it not for the waves of uncertainty unleashed by the
pandemic. Years after the first detected case and the massive fiscal response, it is no longer clear what path Canadian governments are on.
Projected deficits are upended by unexpected revenue windfalls, for
example, as both the federal government and the provinces registered
surpluses during 2022 that none anticipated. Are these short-term reprieves from an otherwise dire situation? Do they signal that governments are extracting too much from the economy and that they should
either return some cash to citizens (as in Alberta and Saskatchewan) or
pay down the debt? Huge amounts of accumulated debt and unstable
revenues create new challenges of interpretation and reaction that will
test standard assumptions. One thing is clear, however: the debt is a
useful foil for laying blame at the feet of incumbents, who are expected
to do a better job of generating believable economic forecasts just as the
task becomes increasingly difficult for anyone to manage.

Pressing Needs

In preceding chapters, we made three key arguments: our political
system tends to reward short-term gains, our economic elites cleave
to the status quo, and accountability for economic decisions is difficult
to establish. None of these deficiencies is immutable; all are subject to
some amelioration. It is unlikely, however, that tinkering with current

institutions will be enough. Many – probably most – of the lessons we might hope to learn from the pandemic bear on better preparation, more consistent messaging, and a superior understanding of the full implications of massive infection. But what about the bigger picture of government policy? What are the chances we will learn something more than how to better manage infectious disease and its economic consequences?

A Better Definition of Prosperity and Well-Being

The need to measure "the economy" became particularly pressing when the economy began to grow in the late nineteenth century, and particularly after the First World War and the Great Depression, when governments began to assume responsibility for economic management. It is difficult to manage something that cannot be measured – hence the need for a straightforward way to sum up the totality of economic activity. Since the 1940s, the conventional way of doing so has been to use the concept of gross national (now domestic) product. There are different ways of calculating GDP, but the most common involves tallying expenditures in the economy according to real or, in the case of government services, imputed prices. This is a non-trivial task, full of disagreements, but by the 1960s conventions had been established, and it was possible to track economic growth and compare economies, even command economies, with one another.

Important to this project of estimating the size of the economy is the idea that there is such a thing as "the economy" in the first place. Initially, measurement enthusiasts did not include government; only market transactions counted. When omitting government from the calculation proved to be unrealistic, GDP measures were amended and expanded to include services of all kinds. Apart from allowing us to track and compare economic growth, this version of the economy – what people are willing to pay for – is congenial to neoclassical economic thinking. It does not, however, capture subjective ideas of value – specifically, estimations of personal and collective well-being. It places emphasis on products and services, but ignores valuable inputs such as childrearing and housekeeping that have no easy or obvious market analogue.

These and other deficiencies sparked an effort to nudge GDP from its central role in evaluating economic health and shift the focus to other summary measures, particularly those based on a determination of overall happiness (Sen et al., 2010). Unlike GDP, which can grow without limit, happiness has some ceiling – you can be only so happy (Coyle,

2014). Economic growth, with its promise of higher living standards, might bring more happiness, but there is no one-to-one relationship. Besides, to the extent that misery – family breakdown, mental illness – attends an all-out focus on growth, quality-of-life indices that capture subjective assessments would seem to be a useful accompaniment to objective measures such as GDP.

Perhaps the most vexing problem with a focus on GDP is the presumption that "the economy" is experienced the same way by everyone. In fact, when the economy grows or contracts, the impacts are felt differently depending on geography, age, income, and sex. When the state of the economy is presented as an aggregate-level phenomenon, GDP growth becomes "a powerful, positive predictor of news tone," whereas other aggregate measures, including unemployment rates, have the opposite effect (Jacobs et al., 2021, p. 1026). In short, perceptions of how the economy is performing depend, to a large extent, on how the economy is portrayed.

More attention to indices that capture inequality, for example, or that contextualize debt, when combined with quality-of-life measures, could help build a more complete picture of economic performance. The integration of environmental, social, and governance criteria into finance, investment, and governance decisions suggests the value of incorporating alternative measures of economic performance into assessments of what is economically sustainable. At a time when economic growth is slowing and natural capital is being consumed at a rapid rate, we need a different lens on the economy than simply the price (imputed or real) of goods sold in the marketplace. It is too early to claim an end to the dominance of GDP, but a consensus is emerging that we should aim to augment GDP measures with more and broader indicators of economic and social progress.

A Long-Term Policy Focus

Any reading of the fiscal challenges facing Canada cannot fail to be impressed by the attention economic elites lavish on near-term consequences. Shifts in interest rates, budget priorities, and tax changes are scoured for their immediate effects on the investment climate. As we have pointed out, the time frame for fiscal policy measures is quite short – less than two years in most cases – and the political cycle itself is not much longer. As the bracing British study Stagnation Nation puts it, "We are short-term to our core" (Resolution Foundation et al., 2022, p. 13). Of course, economic decisions made now can have lasting and cumulative effects; we do not start from scratch with every adjustment to the levers of fiscal policy. Still, our decision time frame is relatively short, and we tend to evaluate success or failure in terms of those currently affected. It is not that all feedback loops are short – policy changes in education or natural resources and the environment, for example, can extend for generations. But fiscal policy decisionmaking is attuned to immediate reactions, even if the payoffs are felt sometime in the future.

In fiscal policymaking, a great deal of stress is placed on bringing some form of stability to a highly risky environment. Reducing risk, sometimes by sharing it, is part of what governments do in this policy realm. The problem is that some of the fiscal problems we face or some collective challenges that are addressed through fiscal measures (inequality, for example) play out over a long period. The same goes for debt, the policy problem that brings intergenerational equity into sharpest focus. Should we simply concentrate on the here and now, looking after the needs of those who are alive, or should we project our present selves into the future and ask what kind of fiscal environment we are bequeathing to future generations? Or, in the case of debt and inequality, do we simply leave them for someone else?

Our political institutions are attuned to the present because the political project involves the exercise of power, and that is not done in the abstract or in the future. But for most people, the idea of heavily discounting the future is difficult to justify. Philosophically, it is hard to defend the idea that someone's time on Earth is worth less than ours just because it will occur years, decades, or centuries in the future (Cowen, 2018, p. 68). Practically, economic decisions in the present have effects – good and bad – that last for centuries. The effects of colonialism are with us every day; so are Victorian attitudes towards the "deserving poor." On a more positive note, success in securing even low levels of economic growth has enduring positive effects, including reducing risk for future generations.

Because environmental quality and wealth equality have implications for the well-being of future generations, these issues are critical for intergenerational sustainability. We might not be able to predict the next pandemic, but we can reverse the deterioration of our natural environment and reduce the gaps in income and wealth. And we must invest in a growth strategy that can manage all of that. As Don Drummond (2020, p. 2) observed at the beginning of the pandemic, "we have been locked into a path of mediocre productivity and real income gains for far too long."

If we are to achieve these goals, we must embrace the idea of long termism and carve out deliberative space to understand the generational effects of today's decisions. When near-term costs have long-term benefits, estimating these benefits is vital in persuading people to absorb the costs. If near-term benefits, such as deficit spending, have long-term risks, it is equally important that those who bear these risks be represented even though they are not present and, in many cases, do not exist.

In principle, institutions designed to extract political accountability could ensure that long-term effects are better appreciated. But, as we explained in Chapter 7, these institutions are relatively weak, both because of the distribution of power within them and because they are organized around achieving short-term political advantage. Making space for the longer term means, first, embracing cost-benefit analysis. For all its limitations, the calculation of costs and benefits, both their size and on whom they fall, is a fundamental requirement of policymaking. If we can afford to have independent budget officers, we should be capable of creating future policy impact scenarios that provide accurate estimates of costs and adequate provision for compensation. To be sure, politicians engage in this kind of calculation themselves, but they do so by relying on their own impressionistic ideas of costs and benefits and their own, implicit, discount rates. We can do better.

Robust State Capacity

Although markets are undeniably effective in fostering innovation, they need to be enabled, supported, and restrained by a strong and capable public sector (Lindsey & Hammond, 2020). At its core, state capacity is "the ability of a state to collect taxes, enforce law and order, and provide public goods" (Lindsey, 2021). It sounds simple, but, as we are aware, or should be, managing the modern state is actually exceedingly difficult. For much of what the state provides, there is no agreed-upon metric to measure success, and much of what the state is expected to do – reduce uncertainty, create a positive investment climate, and provide public goods such as education and health care – is fundamentally problematic. When neither inputs nor outputs are easily measured, as with critical features of economic policymaking, success is elusive by definition. The fact that the state cannot go out of business is enough to persuade critics that it will be hopelessly inept, corrupt, and bloated.

If there were easy fixes to the challenges of managing a modern economy, they would have been implemented by now. And many have been tried. From privatization to lean technologies to "nudge" methods, governments have adopted a variety of techniques to improve performance, all with mixed results. Reorganization, a familiar and favourite tool in the reformist toolkit, is constantly employed to better meet a changing organizational environment.

In Canada these experiments need to continue. In a world with growing externalities, interdependency, uncertainties, risks, and other collective problems, governments have no choice but to try new adaptive techniques that move the state beyond rigid rules and suffocating hierarchies. Above all, at the elite level, excellent advice and sound judgment are essential. The good news is that, in the realm of fiscal policy, the level of available expertise is exceptionally high. The Canadian economic elite is pragmatic, results oriented, and familiar with conventional economic reasoning. Most of all, whether members of this elite are elected, part of the bureaucracy, or simply advisors, a strong ethos of public service permeates their approach to their jobs. As we indicated in the opening chapters, the concept of public interest plays a large role in contemporary judgments about what is desirable, feasible, and sustainable.

Apart from the very real difficulties that attend the design and delivery of programs, the biggest challenge at the most senior levels of economic policymaking is the canvassing and nurturing of new ideas. Public servants provide the intellectual ballast needed to keep the focus on agreed-upon outcomes, discourage dangerous departures from strategic plans, and provide critical feedback in real time. They and their professional economist colleagues can feed ideas to the political level, but the energy and commitment must be delivered by those engaged in political competition. When competition is drained of intellectual content and debate deteriorates into sloganeering or performative denunciations, the politics of economic policy become empty and ritualistic. Even budget debates, the core of fiscal policy, end up as fodder for tired, prepackaged, and predictable monologues. In short, the demand for "state capacity," an understandable and desperately needed ingredient for economic success, will not be enough without better politics. Better prepared politicians are a start, but if political competition chokes out dialogue and becomes merely a communications battle, the prospect for serious success recedes.

Stronger Democratic Accountability

The major institutions of electoral and representative democracy in Canada continue to struggle to deliver accountability for the most critical economic policy decisions. The connection between announced budget priorities and budgetary outcomes typically is weak (Robson &

Dahi, 2023), and so is the ability of legislatures to command the attention of executives. It is, to be sure, difficult to explain and justify complex economic decisions, and economic sophistication among elected representatives cannot be assumed. But when politics is associated exclusively with strategic manoeuvring, duplicity, and compromised principles, most Canadians will shun its practitioners and discount the accountability it offers.

The weakness of political accountability helps explain the growing importance of formal accountability and the offices that deliver it – auditors, electoral officers, privacy commissioners, budget officers, and the like. They can claim to be concerned with both the inputs and the outputs of the system, its overall direction and performance. But their major claim to legitimacy is their impartiality. Unlike democratic institutions, which organize a political process defined by partisanship, these institutions are committed to delivering good government even if the democratic inputs are flawed, as they often are.

The problem is that these offices cannot be expected to deliver accountability on their own. If the relevance of electoral and representative institutions continues to be lost on Canadians, there is a significant risk that populist messages, aimed at dismantling or circumventing existing institutions, will receive an increasingly receptive audience. Just because the rule of law continues to be enforced and expert judgments continue to be rendered does not mean citizens will be happy with their political institutions. Improvements in economic performance undoubtedly would help, but the relationship between a strong economy and support for democratic institutions is by no means automatic and, as we have argued, a strong economy is not something that can simply be ordered up by economic elites.

Without a reservoir of trust, the legitimacy of governments is in constant danger of eroding, which is why some have argued that we should invest less in improving the input processes of democracy – elections, opinion canvassing, parliamentary debate – as a means of shoring up support for the political system, and more on the institutions of formal accountability – judges, bureaucrats, and official guardians (Rothstein, 2011). For Canada, that would be a mistake. Canada's democratic institutions were built for another time, but their basic representative architecture is worthy of retaining, just not necessarily in their current form.

We need, for example, a new, more equitable allocation of seats in the House of Commons, and the introduction of proportional representation is long overdue. A serious conversation about compulsory voting would also be welcome. Regional resentments, a constant and serious threat to the country's political viability, need to be channelled away from echo chambers and into forums that are not designed to be consistently confrontational. A much larger Senate (to enhance representativeness) selected by lottery (to improve impartiality and political equality) might seem like an outrageous proposition, but it would enhance Parliament's democratic credentials and act as a counterbalance to the appropriately partisan House of Commons (Abizadeh, 2021).

For fiscal and monetary policy, we need new advisory institutions. Over the past several decades, the Department of Finance Canada in Ottawa has strengthened its monopoly on the definition of good economic policy and the Prime Minister's Office has become an instrument of orthodoxy enforcement. External advice is available, and occasionally seconded, but it most often takes the form of consulting contracts for specific projects. Canada has not risked a Royal Commission on the country's economic prospects since the Macdonald Royal Commission presented its report in 1984.

The moment is ripe for a comprehensive examination of many contentious economic topics, including defence procurement, reforms to the tax system, the reduction and removal of interprovincial trade barriers, and the transition to new energy sources. Why invite a potentially disruptive report in the middle of an era of increasing uncertainty? The answer is that, although the existing talent in federal and provincial bureaucracies can be counted on to manage the short-term exigencies of revenue and expenditure fluctuations, the public service alone cannot be expected to fashion a plan for a more prosperous and stable future. The future is simply not something that the economic elite is prepared or willing to attend to, as harsh as that might sound.

Canada no longer has an Economic Council, but relies instead on self-organizing groups of academics and commentators passionate about various aspects of public finance. It is past time to draw more explicitly and publicly on the very substantial expertise that Canada possesses and mix it with the perspectives of both conservative and progressive critics. If Parliament can be made a sponsor or a participant in the resulting consultations, so much the better. Otherwise, stale moralizing and predictable positioning will continue to turn off the majority of Canadians.

Conclusion

The pandemic has alerted us to the fragility of our economic assumptions and focused our attention on some immediate challenges. The rare and rapid changes in the economy during the crisis helped economists and policymakers better understand the nature of economic business cycles and the effects and limitations of monetary and fiscal policy. But the lessons of the pandemic cannot end with demand-side stimulus and interest-rate manipulation, as important as these are. The pandemic revealed serious supply-side problems, the imperative of addressing inequalities, and the challenge of designing sound fiscal and monetary policies in an era of profound uncertainty. Under these conditions, realism means confronting the long-term problems that the pandemic revealed and adapting political institutions to new realities.

The idea of a reset is threatening, and not just to adherents of globalist conspiracies. It throws many settled understandings into question, perhaps too many. Those unnerved by the startling confluence of stagnation, inflation, debt, and inequality can take some comfort in the ability of our institutions to slow down adjustments and subject new ideas to ample scrutiny. On the other hand, those desperate to challenge the assumptions and beliefs of the current economic elite will need to be persistent and courageous. Unfortunately, the courage needed to confront these challenges honestly is in short supply, while ritualistic denunciations are abundant. Our institutions can help protect us from radical excess, but they cannot manufacture courage. Courage is a personal, behavioural trait that citizens need to recognize, nourish, and respect. That means attracting and rewarding leaders – elites, if you will – who are public spirited, mindful, and better prepared. Otherwise, the risks we are so committed to avoiding simply will swamp us.

Appendix 1: Interview Questions

Interview Questions (October 2020)

1 Experience with COVID-19 and concerns about global warming have suggested to some that we are entering a period in which governments should play a larger role in rebuilding and steering the economy. Do you share that view?

2 What should be Canada's main economic priorities as we recover from the pandemic?
  • Protecting the income of citizens
  • Controlling inflation
  • Controlling the size of the government
  • Reducing income disparities
  • Stimulating economic growth
  • Other

3 Going forward, what do you think should be the fiscal policy anchor for the federal government? Should the provinces have the same fiscal anchor?
  • A balanced budget
  • A low, stable inflation rate
  • An upper limit on all spending programs
  • A fixed amount spent on interest on the debt
  • A low debt-to-GDP ratio
  • A triple A credit rating

4 Following the Great Recession, some economists urged governments to pursue austerity policies to deal with the public debt problem. What do you think should be the direction of fiscal policy in the post-pandemic era?

5 Given our experience with the pandemic, are you satisfied that the current division of powers between federal and provincial governments serves our collective interest? What about local government?

6 What are your views on programs like equalization and the Fiscal Stabilization Program? Do they need to be tweaked or fundamentally reformed?

7 During the pandemic, central banks in Canada and elsewhere greatly increased their purchases of government debt. What should be the role of Bank of Canada after the pandemic?

8 Modern monetary theory claims that concerns about the national debt are not just overblown, but rest on a misunderstanding of how the financial system operates. Do you have any views on modern monetary theory?

9 Is this the time to make some major shifts in our budget priorities?

10 Are there clear criteria that should be used to evaluate alternative spending options?

11 Does Parliament play a role in fiscal accountability?

12 Some critics have argued that electoral cycles induce myopia in politicians; they pay too much attention to the short term, not enough to the long term. Do you share that concern?

13 Some governments have affirmed a commitment to "growth friendly" adjustment paths coming out of the COVID-19 crisis. Is this the right way to think about economic sustainability?

14 Could you tell us where you obtain your most reliable information on current developments in economic policy? What about the long term: are there any specific sources that are consistent reference points?

Interview Questions (January 2021)

1 Experience with COVID-19 and concerns about global warming have suggested to some that we are entering a period in which governments should play a larger role in rebuilding and steering the economy. Do you share that view?

2 What should be Canada's main economic priorities as we recover from the pandemic?
- Protecting the income of citizens
- Controlling inflation
- Controlling the size of the government
- Reducing income disparities
- Stimulating economic growth
- Other

3 Going forward, what do you think should be the fiscal policy anchor for the federal government? Should the provinces have the same fiscal anchor?

- A balanced budget
- A low, stable inflation rate
- An upper limit on all spending programs
- A fixed amount spent on interest on the debt
- A declining debt-to-GDP ratio
- A triple A credit rating

4 What, if anything, needs to be done to place federal-provincial financial relations on a sound footing?

5 What are your views on programs like equalization, Canada Health Transfer, and the Fiscal Stabilization Program? Do they need to be tweaked or fundamentally reformed?

6 During the pandemic, central banks in Canada and elsewhere greatly increased their purchases of government debt. What should be the role of Bank of Canada after the pandemic?

7 Modern monetary theory claims that concerns about the national debt are not just overblown, but rest on a misunderstanding of how the financial system operates. Do you have any views on modern monetary theory?

8 The programs of income support provided by the federal government at the outset of the pandemic have been described by some as poorly targeted and overly generous. Do you share that assessment?

9 Following the Great Recession, some economists urged governments to pursue austerity policies to deal with the public debt problem. Will austerity be necessary as we emerge from COVID-19?

10 Would a systematic review of current spending programs enhance confidence in the management of public finances?

11 Some critics have argued that politicians pay too much attention to the short term, not enough to the long term. Do you share that concern?

12 Is there a role for Parliament and provincial legislatures in fiscal accountability?

13 Thinking of economic policy in general, how would you define "sustainability"?

14 Could you tell us where you obtain your most reliable information on current developments in economic policy? What about the long term: are there any specific sources that are consistent reference points?

Interview Questions for Independent Agencies (February 2021)

1 What will you consider when you assess the performance of governments as we recover from the pandemic?

- Protecting the income of citizens
- Controlling inflation
- Controlling the size of the government
- Reducing income disparities
- Stimulating economic growth
- Other

2 Among the following indicators, which are the most relevant for your assessment of the fiscal sustainability of a government?
  - Annual budget balance
  - Net-debt-to-GDP ratio
  - Ratio of debt interest payments to government revenue
  - Growth rate of per capita government expenditure

3 Is the environmental, social, and governance framework a significant advance in guiding the evaluation of sustainability?

4 What, if anything, needs to be done to place federal-provincial financial relations on a sound and sustainable footing?

5 Do credit-rating agencies have a role in helping government achieve fiscal sustainability or is their job simply to evaluate financial plans?

6 In your view, what are the key indicators of a transparent government budgeting process?

7 What type of mechanisms can help enhance transparency and accountability of government budgeting?

8 What is the primary role of the independent auditor (i.e., auditor general or provincial auditor) in securing fiscal accountability?

9 The programs of income support provided by the federal government at the outset of the pandemic have been described by some as poorly targeted and overly generous. Do you share that assessment?

10 How important are cost considerations in the evaluation of government programs?

Appendix 2: A Survey of Canadians' Opinions on the Post-Pandemic Economy and Fiscal Policy

To learn what Canadians themselves think our priorities should be, we conducted a national survey in January 2021. Our 563 respondents were randomly chosen by EKOS Research Associates. The resulting sample is consistent with the distribution of Canadian adults across age, gender, and household-income groups in the 2016 census. It also corresponds to the rural-urban division and province of residence of Canadian adults. The margin of error of the sampling at the national level is +/–4.13 per cent (19 times out of 20). Table B.1 describes the distribution.

Table B.1. Distribution of Survey Respondents (n = 563)

Age	n (%)	Gender	n (%)	Household income	n (%)	Region	n (%)
Non-senior (18–64)	410 (73%)	Women	272 (48%)	Low	136 (22%)	West	180 (32%)
		Men	277 (49%)	Middle	196 (35%)	Central	323 (57%)
Senior (65+)	153 (27%)			High	175 (31%)	East	59 (11%)
		Other	14 (3%)	Don't know	66 (15%)	Other	1

Notes: For region, "West" consists of British Columbia, Alberta, Saskatchewan, and Manitoba; "Central" is Ontario and Quebec; "East" is New Brunswick, Nova Scotia, Prince Edward Island, and Newfoundland and Labrador; "Other" refers to the territories.

Survey Questionnaire

1 How familiar are you with government fiscal policy, including, for example, taxation, spending programs, and government debt?

2 Which of the following should be Canada's policy priorities as we recover from the pandemic? Please rank them in order

of importance, with 1 = the most important and 5 = the least important.

Protecting the income of citizens
Controlling increases in the cost of goods and services
Reducing the level of government debt
Reducing income inequalities
Creating jobs

3 Please choose the response – strongly agree, agree, neutral, disagree, strongly disagree – that best represents your views on each question in this section:

Strongly agree
Agree
Neutral
Disagree
Strongly disagree
I do not know

a. After the pandemic, governments should play a larger role than before in shaping the economy.
b. Businesses that receive COVID-19 bailouts should comply with government requirements on climate change.
c. After the pandemic, governments should quickly end the emergency income-support programs.
d. Governments should not be expected to help private companies become more competitive.
e. Financial support from the federal government to the provinces should have no strings attached. That is, support should not require the provinces to do certain things.
f. Even if provinces make poor decisions, the federal government should never allow a province to declare bankruptcy.
g. Politicians should never tell the Bank of Canada what to do.
h. The COVID-19 experience shows us that we have a high level of expert knowledge inside governments in Canada.
i. Most politicians do not understand how our economic system works.
j. Most economists do not understand how our political system works.
k. Governments would run better if left up to successful business people.
l. Elections are the only effective way to protect against the abuse of power by governments.

m. In Parliament the Opposition has succeeded in holding the federal government accountable during the COVID-19 pandemic.
n. Independent audits cannot protect us from government programs that end up wasting money.
o. Government budget information is too complex for the average voter to understand.
p. Government budget information is too complex for the average Member of Parliament to understand.
q. All the provinces should be required to balance their budgets.
r. The federal government should be required to balance its budget.
s. The federal government's debt level after COVID-19 is a more serious problem than most people recognize.
t. The more money governments borrow, the less money is available for private companies to invest.
u. Countries like Canada that can borrow in their own currency can safely print money to fund their spending programs.

4 How often can you trust the federal government in Ottawa to do what is right?

All of the time
Most of the time
About half the time
Sometimes
Never

5 How often can you trust the government in your province to do what is right?

All of the time
Most of the time
About half the time
Sometimes
Never

6 Each of the following budget-management goals has recently been recommended by different economists. Please rank in order of importance with 1 = the most important and 6 = the least important.

A balanced budget
A low, stable inflation rate
An upper limit on all spending programs
A declining level of debt
An excellent credit rating
Full employment

7 All of the areas listed below have been described as worthy of additional investment by the federal government. Please select the three priorities that you believe deserve the most support.

Public health
Childcare support
Early childhood education
A Universal Basic Income
Climate change and a green economy
Broadband expansion and digitization
Physical infrastructure
A strong Canadian supply chain
Oil and gas pipelines
Post-secondary education
Job training
Technology and innovation
Agricultural research

8 All of the areas listed below have been described as worthy of additional investment by the federal government. Please select the three priorities that you believe deserve the least support.

Public health
Childcare support
Early childhood education
A Universal Basic Income
Climate change and a green economy
Broadband expansion and digitalization
Physical infrastructure
A strong Canadian supply chain
Oil and gas pipelines
Post-secondary education
Job training
Technology and innovation
Agricultural research

References

Aberbach, J.D., Rockman, B.A., & Putnam, R.D. (1981). *Bureaucrats and politicians in western democracies*. Harvard University Press.

Abizadeh, A. (2021). Representation, bicameralism, political equality, and sortition: Reconstituting the second chamber as a randomly selected assembly. *Perspectives on Politics, 19*(3), 791–806. https://doi.org/10.1017/S1537592719004626

Acemoglu, D., Naidu, S., Restrepo, P., & Robinson, J.A. (2019). Democracy does cause growth. *Journal of Political Economy, 127*(1), 47–100. https://doi.org/10.1086/700936

Advisory Council on Economic Growth. (2016, 20 October). *Attracting the talent Canada needs through immigration*. https://www.budget.gc.ca/aceg-ccce/pdf/immigration-eng.pdf

Alesina, A., Favero, C., & Giavazzi, F. (2019). Effects of austerity: Expenditure- and tax-based approaches. *Journal of Economic Perspectives, 33*(2), 141–62. https://doi.org/10.1257/jep.33.2.141

Alesina, A., & Passalacqua, A. (2016). The political economy of government debt. In J.B. Taylor & H. Uhlig (Eds.), *Handbook of macroeconomics* (vol. 2, pp. 2599–651). Elsevier. https://doi.org/10.1016/bs.hesmac.2016.03.014

Anderson, B., & Coletto, D. (2020, 19 November). Wealth tax? Canadians like the idea. Abacus Data. https://abacusdata.ca/wealth-tax-canada-poll/

Appelbaum, B. (2019). *The economists' hour: How the false prophets of free markets fractured our society*. Picador.

Arias, E., & Stasavage, D. (2019). How large are the political costs of fiscal austerity? *Journal of Politics, 81*(4), 1517–22. https://doi.org/10.1086/704781

Ascah, R. (1999). *Politics and public debt: The Dominion, the banks and Alberta's social credit*. University of Alberta Press.

Atkinson, A.B. (2014). After Piketty? *British Journal of Sociology, 65*(4), 619–38. https://doi.org/10.1111/1468-4446.12105

Atkinson, M.M. (2011). Discrepancies in perceptions of corruption, or why is Canada so corrupt? *Political Science Quarterly, 126*(3), 445–64. https://doi .org/10.1002/j.1538-165X.2011.tb00708.x

Atkinson, M.M., & Coleman, W.D. (1985). Bureaucrats and politicians in Canada: An examination of the political administration model. *Comparative Political Studies, 18*(1), 58–80. https://doi.org/10.1177/0010414085018001003

Atkinson, M.M., & Mou, H. (2021, 17 March). The post-pandemic economy: What do Canadians want? *JSGS Policy Brief.* Johnson Shoyama Graduate School of Public Policy. https://www.schoolofpublicpolicy.sk.ca /research-ideas/publications-and-policy-insight/policy-brief/the-post -pandemic-economy.php

Atkinson, M.M., Mou, H., & Bruce, P. (2016). Fiscal rules in the Canadian provinces: Abject failure or qualified success? *Canadian Public Administration, 59*(4), 495–515. https://doi.org/10.1111/capa.12191

Autor, D.H. (2014). Skills, education, and the rise of earnings inequality among the "other 99 per cent." *Science, 344*(6186), 843–51. https://doi .org/10.1126/science.1251868

Baccaro, L., Blyth, M., & Pontusson, J. (2022). Introduction: Rethinking comparative capitalism. In L. Baccaro, M. Blyth, & J. Pontusson (Eds.), *Diminishing returns: The new politics of growth and stagnation* (pp. 1–50). Oxford University Press.

Baily, M.N. (2023, Spring). Lessons from a career in productivity research: Some answers, a glimpse of the future and much left to learn. *International Productivity Monitor, 44*, 120–49.

Baker, M., Gruber, J., & Milligan, K. (2008). Universal child care, maternal labor supply, and family well-being. *Journal of Political Economy, 116*(4), 709–45. https://doi.org/10.1086/591908

Banerjee, A.V., & Duflo, E. (2003). Inequality and growth: What can the data say? *Journal of Economic Growth, 8*(3), 267–99. https://doi.org/10.1023 /A:1026205114860

Banerjee, A.V., & Duflo, E. (2019). *Good economics for hard times.* PublicAffairs.

Bank of Canada. (n.d.). *Selected benchmark bond yields.* Retrieved 14 August 2023 from https://www.bankofcanada.ca/rates/interest-rates/canadian-bonds/

Bank of Canada. (2015, December). *Framework for conducting monetary policy at low interest rates.* https://www.bankofcanada.ca/wp-content /uploads/2015/12/framework-conducting-monetary-policy.pdf

Bank of Canada. (2020, 10 December). *How quantitative easing works.* https:// www.bankofcanada.ca/2020/12/how-quantitative-easing-works/

Bank of Canada. (2021, December). *Monetary policy framework renewal.* https:// www.bankofcanada.ca/wp-content/uploads/2021/12/Monetary-Policy -Framework-Renewal-December-2021.pdf

Bansak, K., Bechtel, M.M., & Margalit, Y. (2021). Why austerity? The mass politics of a contested policy. *American Political Science Review, 115*(2), 486–505. https://doi.org/10.1017/S0003055420001136

Banting, K. (1982). *The welfare state and Canadian federalism* (1st ed.). McGill-Queen's University Press.

Banting, K. (2005). Canada: Nation-building in a federal welfare state. In H. Obinger, S. Leibfried, & F.G. Castles (Eds.), *Federalism and the welfare state: New world and European experiences* (pp. 89–137). Cambridge University Press. https://doi.org/10.1017/CBO9780511491856.005

Banting, K. (2006). Disembedding liberalism? The new social policy paradigm in Canada. In D. Green & J. Kesselman (Eds.), *Dimensions of inequality in Canada* (pp. 417–52). UBC Press.

Banting, K., & Myles, J. (2013). Introduction: Inequality and the fading of redistributive politics. In K. Banting & J. Myles (Eds.), *Inequality and the fading of redistributive politics* (pp. 1–39). UBC Press.

Banting, K., & Thompson, D. (2021). The puzzling persistence of racial inequality in Canada. *Canadian Journal of Political Science, 54*(4), 870–91. https://doi.org/10.1017/S0008423921000585

Barber, B. (1984). *Strong democracy: Participatory politics for a new age.* University of California Press.

Barro, R.J. (1979). On the determination of public debt. *Journal of Political Economy, 87*(5), 940–71. https://doi.org/10.1086/260807

Barro, R.J. (1999). *Inequality, growth, and investment* (NBER Working Paper No. 7038). National Bureau of Economic Research. https://www.nber.org/system/files/working_papers/w7038/w7038.pdf

Barzelay, M. (1996). Performance auditing and the New Public Management: Changing roles and strategies of central audit institutions. In *Performance auditing and the modernisation of government* (pp. 15–56). Organisation for Economic Co-operation and Development.

Bateman, W. (2020). *Public finance and parliamentary constitutionalism.* Cambridge University Press. https://doi.org/10.1017/9781108784283

Baumgartner, F.R., & Jones, B.D. (2002). Positive and negative feedback in politics. In F.R. Baumgartner & B.D. Jones (Eds.), *Policy dynamics* (pp. 3–28). University of Chicago Press.

Baumol, W.J. (1967). Macroeconomics of unbalanced growth: The anatomy of urban crisis. *American Economic Review, 57*(3), 415–26. https://www.jstor.org/stable/1812111

Baumol, W.J. (1993). Social wants and dismal science: The curious case of the climbing costs of health and teaching. *Proceedings of the American Philosophical Society, 137*(4), 612–37. https://www.jstor.org/stable/987077

Béland, D., & Lecours, A. (2014). Accommodation and the politics of fiscal equalization in multinational states: The case of Canada. *Nations and Nationalism, 20*(2), 337–54. https://doi.org/10.1111/nana.12049

Béland, D., Lecours, A., Marchildon, G.P., Mou, H, & Olfert, R. (2017). *Fiscal federalism and equalization policy in Canada: Political and economic dimensions.* University of Toronto Press.

Béland, D., Lecours, A., Paquet, M., & Tombe, T. (2020). A critical juncture in fiscal federalism? Canada's response to COVID-19. *Canadian Journal of Political Science, 53*(2), 239–43. https://doi.org/10.1017/S0008423920000323

Béland, D., & Marier, P. (2022). The magic is in the mix: How the Guaranteed Income Supplement and Old Age Security interact in Canada's pension system to tackle successfully poverty in old age. In E. Lindquist, M. Howlett, G. Skogstad, G. Tellier, & P. t' Hart (Eds.), *Policy success in Canada: Cases, lessons, and challenges* (pp. 206–24). Oxford University Press.

Berdahl, L. (2012). (Sub) national economic union: Institutions, ideas, and internal trade policy in Canada. *Publius: The Journal of Federalism, 43*(2), 275–96. https://doi.org/10.1093/publius/pjs036

Bernanke, B.S. (2012). The Great Moderation. In R. Leeson, E.F. Koenig & G.A. Kahn (Eds.), *The Taylor rule and the transformation of monetary policy* (pp. 145–62). Hoover Institution.

Bilbiie, F., Monacelli, T., & Perotti, R. (2021). Fiscal policy in Europe: Controversies over rules, mutual insurance, and centralization. *Journal of Economic Perspectives, 35*(2), 77–100. https://doi.org/10.1257/JEP.35.2.77

Bird, R.M., & Tassonyi, A. (2003). Constraining subnational fiscal behavior in Canada: Different approaches, similar results? In J.A. Rodden, G.S. Eskeland, & J. Litvack (Eds.), *Fiscal decentralization and the challenge of hard budget constraints* (pp. 85–132). MIT Press.

Blanchard, O. (2019). Public debt and low interest rates. *American Economic Review, 109*(4), 1197–229. https://doi.org/10.1257/aer.109.4.1197

Blanchard, O.J., & Das, M. (2017). *A new index of debt sustainability* (NBER Working Paper No. 24068). National Bureau of Economic Research. https://doi.org/10.3386/w24068

Blanchard, O.J., & Summers, L. (2017, 8 October). *Rethinking stabilization policy. Back to the future.* Peterson Institute for International Economics. https://www.piie.com/sites/default/files/documents/blanchard-summers20171012paper.pdf

Blinder, A.S. (2000). Central-bank credibility: Why do we care? How do we build it? *American Economic Review, 90*(5), 1421–31. https://doi.org/10.1257/aer.90.5.1421

Blinder, A.S. (2018). *Advice and dissent: Why America suffers when economics and politics collide.* Basic Books.

Blinder, A.S. (2022). *A monetary and fiscal history of the United States, 1961–2021*. Princeton University Press. https://doi.org/10.2307/j.ctv2h439tc

Bloch, D., & Fall, F. (2015, July). *Government debt indicators: Understanding the data* (OECD Economics Department Working Paper No. 1228). Organisation for Economic Co-operation and Development. https://doi.org/10.1787/5jrxv0ftbff2-en

Blöndal, J.R. (2001). Budgeting in Canada. *OECD Journal on Budgeting, 1*(2), 39–82. https://www.oecd.org/canada/40140423.pdf

Blöndal, J.R. (2003). Accrual accounting and budgeting: Key issues and recent developments. *OECD Journal on Budgeting, 3*(1), 43–59. https://www.oecd.org/gov/budgeting/42187847.pdf

Blyth, M. (2013). *Austerity: The history of a dangerous idea*. Oxford University Press.

Boadway, R. (2004). What do we get for public indebtedness? In C. Ragan & W. Watson (Eds.), *Is the debt war over?* (pp. 133–60). Institute for Research on Public Policy.

Boadway, R. (2005). National taxation, fiscal federalism and global taxation. In A.B. Atkinson (Ed.), *New sources of development finance* (pp. 210–37). Oxford Scholarship Online. https://doi.org/10.1093/0199278555.001.0001

Boadway, R. (2011). Rethinking tax-transfer policy for the 21st century Canada. In F. Gorbet & A. Sharpe (Eds.), *New directions for intelligent government in Canada: Papers in honour of Ian Stewart* (pp. 163–203). Centre for the Study of Living Standards.

Boadway, R., & Cuff, K. (2013). The recent evolution of tax-transfer policies. In K. Banting & J. Myles (Eds.), *Inequality and the fading of redistributive politics* (pp. 335–58). UBC Press.

Boadway, R., & Pestieau, P. (2019). *Over the top: Why an annual wealth tax for Canada is unnecessary* (Commentary No. 546). C.D. Howe Institute. https://www.cdhowe.org/sites/default/files/attachments/research_papers/mixed/Commentary%20546.pdf

Booth, W.J. (1994). On the idea of the moral economy. *American Political Science Review, 88*(3), 653–67. https://doi.org/10.2307/2944801

Borowiak, C.T. (2011). *Accountability and democracy: The pitfalls and promise of popular control*. Oxford University Press.

Bourgon, J. (2009, 10 September). *Program review: The Government of Canada's experience eliminating the deficit, 1994–1999 – A Canadian case study*. Centre for International Governance Innovation. https://www.cigionline.org/publications/program-review-government-canadas-experience-eliminating-deficit-1994-1999-canadian/

Bovens, M. (2007). Analysing and assessing accountability: A conceptual framework. *European Law Journal, 13*(4), 447–68. https://doi.org/10.1111/j.1468-0386.2007.00378.x

Boychuk, G.W. (2013). Territorial politics and the new politics of redistribution. In K. Banting & J. Myles (Eds.), *Inequality and the fading of redistributive politics* (pp. 234–55). UBC Press.

Boyer, R. (2012). The four fallacies of contemporary austerity policies: The lost Keynesian legacy. *Cambridge Journal of Economics, 36*(1), 283–312. https://doi.org/10.1093/cje/ber037

Brethour, P. (2021, 21 March). Thousands of CRA accounts affected by CERB-related hacking. *Globe and Mail.* https://www.theglobeandmail.com/business/article-identity-fraud-complaints-nearly-doubled-in-2020-over-2019/

Breton, C., & Parkin, A. (2022, 10 May). *Federal transfers to provinces: Public preferences.* Centre of Excellence on the Canadian Federation. https://centre.irpp.org/research-studies/federal-transfers-to-provinces-public-preferences/

Brewer, S. (1998). Scientific expert testimony and intellectual due process. *Yale Law Journal, 107*(6), 1535–681. https://doi.org/10.2307/797336

Bricker, D., & Ibbitson, J. (2019). *Empty planet: The shock of global population decline.* Signal.

Brossard, R. (2021, 25 March). Taxpayers Federation slams Legault government for delaying balanced budgets. [News release]. *Canadian Taxpayers Federation.* https://www.taxpayer.com/newsroom/taxpayers-federation-slams-legault-government-for-delaying-balanced-budgets

Brown, D.M. (2020). Fiscal federalism: The importance of balance. In H. Bakvis & G. Skogstad (Eds.), *Canadian federalism: Performance, effectiveness, and legitimacy* (4th ed., pp. 251–81). University of Toronto Press. https://doi.org/10.3138/9781487570460-012

Brynjolfsson, E., & McAfee, A. (2014). *The second machine age: Work, progress, and prosperity in a time of brilliant technologies.* W.W. Norton.

Buchanan, J.M. (1997). The balanced budget amendment: Clarifying the arguments. *Public Choice, 90*(1–4), 117–38. https://doi.org/10.1023/A:1004969320944

Buhr, N. (2012). Accrual accounting by Anglo-American governments: Motivations, developments, and some tensions over the last 30 years. *Accounting History, 17*(3–4), 287–309. https://doi.org/10.1177/1032373212443956

Busby, C., Chejfec, R., & Tamburri, R. (2022, 10 May). How to fix Canada's broken Employment Insurance program. *Policy Options.* Institute for Research on Public Policy. https://policyoptions.irpp.org/magazines/may-2022/employment-insurance-solutions/

Cairns, A. (1979). The other crisis of Canadian federalism. *Canadian Public Administration, 22*(2), 175–95. https://doi.org/10.1111/j.1754-7121.1979.tb01811.x

Campagnolo, Y. (2021). *Behind closed doors: The law and politics of cabinet secrecy.* UBC Press.

Canada. (2014). *Action for seniors.* https://www.canada.ca/content/dam/canada/employment-social-development/migration/documents/Eng/report/pdf/action_report_for_seniors.pdf

Canada. (1867). *The Constitution Act, 1867*, 30 & 31 Vict, c 3.

Canada. (1977). *Federal-Provincial Fiscal Arrangements and Established Programs Financing Act, 1977*, SOR/78-587.

Canada. (1982). *The Constitution Act, 1982*, Schedule B to the *Canada Act 1982* (UK), 1982, c 11.

Canada. (1985a). *Auditor General Act*, RSC, 1985, c A-17.

Canada. (1985b). *Financial Administration Act*, RSC, 1985, c F-11.

Canada. (1985c). *Parliament of Canada Act*, RSC, 1985, c. P-1.

Canada. (2006a). *Conflict of Interest Act*, SC 2006, c 9, s 2 (assented 12 December 2006).

Canada. (2006b). *Federal Accountability Act*, SC 2006, c 9 (assented 12 December 2006).

Canada. (2015, 4 December). *Making real change happen: Speech from the Throne to open the first session of the forty-second Parliament of Canada.* Governor General. https://www.canada.ca/content/dam/pco-bcp/documents/pm/speech_from_the_throne.pdf

Canada. (2020a). *An Act to amend the Financial Administration Act (special warrant)*, SC 2020, c 4 (assented 13 March 2020).

Canada. (2020b). *Public Health Events of National Concern Payments Act*, SC 2020, c 5, s 9 (assented 25 March 2020).

Canada. (2022, 25 May). *Shared health priorities and safe long-term care fund.* Health Canada. https://www.canada.ca/en/health-canada/corporate/transparency/health-agreements/shared-health-priorities.html

Carmichael, K., Dahir, N.L., & Page, K. (2020, 10 September). *A basic primer on federal government debt: Definitions, numbers, and issues.* Finances of the Nation. https://financesofthenation.ca/2020/09/10/a-basic-primer/

Carney, M. (2021). *Value(s): Building a better world for all.* Signal/McClelland & Stewart.

Cave, D., Bubola, E., & Sang-Hun, C. (2021, 22 May). Long slide looms for world population, with sweeping ramifications. *New York Times.* https://www.nytimes.com/2021/05/22/world/global-population-shrinking.html

CBC News. (2004, 11 February). *Auditor general gives details of 'scandalous' sponsorship program.* https://www.cbc.ca/news/canada/auditor-general-gives-details-of-scandalous-sponsorship-program-1.506377

C.D. Howe Institute. (2021, 17 February). *Stimulus spending if necessary, but not necessarily stimulus spending* (Communiqué No. 4). Fiscal and Tax Working

Group. https://www.cdhowe.org/sites/default/files/attachments
/communiques/mixed/CWGR_2021_0217_0.pdf

Chaplin, S. (2020). Protecting parliamentary democracy in 'plague' times: Accountability and democratic institutions during the pandemic. *Commonwealth Law Bulletin, 46*(1), 110–23. https://doi.org/10.1080 /03050718.2020.1762235

Chetty, R., Grusky, D., Hell, M., Hendren, N., Manduca, R., & Narang, J. (2016, December). *The fading American dream: Trends in absolute income mobility since 1940* (NBER Working Paper No. 22910). National Bureau of Economic Research. https://www.nber.org/system/files/working_papers/w22910 /w22910.pdf

Cingano, F. (2014, December). *Trends in income inequality and its impact on economic growth* (OECD Social, Employment and Migration Working Paper No. 163). Organisation for Economic Co-operation and Development. https://doi.org/10.1787/5jxrjncwxv6j-en

Clark, I.D., & Swain, H. (2005). Distinguishing the real from the surreal in management reform: Suggestions for beleaguered administrators in the government of Canada. *Canadian Public Administration, 48*(4), 453–76. https://doi.org/10.1111/j.1754-7121.2005.tb01198.x

Clemens, J., Palacios, M., & Li, N. (2020, 27 August). *Poor CERB targeting wastes billions*. Fraser Institute. https://www.fraserinstitute.org/article /poor-cerb-targeting-wastes-billions

Coleman, W.D. (1991). Monetary policy, accountability, and legitimacy: A review of the issues in Canada. *Canadian Journal of Political Science, 24*(4), 711–34. https://doi.org/10.1017/S0008423900005631

Conference Board of Canada. (2021). *Challenges ahead: Canada's post-pandemic fiscal prospects*. https://www.conferenceboard.ca/product/challenges -ahead-canadas-post-pandemic-fiscal-prospects/

Congressional Budget Office. (2021). *CBO's appropriation request for fiscal year 2022*. Congressional Budget Office. https://www.cbo.gov/system /files/2021-04/57087-Budget-Senate.pdf

Corak, M. (2013). Income inequality, equality of opportunity, and intergenerational mobility. *Journal of Economic Perspectives, 27*(3), 79–103. https://doi.org/10.1257/jep.27.3.79

Cottarelli, C. (2017). *What we owe: Truths, myths and lies about public debt.* Brookings Institution Press.

Cowen, T. (2018). *Stubborn attachments: A vision for a society of free, prosperous, and responsible individuals.* Stripe Press.

Coyle, D. (2014). *GDP: A brief but affectionate history* (Rev. and expanded ed.). Princeton University Press.

Coyne, A. (2012, 30 April). Bill C-38 shows us how far Parliament has fallen. *National Post.* https://nationalpost.com/opinion/andrew-coyne-bill -c-38-shows-us-how-far-parliament-has-fallen

Coyne, A. (2023, 26 January). How Ottawa can help fix health care: first, send less money. *Globe and Mail*. https://www.theglobeandmail.com/opinion/article-how-ottawa-can-help-fix-health-care-first-send-less-money/

CPA Canada. (2021). *Implementation tool for auditors – Canadian Auditing Standards (CAS)*. Chartered Professional Accountants.

Cross, P. (2020, 30 July). Ottawa's anti-business bias evident in emergency aid programs. *Financial Post*. https://financialpost.com/opinion/philip-cross-ottawas-anti-business-bias-evident-in-emergency-aid-programs

Cross, P. (2021, March). *Will Canada's rapidly expanding money supply result in higher inflation?* [Commentary]. Macdonald-Laurier Institute. https://www.macdonaldlaurier.ca/files/pdf/20210309_Quantitative_easing_2020_Cross_COMMENTARY_FWeb.pdf

Crouch, C. (2004). *Post-democracy*. Polity Press.

Curry, B. (2021a, 10 May). Size of federal budget deficit concerns 74% of Canadians, according to Nanos poll. *Globe and Mail*. https://www.theglobeandmail.com/politics/article-size-of-federal-budget-deficit-concerns-74-per-cent-of-canadians/

Curry, B. (2021b, 2 December). Ottawa yet to account for $600-billion in public spending. *Globe and Mail*. https://www.theglobeandmail.com/politics/article-how-did-ottawa-spend-more-than-600-billion-last-year/

Curry, B., & Fife, R. (2020, 25 March). House approves emergency bill to respond to coronavirus economic fallout. *Globe and Mail*. https://www.theglobeandmail.com/politics/article-house-approves-emergency-bill-to-respond-to-coronavirus-economic/

Daly, H.E. (1996). *Beyond growth: The economics of sustainable development* (3rd ed). Beacon Press.

Davies, J.B., & Di Matteo, L. (2021). Long run Canadian wealth inequality in international context. *Review of Income and Wealth, 67*(1), 134–64. https://doi.org/10.1111/roiw.12453

Debrun, X., Moulin, L., Turrini, A., Ayuso-i-Casals, J., Manmohan S., K., Drazen, A., & Fuest, C. (2008). Tied to the mast? National fiscal rules in the European Union. *Economic Policy, 23*(54), 298–362. https://doi.org/10.1111/j.1468-0327.2008.00199.x

DeLong, J.B. (2022). *Slouching towards utopia: An economic history of the twentieth century*. Basic Books.

Department of Finance Canada. (2020, 25 March). *Government introduces Canada Emergency Response Benefit to help workers and businesses* [News release]. Government of Canada. https://www.canada.ca/en/department-finance/news/2020/03/introduces-canada-emergency-response-benefit-to-help-workers-and-businesses.html

Department of Finance Canada. (2021a). *Budget 2021*. Government of Canada. Last modified 19 April 2021 from https://www.budget.gc.ca/2021/home-accueil-en.html

Department of Finance Canada. (2021b). *Budget 2021: Address by the Deputy Prime Minister and Minister of Finance.* Government of Canada. Last modified 23 April 2021 from https://www.canada.ca/en/department-finance/news /2021/04/budget-2021-address-by-the-deputy-prime-minister-and -minister-of-finance.html

Department of Finance Canada. (2021c). *A Canada-wide early learning and child care plan.* Government of Canada. Last modified 16 December 2021 from https://www.canada.ca/en/department-finance/news/2021/12/a -canada-wide-early-learning-and-child-care-plan.html

Department of Finance Canada. (2021d). *Economic and fiscal update 2021.* Government of Canada. https://budget.gc.ca/efu-meb/2021/report -rapport/EFU-MEB-2021-EN.pdf

Department of Finance Canada. (2021e). *Fiscal reference tables 2021.* Government of Canada. https://www.canada.ca/en/department-finance /services/publications/fiscal-reference-tables/2021.html

Department of Finance Canada. (2022a). *Annual financial report of the Government of Canada fiscal year 2020-2021.* Government of Canada. Last modified 1 March 2022 from https://www.canada.ca/en/department -finance/services/publications/annual-financial-report/2021/report. html#_Toc55397353

Department of Finance Canada. (2022b). *Fall economic statement 2022: Building an economy that works for everyone.* Government of Canada. https://www .budget.canada.ca/fes-eea/2022/home-accueil-en.html

Department of Finance Canada. (2022c). *Fiscal reference tables 2022.* Government of Canada. https://www.canada.ca/content/dam/fin /publications/frt-trf/2022/frt-trf-22-eng.pdf

Department of Finance Canada. (2022d). *Major federal transfers.* Government of Canada. Last modified 16 December 2022 from https://www.canada .ca/en/department-finance/programs/federal-transfers/major-federal -transfers.html#Newfoundland

Department of Finance Canada. (2023). *Budget 2023: A made-in-Canada plan.* Government of Canada. https://www.budget.canada.ca/2023/pdf /budget-2023-en.pdf

DeRosa, K. (2022, 9 November). Failed talks over health care cash raise prospect of individual deals between Ottawa and provinces. *Vancouver Sun.* https://vancouversun.com/news/failed-talks-over-health-care-cash-raise -prospect-of-individual-deals-between-ottawa-and-provinces

Deslauriers, J., Gagné, R., Gouba, F., & Paré, J. (2020, August). *Taxing the rich: An inconvenient truth.* Centre for Productivity and Prosperity Walter J. Somers Foundation HEC Montreal. https://cpp.hec.ca/en/wp-content /uploads/sites/2/2020/08/PP-2019-08_ANG.pdf

Diamond, M. (1973). The ends of federalism. *Publius, 3*(2), 129–52. https:// doi.org/10.1093/oxfordjournals.pubjof.a038276

Dionne-Simard, D., & Miller, J. (2019, 11 September). *Maximum insights on minimum wage workers: 20 years of data. Labour Statistics: Research Papers.* Statistics Canada. https://www150.statcan.gc.ca/n1/pub/75-004-m/75-004-m2019003-eng.htm

Dobell, R., & Zussman, D. (2018). Sunshine, scrutiny, and spending review in Canada, Trudeau to Trudeau: From program evaluation and policy to commitment and results. *Canadian Journal of Program Evaluation, 32*(3), 371–93. https://doi.org/10.3138/cjpe.43184

Dodge, D. (2020, 14 September). *Two mountains to climb: Canada's twin deficits and how to scale them.* Public Policy Forum. https://ppforum.ca/publications/two-mountains-to-climb-canadas-twin-deficits-and-how-to-scale-them/

Dodge, D., & Dion, R. (2016, 19 October). Economic performance and policy during the Harper years. *Policy Options.* Institute for Research on Public Policy. https://policyoptions.irpp.org/magazines/october-2016/economic-performance-and-policy-during-the-harper-years/

Dodge, D., & Dion, R. (2023, 23 January). *Assessing the potential risks to the sustainability of the Government of Canada's current fiscal plan: Explainer of key findings.* Business Council of Canada. https://thebusinesscouncil.ca/report/assessing-the-potential-risks-to-the-sustainability-of-the-government-of-canadas-current-fiscal-plan/

Doern, G.B., Maslove, A.M., & Prince, M.J. (2013). *Canadian public budgeting in the age of crises: Shifting budgetary domains and temporal budgeting.* McGill-Queen's University Press.

Drummond, D. (2020, 20 October). *Canada's foggy economic and fiscal future* [E-brief]. C.D. Howe Institute. https://www.cdhowe.org/sites/default/files/attachments/research_papers/mixed/E-brief_308_0.pdf

Dubnick, M.J., & O'Brien, J.P. (2011). Rethinking the obsession: Accountability and the financial crisis. In M.J. Dubnick & H.G. Frederickson (Eds.), *Accountable governance: Promises and problems* (pp. 282–301). M.E. Sharpe.

Dworkin, R. (2002). *Sovereign virtue: The theory and practice of equality.* Harvard University Press.

Efford, D. (1996, July). *The case for accrual recording in the IMF'S Government Finance Statistics System* (IMF Working Paper No. 96/73). International Monetary Fund. https://www.elibrary.imf.org/view/journals/001/1996/073/001.1996.issue-073-en.xml

Eich, S. (2022). *The currency of politics: The political theory of money from Aristotle to Keynes.* Princeton University Press.

Eichengreen, B., El-Ganainy, A., Esteves, R., & Mitchener, K.J. (2021). *In defense of public debt.* Oxford University Press.

Eichengreen, B., & von Hagen, J. (1995, September). *Fiscal policy and monetary union: Federalism, fiscal restrictions and the no-bailout rule* (Working Paper No. C95-056). Center for International and Development Economics Research

(CIDER). University of California-Berkeley. https://doi.org/10.22004/ag.econ.233417

Elkjær, M.A., & Iversen, T. (2022). The democratic state and redistribution: Whose interests are served? *American Political Science Review*, 1–16. https://doi.org/10.1017/S0003055422000867

Engler, S., & Weisstanner, D. (2021). The threat of social decline: Income inequality and radical right support. *Journal of European Public Policy*, *28*(2), 153–73. https://doi.org/10.1080/13501763.2020.1733636

Epley, N., & Gilovich, T. (2016). The mechanics of motivated reasoning. *Journal of Economic Perspectives*, *30*(3), 133–40. https://doi.org/10.1257/jep.30.3.133

Esping-Andersen, G. (1990). The three political economies of the welfare state. *International Journal of Sociology*, *20*(3), 92–123. https://doi.org/10.1080/15579336.1990.11770001

European Central Bank. (2014, 14 June). Economic and monetary developments. *Monthly Bulletin*. https://www.ecb.europa.eu/pub/pdf/other/mb201406_focus08.en.pdf

FAO. (2021). *2020-21 annual report*. Financial Accountability Office of Ontario. https://www.fao-on.org/web/default/files/publications/Annual%20Report%202020-21/2020-21%20Annual%20Report-EN.pdf

Fernandez, R., & Rodrik, D. (1991). Resistance to reform: Status quo bias in the presence of individual- specific uncertainty. *American Economic Review*, *81*(5), 1146–55. https://doi.org/10.2307/2006910

Fiedler, F. (2004). The independence of supreme audit institutions. In *INTOSAI: 50 Years (1953-2003)*. https://www.intosai.org/fileadmin/downloads/documents/open_access/INTOSAI_Publications/Publication_50y_INTOSAI/INTOSAI_50th_Anniv_EN.pdf

Fife, R., & Chase, S. (2021, 13 December). Michael Sabia was greeted as a game changer as Canada's deputy finance minister. A year later, he has made little headway. *Globe and Mail*. https://www.theglobeandmail.com/politics/article-michael-sabia-was-greeted-as-a-game-changer-as-canadas-deputy-finance/

Fischer, S., & Easterly, W. (1990). The economics of the government budget constraint. *World Bank Research Observer*, *5*(2), 127–42. https://doi.org/10.1093/wbro/5.2.127

Fortin, N., Green, D.A., Lemieux, T., Milligan, K., & Riddell, W.C. (2012). Canadian inequality: Recent developments and policy options. *Canadian Public Policy/Analyse de politiques*, *38*(2), 121–45. https://doi.org/10.3138/cpp.38.2.121

Frank, R.H. (2016). *Success and luck: Good fortune and the myth of meritocracy*. Princeton University Press. https://doi.org/10.2307/j.ctvc77k7k

Fullwiler, S.T. (2016). The debt ratio and sustainable macroeconomic policy. *World Economic Review*, *7*, 12–42. http://wer.worldeconomicsassociation.org/files/WEA-WER-7-Fullwiler.pdf

Furman, J., & Orszag, P. (2019). Are slower productivity and higher inequality related? In A.S. Posen, & J. Zettelmeyer (Eds.), *Facing up to low productivity growth* (pp. 245–62). Peterson Institute of International Economics Press.

G7 Health Ministers. (2021, 4 June). *G7 health ministers' declaration.* https://assets.publishing.service.gov.uk/government/uploads/system/uploads/attachment_data/file/992268/G7-health_ministers-communique-oxford-4-june-2021_5.pdf

G7 Panel on Economic Resilience. (2021). *Global economic resilience: Building forward better.* https://rooseveltinstitute.org/wp-content/uploads/2022/09/GlobalEconomic-ResilienceBuilding-ForwardBetter_202110.pdf

Galbraith, J.K. (2012). *Inequality and instability: A study of the world economy just before the great crisis.* Oxford University Press. https://doi.org/10.1093/acprof:osobl/9780199855650.003.0005

Gallant, C. (2021, 10 July). Minister, job agency blames CERB for vacancies. *Medicine Hat News.* https://medicinehatnews.com/news/local-news/2021/07/10/minister-job-agency-blame-cerb-for-vacancies/

Gay, O., & Winetrobe, B.K. (2008). Introduction: Watchdogs in need of support. In O. Gay & B.K. Winetrobe (Eds.), *Parliament's watchdogs: At the crossroads.* UK Study of Parliament Group, Constitutional Unit, University College London. https://discovery.ucl.ac.uk/id/eprint/19571/1/19571.pdf.

Gbohoui, W., & Medas, P. (2020, 29 April). *Fiscal rules, escape clauses, and large shocks.* International Monetary Fund.

GC InfoBase. (2022). *Voted and statutory split (2022-23).* https://www.tbs-sct.canada.ca/ems-sgd/edb-bdd/index-eng.html#infographic/gov/gov/financial/.-.-(panel_key.-.-'in_year_voted_stat_split)

Geist, M. (1997). Balanced budget legislation: An assessment of the recent Canadian experience. *Ottawa Law Review, 29*(1), 1–38. https://ssrn.com/abstract=2723525

Gerstle, G. (2022). *The rise and fall of the neoliberal order: America and the world in the free market era.* Oxford University Press.

Gilens M., & Page, B. (2014). Testing theories of American politics: Elites, interest groups and average citizens. *Perspectives on Politics, 12*(3), 564–81. https://doi.org/10.1017/S1537592714001595

Goldin, C., & Katz, L.F. (2007, December). *Long-run changes in the U.S. wage structure: Narrowing, widening, polarizing* (NBER Working Paper No. 13568). National Bureau of Economic Research. https://doi.org/10.3386/w13568

Good, D.A. (2013). The new bureaucratic politics of redistribution. In K. Banting & J. Myles (Eds.), *Inequality and the fading of redistributive politics* (pp. 210–33). UBC Press.

Good, D.A. (2014). *The politics of public money* (2nd ed.). University of Toronto Press.

Goodhart, C., & Pradhan, M. (2020). *The great demographic reversal: Ageing societies, waning inequality, and an inflation revival*. Palgrave Macmillan.

Goodman, P. (2022). *Davos man: How the billionaires devoured the world*. Custom House.

Gordon, R.J. (2015). Secular stagnation: A supply-side view. *American Economic Review, 105*(5), 54–9. https://doi.org/10.1257/aer.p20151102

Gordon, R.J. (2016). *The rise and fall of American growth: The U.S. standard of living since the civil war*. Princeton University Press.

Gosselin, J.S., Godbout, L., Gagné-Dubé, T., & St-Cerny, S. (2020, 1 June). *Chronology of the economic response of the governments of Canada and the provinces to the COVID-19 crisis*. Finances of the Nation. https://financesofthenation.ca/2020/06/01/fotn-papers-godbout-chronology-of-the-economic-responce/

Graeber, D. (2018). *Bullshit jobs: A theory*. Simon & Schuster.

Gray, G. (1991). *Federalism and health policy: The development of health systems in Canada and Australia*. University of Toronto Press.

Green, D.A., Kesselman, J.R., & Tedds, L.M. (2020, 28 December). *Covering all the basics: Reforms for a more just society – Final report of the British Columbia expert panel on basic income*. https://bcbasicincomepanel.ca/wp-content/uploads/2021/01/Final_Report_BC_Basic_Income_Panel.pdf

Greenwald, D.L., Lettau, M., & Ludvigson, S.C. (2019, April). *How the wealth was won: Factors shares as market fundamentals* (NBER Working Paper No. 25769). National Bureau of Economic Research. https://doi.org/10.3386/w25769

Hacker, J.S. (2019). *The great risk shift: The new economic insecurity and the decline of the American dream* (2nd ed.). Oxford University Press.

Hacker, J.S., & Pierson, P. (2014). After the "master theory": Downs, Schattschneider, and the rebirth of policy-focused analysis. *Perspectives on Politics, 12*(3), 643–62. https://doi.org/10.1017/S1537592714001637

Hacker, J.S., & Pierson, P. (2016). *American amnesia: How the war on government led us to forget what made America prosper*. Simon & Schuster.

Haffert, L. (2019). Permanent budget surpluses as a fiscal regime. *Socio-Economic Review, 17*(4), 1043–63. https://doi.org/10.1093/ser/mwx050

Hall, C. (2017, 17 May). *Auditor general's complaint leads to cabinet order for release of Finance documents*. CBC News. https://www.cbc.ca/news/politics/auditor-general-canada-finance-department-1.4120542

Hallerberg, M., Strauch, R., & von Hagen, J. (2007). The design of fiscal rules and forms of governance in European Union countries. *European Journal of Political Economy, 23*(2), 338–59. https://doi.org/10.1016/j.ejpoleco.2006.11.005

Han, K.J. (2016). Income inequality and voting for radical right-wing parties. *Electoral Studies, 42*, 54–64. https://doi.org/10.1016/j.electstud.2016.02.001

Hanniman, K. (2018). Is Canadian federalism market-preserving? The view from the bond markets. In E. Goodyear-Grant, J. Myles, W. Kymlicka, & R. Johnston (Eds.), *Federalism and the welfare state in a multicultural world* (pp. 49–72). McGill-Queen's University Press.

Hanniman, K. (2020a). Are transfer-dependent governments more creditworthy? Reassessing the fiscal federal foundations of subnational default risk. *British Journal of Political Science, 50*(4), 1381–403. https://doi .org/10.1017/S000712341800042X

Hanniman, K. (2020b). COVID-19, fiscal federalism and provincial debt: Have we reached a critical juncture? *Canadian Journal of Political Science, 53*(2), 279–85. https://doi.org/10.1017/S0008423920000621

Harell, A., Soroka, S., & Ladner, K. (2014). Public opinion, prejudice and the racialization of welfare in Canada. *Ethnic and Racial Studies, 37*(14), 2580–97. https://doi.org/10.1080/01419870.2013.851396

Harmes, A. (2007). The political economy of open federalism. *Canadian Journal of Political Science, 40*(2), 417–37. https://doi.org/10.1017/S0008423907070114

Harris, K. (2020, 18 March). *Trudeau unveils $82B COVID-19 emergency response package for Canadians, businesses.* CBC News. https://www.cbc.ca/news /politics/economic-aid-package-coronavirus-1.5501037

Harrison, K. (2006). Provincial interdependence: Concepts and theories. In K. Harrison (Ed.), *Racing to the bottom? Provincial interdependence in the Canadian federation* (pp. 1–23). UBC Press.

Hauser, A. (2021, 7 January). *From lender of last resort to market maker of last resort via the dash for cash: Why central banks need new tools for dealing with market dysfunction* [Speech]. Bank of England. https://www.bankofengland.co.uk/-/ media/boe/files/speech/2021/january/why-central-banks-need-new-tools -for-dealing-with-market-dysfunction-speech-by-andrew-hauser.pdf

Hayek, F. (1945). The use of knowledge in society. *American Economic Review, 35*(4), 519–30. https://www.jstor.org/stable/1809376

Hayne, C., & Salterio, S.E. (2014). Accounting and auditing. In M. Bovens, R.E. Goodin, & T. Schillemans (Eds.), *The Oxford handbook of public accountability* (pp. 421–40). Oxford University Press.

Heaman, E. (2017). *Tax, order, and good government: A new political history of Canada, 1867–1917.* McGill-Queen's University Press.

Heath, J. (2020). *The machinery of government: Public administration and the liberal state.* Oxford Scholarship Online. https://doi.org/10.1093/oso /9780197509616.001.0001

Helliwell, J.F., & Huang, H. (2014). New measures of the costs of unemployment: Evidence from the subjective well-being of 3.3 million Americans. *Economic Inquiry, 52*(4), 1485–502. https://doi.org/10.1111/ecin.12093

Hemerijck, A. (2018). Social investment as a policy paradigm. *Journal of European Public Policy, 25*(6), 810–27. https://doi.org/10.1080/13501763.2017.1401111

Hildebrand, P. (2022, 27 January). The old inflation playbook no longer applies. *Financial Times*. https://www.ft.com/content/1e59e952-c5cf-4c8e-983a-560170c87cda

Himelfarb, A. (2019). Trust, taxes, and democracy in Canada. In D. McGrane, J. Whyte, R.J. Romanow, & R. Isinger (Eds.), *Back to Blakeney: Revitalizing the democratic state* (pp. 121–34). University of Regina Press.

Hinkel, J. (2021). *Less is more: How degrowth will save the world*. Penguin.

Hirschman, A. (1982). *Shifting involvements: Private interests and public actions*. Princeton University Press.

Hogg, P. (2001). *Constitutional Law of Canada* (Student edition). Carswell.

Homer-Dixon, T. (2020). *Commanding hope: The power we have to renew a world in peril*. Knopf Canada.

Homer-Dixon, T., Renn, O., Rockström, J., Donges, J.F., & Janzwood, S. (2022, 8 March). A call for an international research program on the risk of a global polycrisis (Technical Paper No. 2022-3). Cascade Institute. https://cascadeinstitute.org/technical-paper/a-call-for-an-international-research-program-on-the-risk-of-a-global-polycrisis/

Hood, C. (2011). *The blame game: Spin, bureaucracy, and self-preservation in government*. Princeton University Press.

Hotchkiss, M. (2014, 23 April). *Not just the poor live hand-to-mouth*. Office of Communications, Princeton University. https://www.princeton.edu/news/2014/04/23/not-just-poor-live-hand-mouth

Huddleston, T., Jr. (2020, 9 April). *Ray Dalio predicts a coronavirus depression: "This is bigger than what happened in 2008."* CNBC Make It. https://www.cnbc.com/2020/04/09/ray-dalio-predicts-coronavirus-depression-this-is-bigger-than-2008.html

IMF (International Monetary Fund). (2021a). *Policy responses to COVID-19: Policy tracker*. International Monetary Fund. https://www.imf.org/en/Topics/imf-and-covid19/Policy-Responses-to-COVID-19#C

IMF. (2021b, 18 March). *Canada: 2021 Article IV consultation – Press release and staff report* (IMF Country Report No. 21/54). International Monetary Fund. https://www.imf.org/en/Publications/CR/Issues/2021/03/17/Canada-2021-Article-IV-Consultation-Press-Release-and-Staff-Report-50273

IMF. (2021c, June). *Fiscal monitor database of country fiscal measures in response to the COVID-19 pandemic*. International Monetary Fund. https://www.imf.org/en/Topics/imf-and-covid19/Fiscal-Policies-Database-in-Response-to-COVID-19

IMF. (2021d, October). *Fiscal Monitor*. International Monetary Fund. https://www.imf.org/external/datamapper/GGXWDN_G01_GDP_PT@FM/CAN/JPN/USA/ADVEC

IMF. (2021e, October). *World Economic Outlook Database*. International Monetary Fund. https://www.imf.org/en/Publications/WEO/weo-database/2021/October/download-entire-database

Industry Strategy Council. (2020). *Restart, recover and reimagine prosperity for all Canadians: An ambitious growth plan for building a digital, sustainable and innovative economy*. Industry, Science and Economic Development Canada. https://www.ic.gc.ca/eic/site/062.nsf/vwapj/00118a_en.pdf/$file/00118a_en.pdf

Institute on Governance, & Brian Mulroney Institute of Government. (2022). *Top of mind: Answering the call, adapting to change – 2022 Summary report.* https://iog.ca/wp-content/uploads/2022/05/Top-of-Mind-Summary-Report-EN.pdf

International Energy Agency. (2021). *World energy outlook 2021.* https://iea.blob.core.windows.net/assets/4ed140c1-c3f3-4fd9-acae-789a4e14a23c/WorldEnergyOutlook2021.pdf

INTOSAI. (2021, August). *Performance audit ISSAI implementation handbook – Version 1.* International Organization of Supreme Audit Institutions. https://www.idi.no/elibrary/professional-sais/issai-implementation-handbooks/handbooks-english/performance-audit-v1-2021/1330-idi-performance-audit-issai-implementation-handbook-v1-en/file

ISED Canada. (2021). *About Canada's global innovation clusters.* Innovation, Science and Economic Development Canada. Last modified 22 June 2021 from https://ised-isde.canada.ca/site/global-innovation-clusters/en/about-canadas-innovation-clusters-initiative

Ivison, J. (2021, 1 March). Trudeau's COVID response shows money can buy the affection of voters. *National Post.* https://nationalpost.com/opinion/john-ivison-trudeaus-covid-response-shows-money-can-buy-the-affection-of-voters

Jacobs, A.M., Matthews, J.S., Hicks, T., & Merkley, E. (2021). Whose news? Class-biased economic reporting in the United States. *American Political Science Review, 115*(3), 1016–33. https://doi.org/10.1017/S0003055421000137

Jacques, O., Béland, D., & Lecours, A. (2021, 13 October). Alberta, Quebec, and the politics of equalization. *Policy Options.* Institute for Research on Public Policy. https://policyoptions.irpp.org/magazines/october-2021/alberta-quebec-and-the-politics-of-equalization/

Jacques, O., & Bélanger, É. (2022). Deficit or austerity bias? The changing nature of Canadians' opinion of fiscal policies. *Canadian Journal of Political Science, 55*(2), 404–17. https://doi.org/10.1017/S0008423922000038

Jakobsen, K., Jakobsen, K., Kleven, H., & Zucman, G. (2019). Wealth taxation and wealth accumulation: Theory and evidence from Denmark. *Quarterly Journal of Economics, 135*(1), 329–88. https://doi.org/10.1093/qje/qjz032

Janigan, M. (2020). *The art of sharing: The richer versus the poorer provinces since Confederation.* McGill-Queen's University Press.

Jeffrey, B. (2013). The Parliamentary Budget Officer two years later: A progress report. *Canadian Parliamentary Review, 33*(4), 37–45. http://www.revparl.ca/33/4/33n4_10e_Jeffrey.pdf

Jenson, J. (2013). Historical transformations of Canada's social architecture: Institutions, instruments, and ideas. In K. Banting & J. Myles (Eds.), *Inequality and the fading of redistributive politics* (pp. 43–64). UBC Press.

Jenson, J., & Saint-Martin, D. (2006). Building blocks for a new social architecture: The LEGO™ paradigm of an active society. *Policy & Politics, 34*(3), 429–51. https://doi.org/10.1332/030557306777695325

Johnson, D. (2004). Does the debt matter? In C. Ragan & W. Watson (Eds.), *Is the debt war over?* (pp. 133–60). Institute for Research on Public Policy.

Kahneman, D., & Klein, G. (2009). Conditions for intuitive expertise: A failure to disagree. *American Psychologist, 64*(6), 515–26. https://doi.org/10.1037/a0016755

Kahneman, D., & Tversky, A. (1984). Choices, values, and frames. *American Psychologist, 39*(4), 341–50. https://doi.org/10.1037/0003-066X.39.4.341

Karaguesian, J. (2023, 27 March). Canada needs a new economic vision, and new policies to go with it (IRPP working paper). *Policy Options.* Institute for Research on Public Policy. https://policyoptions.irpp.org/magazines/march-2023/economy-industrial-policy/

Keech, W.R. (2013). *Economic politics in the United States: The costs and risks of democracy.* Cambridge University Press.

Kellock, B., & LeRoy, S. (2007, 11 October). *Questioning the legality of the federal spending power.* Fraser Institute. https://www.fraserinstitute.org/studies/questioning-the-legality-federal-spending-power

Kelton, S. (2020). *The deficit myth: Modern Monetary Theory and the birth of the people's economy.* PublicAffairs.

Kernaghan, K., & Langford, J.W. (2014). *The responsible public servant* (2nd ed.). Institute of Public Administration of Canada.

Khan, A., & Mayes, S. (2009). *Transition to accrual accounting.* International Monetary Fund Technical Notes and Manuals. https://www.imf.org/external/pubs/ft/tnm/2009/tnm0902.pdf

King, M. (2016). *The end of alchemy: Money, banking, and the future of the global economy.* W.W. Norton.

Knight, F. (1921). *Risk, uncertainty, and profit.* Harper Torchbooks.

Kopits, G., & Symansky, S. (1998). *Fiscal Policy Rules.* International Monetary Fund. https://doi.org/10.5089/9781557757043.084

Kroeger, A. (1996). A retrospective on policy development in Ottawa. *Canadian Public Administration, 39*(4), 457–68. https://doi.org/10.1111/j.1754-7121.1996.tb00145.x

Krueger, A. (1974). The political economy of the rent-seeking society. *American Economic Review, 64*(3), 291–303. https://www.jstor.org/stable/1808883

Krugman, P. (2021, 16 December). The year of inflation infamy. *New York Times.* https://www.nytimes.com/2021/12/16/opinion/inflation-economy-2021.html

Kuznets, S. (1955). Economic growth and income inequality. *American Economic Review, 45*(1), 1–28. https://www.jstor.org/stable/1811579

Landemore, H. (2013). *Democratic reason: Collective intelligence and the rule of the many*. Princeton University Press.

Leeper, E.M. (2010). *Monetary science, fiscal alchemy* (NBER Working Paper No. 16510). National Bureau of Economic Research. https://www.nber.org/system/files/working_papers/w16510/w16510.pdf

Lefebvre, P., & Merrigan, P. (2008). Child-care policy and the labor supply of mothers with young children: A natural experiment from Canada. *Journal of Labor Economics, 26*(3), 519–48. https://doi.org/10.1086/587760

Lerner, A.P. (1943). Functional finance and the federal debt. *Social Research, 10*(1), 38–51. https://www.jstor.org/stable/40981939

Lester, J. (2020, 8 December). *Overcompensation of income losses: A major flaw in Canada's pandemic response*. Finances of the Nation. https://financesofthenation.ca/2020/12/08/overcompensation-of-income-losses-a-major-flaw-in-canadas-pandemic-response/

Levi, M. (1988). *Of rule and revenue*. University of California Press.

Levy, G. (2008). A Parliamentary Budget Officer for Canada. *Canadian Parliamentary Review, 31*(2), 39–44. http://revparl.ca/31/2/31n2_08e_Levy.pdf

Lewis, T. (2003). *In the long run we're all dead: The Canadian turn to fiscal restraint*. UBC Press.

Light, P.C. (2014, July). *A cascade of failures: Why government fails, and how to stop it*. Center for Effective Public Management at Brookings. https://wagner.nyu.edu/files/faculty/publications/Light_Cascade_of_Failures_Why_Govt_Fails.pdf

Limberg, J., & Seelkopf, L. (2022). The historical origins of wealth taxation. *Journal of European Public Policy, 29*(5), 670–88. https://doi.org/10.1080/13501763.2021.1992486

Lindquist, E.A., Howlett, M., Skogstad, G., Tellier, G., & t'Hart, P. (2022). Introduction: Exploring Canadian experiences with policy success. In E.A. Lindquist, M. Howlett, G. Skogstad, G. Tellier, & P. t'Hart (Eds.), *Policy success in Canada: Cases, lessons, challenges* (pp. 1–14). Oxford University Press.

Lindquist, E.A., & Shepherd, R.P. (2023). Spending reviews and the government of Canada: From episodic to institutionalized capabilities and repertoires. *Canadian Public Administration, 66*, 247–67. https://doi.org/10.1111/capa.12532

Lindsey, B. (2021, 18 November). *State capacity: What is it, how we lost it, and how to get it back*. Niskanen Center. https://www.niskanencenter.org/state-capacity-what-is-it-how-we-lost-it-and-how-to-get-it-back/

Lindsey, B., & Hammond, S. (2020). *Faster growth, fairer growth: Policies for a high road, high performance economy*. Niskanen Center. https://www.niskanencenter.org/faster_fairer/agenda.html

Lozano, M., Atkinson, M.M., & Mou, H. (2021). Democratic accountability in times of crisis: Executive power, fiscal policy and COVID-19. *Government and Opposition*, 1–22. https://doi.org/10.1017/gov.2021.24

Lucas, R. (2003). Macroeconomic priorities. *American Economic Review, 93*(1), 1–14. https://doi.org/10.1257/000282803321455133

Macdonald, D. (2022, March). *Disappearing act: The state of provincial deficits in Canada*. Canadian Centre for Policy Alternatives. https://policyalternatives.ca/sites/default/files/uploads/publications/National%20Office/2022/03/Disappearing%20Act.pdf

MacEachen, A.J. (1982, April). *The budget process: A paper on budget secrecy and proposals for broader consultation*. Department of Finance Canada. https://publications.gc.ca/collections/collection_2016/fin/F2-54-1982-eng.pdf

MacNevin, A. (2004). *The Canadian federal-provincial equalization regime: An assessment*. Canadian Tax Foundation.

Madrick, J. (2015). *Seven bad ideas: How mainstream economists have damaged America and the world*. Alfred A. Knopf.

Malloy, J. (2023). *The paradox of parliament*. University of Toronto Press.

Marchildon, G., & Mou, H. (2014). A needs-based allocation formula for Canada Health Transfer. *Canadian Public Policy/Analyse de politiques, 40*(3), 209–23. https://doi.org/10.3138/cpp.2013-052

Martin, C., & Milas, C. (2012). Quantitative easing: A sceptical survey. *Oxford Review of Economic Policy, 28*(4), 750–64. https://doi.org/10.1093/oxrep/grs029

Massicotte, L. (2013). Omnibus bills in theory and practice. *Canadian Parliamentary Review, 36*(1), 13–17. http://revparl.ca/36/1/36n1_13e_Massicotte.pdf

Mayne, J. (2018). Linking evaluation to expenditure reviews: Not realistic nor a good idea. *Canadian Journal of Program Evaluation, 32*(3), 316–26. https://doi.org/10.3138/cjpe.43178

Mazzucato, M. (2018). *The value of everything: Making and taking in the global economy*. PublicAffairs.

McAfee, A. (2019). *More from less: The surprising story of how we learned to prosper using fewer resources – and what happens next*. Scribner.

McAllister, J. (2018). Using GBA+ to analyze federal equalization. In K.A.H. Graham & A.M. Maslove (Eds.), *How Ottawa spends: Next?* (pp. 41–52). Carleton University, School of Public Policy and Administration. http://doi.org/10.22215/hos/2018-19

McIntosh, T. (2021, 28 March). The disingenuous demands of Canada's premiers for $28 billion in health-care funding. *The Conversation*. https://theconversation.com/the-disingenuous-demands-of-canadas-premiers-for-28-billion-in-health-care-funding-157024

McIntosh, T. (2022, 15 May). Canada's premiers are missing a real chance to fix our ailing health-care system. *The Conversation*. https://theconversation

.com/canadas-premiers-are-missing-a-real-chance-to-fix-our-ailing-health
-care-system-182364

McKinsey & Company. (2022, 30 March). *The coronavirus effect on global sentiment* [Survey]. https://www.mckinsey.com/business-functions /strategy-and-corporate-finance/our-insights/the-coronavirus-effect -on-global-economic-sentiment

Mercer, J. (2005). Prospect theory and political science. *Annual Review of Political Science, 8*(1), 1–21. https://doi.org/10.1146/annurev.polisci .8.082103.104911

Microsoft WorkLab (2022, 16 March). *Great Expectations: Making hybrid work work.* https://www.microsoft.com/en-us/worklab/work-trend-index /great-expectations-making-hybrid-work-work

Milligan, K. (2013, August). Income inequality and income taxation in Canada: Trends in the census 1980–2005. *School of Public Policy Publications, University of Calgary, 6*(24), 1–28. https://doi.org/10.11575/sppp.v6i0.42436

Milligan, K. (2016). The tax recognition of children in Canada: Exemptions, credits, and cash transfers. *Canadian Tax Journal, 64*(3), 601–18. https:// financesofthenation.ca/wp-content/uploads/2018/08/16ctj3-fn.pdf

Milligan, K. (2018, 16 April). Resource jobs are sustaining Canada's middle class. Period. *Globe and Mail.* https://www.theglobeandmail.com/opinion /article-resource-jobs-are-sustaining-canadas-middle-class-period/

Milligan, K. (2022). How progressive is the Canadian personal income tax? A Buffett curve analysis. *Canadian Public Policy/Analyse de politiques, 48*(2), 211–24. https://doi.org/10.3138/cpp.2021-087

Minsky, H.P. (1986). *Stabilizing an unstable economy.* Yale University Press.

Mitchell, W., & Fazi, T. (2017). *Reclaiming the state: A progressive vision of sovereignty for a post-neoliberal world.* Pluto Press.

Mitchener, J.K., & Trebesch, C. (2023). Sovereign debt in the twenty-first century. *Journal of Economic Literature, 61*(2), 565–623. https://doi.org/10 .1257/jel.20211362

Mohamed, R. (2022, 11 January). Rahim Mohamed: Quebec's child-care program at 25: A scorecard. *The Line.* https://theline.substack.com/p /rahim-mohamed-quebecs-child-care

Moody's Investor Service. (2022). *Government of Canada – Aaa stable: Update following change to forecasts* [Credit opinion]. https://www.moodys.com /credit-ratings/Canada-Government-of-credit-rating-137160?lang =pt&cy=bra

Morneau, B., & Reynolds, J.L. (2023). *Where to from here? A path to Canadian prosperity.* ECW Press.

Mou, H. (2021, May). *Canada Health Transfer: Background and future.* Canada West Foundation. https://cwf.ca/wp-content/uploads/2021/05/CWF _IFRC_WhatNow_CanadaHealthTransfer.pdf

Mou, H., Atkinson, M.M., & Tapp, S. (2018). Do balanced budget laws matter in recessions? *Public Budgeting & Finance, 38*(1), 28–46. https://doi.org/10.1111/pbaf.12163

Mounk, Y. (2017). *The age of responsibility: Luck, choice and the welfare state.* Harvard University Press.

Mousseau, N., Beaumier, L., & Langlois-Bertrand, S. (2021, 14 October). Canada is aiming for carbon neutrality and that will mean big changes to how we produce and consume energy. *The Conversation.* https://theconversation.com/canada-is-aiming-for-carbon-neutrality-and-that-will-mean-big-changes-to-how-we-produce-and-consume-energy-169511

Munro, D., Ornston, D., & Wolfe, D.A. (2022, 25 May). Breaking Canada's innovation inertia. *Policy Options.* Institute for Research on Public Policy. https://policyoptions.irpp.org/magazines/may-2022/breaking-canadas-innovation-inertia/

Nardi, C. (2020, 29 October). Federal auditor general says her office needs extra $31M to fulfil its government watchdog mandate. *National Post.* https://nationalpost.com/news/politics/canadas-auditor-general-says-her-office-needs-an-extra-31-million-to-properly-fulfill-its-government-watchdog-mandate

Noël, A. (2020). The politics of minimum income protection in the Canadian provinces. *Canadian Journal of Political Science, 53*(2), 399–420. https://doi.org/10.1017/S0008423920000098

Nolan, B., & Valenzuela, L. (2019). Inequality and its discontents. *Oxford Review of Economic Policy, 35*(3), 396–430. https://doi.org/10.1093/oxrep/grz016

OAG (Office of the Auditor General of Canada). (2017, Spring). *2017 Spring Reports of the Auditor General of Canada to the Parliament of Canada: Message from the Auditor General.* https://www.oag-bvg.gc.ca/internet/English/parl_oag_201705_00_e_42222.html

OAG. (2019a). *1510 Selection of Performance Audit Topics.* Retrieved 19 January 2022 from https://www.oag-bvg.gc.ca/internet/methodology/performance-audit/manual/1510.shtm

OAG. (2019b, 13 June). *Budget and Funding of the Office of the Auditor General of Canada.* https://www.oag-bvg.gc.ca/internet/English/osh_20190613_e_43399.html

OAG. (2021a). *COVID-19 pandemic: Report 6 – Canada emergency response benefit.* Reports of the Auditor General of Canada. https://www.oag-bvg.gc.ca/internet/English/parl_oag_202103_01_e_43783.html

OAG. (2021b). *COVID-19 Pandemic: Report 8 – Pandemic preparedness, surveillance, and border control measures.* Reports of the Auditor General of Canada. https://www.oag-bvg.gc.ca/internet/English/parl_oag_202103_03_e_43785.html

OAG. (2021c, 13 April). *Opening statement to the Standing Committee on Public Accounts: March 2021 Reports of the Auditor General of Canada.* https://www.oag-bvg.gc.ca/internet/English/osh_20210413_e_43800.html

OAG. (2021d). *Quarterly Financial Report for the quarter ended 31 December 2020.* https://www.oag-bvg.gc.ca/internet/English/acc_rpt_e_43710.html#hd3a

OAG. (2021e). *Quarterly Financial Report for the quarter ended 30 June 2021.* https://www.oag-bvg.gc.ca/internet/English/acc_rpt_e_43882.html#hd3a

OAG. (2022a). *COVID-19 pandemic: Report 9 – COVID-19 vaccines.* https://www.oag-bvg.gc.ca/internet/docs/parl_oag_202212_09_e.pdf

OAG. (2022b). *COVID-19 pandemic: Report 10 – Specific COVID-19 benefits.* https://www.oag-bvg.gc.ca/internet/docs/parl_oag_202212_10_e.pdf

Oates, W.E. (1972). *Fiscal federalism.* Harcourt Brace Jovanovich.

Oates, W.E. (2008). On the evolution of fiscal federalism: Theory and institutions. *National Tax Journal, 61*(2), 313–34. https://doi.org/10.17310/ntj.2008.2.08

OECD (Organisation for Economic Co-operation and Development). (n.d.-a). *General government debt (indicator).* Organisation for Economic Co-operation and Development. Retrieved 7 September 2022 from https://data.oecd.org/gga/general-government-debt.htm

OECD. (n.d.-b). *Growth in GDP per capita, productivity and ULC: GDP per capita, constant prices* [Data table]. Organisation for Economic Co-operation and Development. Retrieved 3 January 2023 from https://stats.oecd.org/Index.aspx?DataSetCode=PDB_GR

OECD. (n.d.-c). *Income distribution database (IDD)* [Data table]. Organisation for Economic Co-operation and Development. Retrieved 8 August 2022 from https://stats.oecd.org/Index.aspx?DataSetCode=IDD

OECD. (n.d.-d). *Income inequality (indicator)* [Data table]. Organisation for Economic Co-operation and Development. Retrieved 2 August 2022 from https://doi.org/10.1787/459aa7f1-en

OECD. (n.d.-e). *Poverty rate (indicator)* [Data table]. Organisation for Economic Co-operation and Development. Retrieved 3 January 2023 from https://doi.org/10.1787/0fe1315d-en

OECD. (n.d.-f). *Social spending (indicator)* [Data table]. Organisation for Economic Co-operation and Development. Retrieved 29 July 2022 from https://doi.org/10.1787/7497563b-en

OECD. (n.d.-g). *Trust in government (indicator).* Organisation for Economic Co-operation and Development. Retrieved 29 October 2021 from https://doi.org/10.1787/1de9675e-en

OECD. (2020). *Sovereign borrowing outlook for OECD countries 2020: Special COVID-19 edition.* Organisation for Economic Co-operation and Development. https://www.oecd.org/finance/Sovereign-Borrowing-Outlook-in-OECD-Countries-2020.pdf

OECD. (2021a, July). Fiscal balance and debt by level of government. In *Government at a Glance 2021* (pp. 78–9). Organisation for Economic Co-operation and Development. https://doi.org/10.1787/213823a6-en

OECD. (2021b). *Independent fiscal institutions database: Version 2.0*. Organisation for Economic Co-operation and Development. https://www.oecd.org/gov/budgeting/OECD-Independent-Fiscal-Institutions-Database.xlsx

OECD. (2021c, October). *The long game: Fiscal outlooks to 2060 underline need for structural reform* (OECD Economic Policy Paper No. 29). Organisation for Economic Co-operation and Development. https://doi.org/10.1787/a112307e-en

OECD, &UCLG. (2016). *Subnational governments around the world: Structure and finance*. Organisation for Economic Co-operation and Development. https://www.oecd.org/regional/regional-policy/Subnational-Governments-Around-the-World-%20Part-I.pdf

Okun, A.M. (1975). *Equality and efficiency: The big tradeoff*. Brookings Institution Press.

OSB Canada. (2022). *Insolvency statistics in Canada*. Office of the Superintendent of Bankruptcy Canada. https://www.ic.gc.ca/eic/site/bsf-osb.nsf/eng/br02290.html#monthly2022

Osberg, L. (1995). The equity/efficiency trade-off in retrospect. *Canadian Business Economics*, 3(3), 5–19.

Osberg, L. (2000). Poverty in Canada and the United States: Measurement, trends and implications. *Canadian Journal of Economics*, 33(4), 847–77. https://doi.org/10.1111/0008-4085.00045

Osberg, L. (2018). *The age of increasing inequality: The astonishing rise of Canada's 1%*. Lorimer.

Ostrovsky, Y. (2017). *Doing as well as one's parents? Tracking recent changes in absolute income mobility in Canada. Economics Insight*. Statistics Canada. https://www150.statcan.gc.ca/n1/pub/11-626-x/11-626-x2017073-eng.htm

Page, K., & Yalkin, T.R. (2014). Canada: Oversight with qualified independence. In G. Kopits (Ed.), *Restoring public debt sustainability: The role of independent fiscal institutions* (pp. 167–86). Oxford Scholarship Online. https://doi.org/10.1093/acprof:oso/9780199644476.001.0001

Papadia, A., & Truchlewski, Z. (2022). Recessions and tax introductions. In P. Genschel & L. Seelkopf (Eds.), *Global taxation: How modern taxes conquered the world* (pp. 159–77). Oxford University Press.

Parkinson, D. (2020, 25 May). Canadian economy entering 'unknowable times' because of downturn from pandemic, Poloz says. *Globe and Mail*. https://www.theglobeandmail.com/business/article-canadian-economy-entering-unknowable-times-due-to-downturn-from/

Parliament of Canada. (2004, 5 October). *Speech from the Throne to open the First Session Thirty-Eighth Parliament of Canada*. https://lop.parl.ca/sites/ParlInfo/default/en_CA/Parliament/throneSpeech/speech381

Pateman, C. (2012). Participatory democracy revisited. *Perspectives on Politics, 10*(1), 7–19. https://doi.org/10.1017/S1537592711004877

PBO (Parliamentary Budget Office). (2008, 9 October). *Fiscal impact of the Canadian mission in Afghanistan*. Office of the Parliamentary Budget Officer. https://publications.gc.ca/pub?id=9.691552&sl=0

PBO. (2011, 10 March). *An estimate of the fiscal impact of Canada's proposed acquisition of the F-35 Lightning II Joint Strike Fighter*. Office of the Parliamentary Budget Officer. https://publications.gc.ca/pub?id=9.695113&sl=0

PBO. (2020a, 18 June). *Federal debt: Frequently asked questions*. Office of the Parliamentary Budget Officer. https://www.pbo-dpb.ca/en/additional -analyses--analyses-complementaires/BLOG-2021-016--federal-debt -frequently-asked-questions--dette-federale-foire-questions

PBO. (2020b, 6 November). *Fiscal sustainability report 2020: Update*. Office of the Parliamentary Budget Officer. https://www.pbo-dpb.gc.ca/web/default /files/Documents/Reports/RP-2021-033-S/RP-2021-033-S_en.pdf

PBO. (2022a, 19 January). *Economic and fiscal update 2021: Issues for Parliamentarians*. Office of the Parliamentary Budget Officer. https://www .pbo-dpb.ca/en/publications/RP-2122-027-S--economic-fiscal-update-2021 -issues-parliamentarians--mise-jour-economique-budgetaire-2021-enjeux -parlementaires

PBO. (2022b, 28 July). *Fiscal sustainability report 2022*. Office of the Parliamentary Budget Officer. https://www.pbo-dpb.ca/en/publications/RP-2223-012 -S--fiscal-sustainability-report-2022--rapport-viabilite-financiere-2022

PBO. (2022c, 15 November). *Fall economic statement 2022: Issues for Parliamentarians*. Office of the Parliamentary Budget Officer. https://www .pbo-dpb.ca/en/publications/RP-2223-021-S--fall-economic-statement -2022-issues-parliamentarians--enonce-economique-automne-2022-enjeux -parlementaires

Perrin, B. (2015). Bringing accountability up to date with the realities of public sector management in the 21st century. *Canadian Public Administration, 58*(1), 183–203. https://doi.org/10.1111/capa.12107

Persson, T., & Tabellini, G. (1994). Is inequality harmful for growth? *American Economic Review, 84*(3), 600–21. https://www.jstor.org/stable/2118070

Phillips, P.W.B., & Castle, D. (2022). Conclusions and lessons learned. In P.W.B. Phillips & D. Castle (Eds.), *Ideas, institutions, and interests: The drivers of Canadian provincial science, technology, and innovation policy* (pp. 353–83). University of Toronto Press.

Philp, M. (2009). Delimiting democratic accountability. *Political Studies, 57*(1), 28–53. https://doi.org/10.1111/j.1467-9248.2008.00720.x

Pierson, P. (2004). *Politics in time: History, institutions, and social analysis*. Princeton University Press.

Piketty, T. (2014). *Capital in the twenty-first century*. Belknap Press of Harvard University Press.

Piketty, T. (2020). *Capital and ideology*. Belknap Press of Harvard University Press.

Piketty, T., & Saez, E. (2003). Income inequality in the United States, 1913–1998. *Quarterly Journal of Economics, 118*(1), 1–41. https://doi.org/10.1162/00335530360535135

Piketty, T., Saez, E., & Zucman, G. (2018). Distributional national accounts: Methods and estimates for the United States. *Quarterly Journal of Economics, 133*(2), 553–609. https://doi.org/10.1093/qje/qjx043

Platt, B. (2022, 11 May). *Trudeau's Tory rival says he'd fire Bank of Canada governor*. Bloomberg News. https://www.bloomberg.com/news/articles/2022-05-12/trudeau-s-tory-rival-says-he-d-fire-bank-of-canada-governor

Poloz, S. (2022). *The next age of uncertainty: How the world can adapt to a riskier future*. Allen Lane.

Posner, P.L., & Shahan, A. (2014). Audit institutions. In M. Bovens, R.E. Goodin, & T. Schillemans (Eds.), *The Oxford handbook of public accountability* (pp. 488–506). Oxford University Press.

Potter, A. (2021). *On decline: Stagnation, nostalgia, and why every year is the worst one ever*. Biblioasis.

Power, M. (1999). *The audit society: Rituals of verification* (2nd ed.). Oxford University Press Inc.

Prime Minister of Canada. (2016, 20 July). *Families now receiving new Canada Child Benefit* [News release]. https://pm.gc.ca/en/news/news-releases/2016/07/20/families-now-receiving-new-canada-child-benefit

Prime Minister of Canada. (2020a, 11 March). *Prime Minister outlines Canada's COVID-19 response* [News release]. https://pm.gc.ca/en/news/news-releases/2020/03/11/prime-minister-outlines-canadas-covid-19-response

Prime Minister of Canada. (2020b, 11 June). *Prime Minister Trudeau speaks with His Royal Highness The Prince of Wales and the Commonwealth group of Permanent Representatives to the United Nations* [News release]. https://pm.gc.ca/en/news/readouts/2020/06/11/prime-minister-trudeau-speaks-his-royal-highness-prince-wales-and

Prime Minister of Canada. (2021, 28 July). *Securing a strong future for Newfoundland and Labrador* [News release]. https://pm.gc.ca/en/news/news-releases/2021/07/28/securing-strong-future-newfoundland-and-labrador

Przeworski, A. (1999). Minimalist theory of democracy: A defense. In I. Shapiro & C. Hacker-Cordon (Eds.), *Democracy's value* (pp. 23–55). Cambridge University Press.

Przeworski, A., & Limongi, F. (1993). Political regimes and economic growth. *Journal of Economic Perspectives, 7*(3), 51–69. https://doi.org/10.1257/jep.7.3.51

Public Policy Forum. (2018, April). *Independent and accountable – Modernizing the role of agents of Parliament and legislatures*. https://ppforum.ca/wp-content/uploads/2018/04/Independent-and-Accountable-PPF-Report-April-2018.pdf

Ragan, C. (2021, 16 December). *Are dangers lurking within the Bank of Canada's new mandate?* Max Bell School of Public Policy. https://www.mcgill.ca/maxbellschool/article/chris-ragan-dangers-lurking-within-bank-canadas-new-mandate

Rawls, J. (2005). *A theory of justice.* Belknap Press of Harvard University Press.

Rayment, E., & VandenBeukel, J. (2020). Pandemic parliaments: Canadian legislatures in a time of crisis. *Canadian Journal of Political Science, 53*(2), 379–84. https://doi.org/10.1017/S0008423920000499

Reinhart, C.M., Reinhart, V.R., & Rogoff, K.S. (2012). Public debt overhangs: Advanced-economy episodes since 1800. *Journal of Economic Perspectives, 26*(3), 69–86. https://doi.org/10.1257/jep.26.3.69

Reinhart, C.M., & Rogoff, K.S. (2010). Growth in a time of debt. *American Economic Review, 100*(2), 573–8. https://doi.org/10.1257/aer.100.2.573

Resolution Foundation, & Centre for Economic Performance, LSE. (2022, 13 July). *Stagnation nation: Navigating a route to a fairer and more prosperous Britain.* Resolution Foundation. https://economy2030.resolutionfoundation.org/wp-content/uploads/2022/07/Stagnation_nation_interim_report.pdf

Richards, J. (2010, June). *Reducing lone-parent poverty: A Canadian success story* (Commentary No. 305). C.D. Howe Institute. https://www.cdhowe.org/sites/default/files/attachments/research_papers/mixed//commentary_305.pdf

Riker, W. (1964). *Federalism: Origin, operation, significance.* Little, Brown.

Rivlin, A.M. (2014). Politics and independent analysis. In G. Kopits (Ed.), *Restoring public debt sustainability: The role of independent fiscal institutions* (pp. 19–31). Oxford Scholarship Online. https://doi.org/10.1093/acprof:oso/9780199644476.001.0001

Robson, W.B.P., & Laurin, A. (2022, 22 April). Building back bigger: How Ottawa grew under cover of COVID. *Financial Post.* https://financialpost.com/opinion/opinion-building-back-bigger-how-ottawa-grew-under-cover-of-covid

Robson, W.B.P., & Dahi, N. (2023, July). *Fiscal COVID: The pandemic's impact on government finances and accountability in Canada* (Commentary No. 643). C.D. Howe Institute. https://www.cdhowe.org/sites/default/files/2023-07/Commentary_643.pdf

Robson, W.B.P., & Mahboubi, P. (2018, 13 March). *Inflated expectations: More immigrants can't solve Canada's aging problem on their own* [E-brief]. C.D. Howe Institute. https://www.cdhowe.org/sites/default/files/attachments/research_papers/mixed/March%209%20e-brief_274%20Web.pdf

Rodden, J.A. (2019). Decentralized rule and revenue. In J.A. Rodden & E. Wibbels (Eds.), *Decentralized governance and accountability: Academic research and the future of donor programming* (pp. 91–114). Cambridge University Press.

Rodden, J.A., & Wibbels, E. (2002). Beyond the fiction of federalism: Macroeconomic management in multitiered systems. *World Politics, 54*(4), 494–531. https://doi.org/10.1353/wp.2002.0016

Rosanvallon, P. (2011). *Democratic legitimacy: Impartiality, reflexivity, proximity.* Princeton University Press.

Rosenberg, S.W. (2007). Rethinking democratic deliberation: The limits and potential of citizen participation. *Polity, 39*(3), 335–60. https://doi.org/10.1057/palgrave.polity.2300073

Rothstein, B. (2011). *The quality of government: Corruption, social trust, and inequality in international perspective.* University of Chicago Press.

Saint-Martin, D. (2004). Managerialist advocate or "control freak"? The Janus-faced Office of the Auditor General. *Canadian Public Administration, 47*(2), 121–40. https://doi.org/10.1111/j.1754-7121.2004.tb01180.x

Samuelson, W., & Zeckhauser, R. (1988). Status quo bias in decision making. *Journal of Risk and Uncertainty, 1,* 7–59. https://doi.org/10.1007/BF00055564

Sandbu, M. (2022, 19 July). The investment drought of the past two decades is catching up with us. *Financial Times.* https://www.ft.com/content/3a8731bc-aad3-42ca-b99e-b3a553974ccf

Santor, E., & Suchanek, L. (2016, Spring). A new era of central banking: Unconventional monetary policies. *Bank of Canada Review.* https://www.bankofcanada.ca/wp-content/uploads/2016/05/boc-review-spring16-santor.pdf

Saunders, D. (2017). *Maximum Canada: Why 35 million Canadians are not enough.* Knopf Canada.

Savoie, D.J. (1999). *Governing from the centre: The concentration of power in Canadian politics.* University of Toronto Press.

Savoie, D.J. (2015, 22 August). How government went off the rails. *National Post.* https://nationalpost.com/opinion/donald-savoie-how-government-went-off-the-rails

Savoie, D.J. (2019). *Democracy in Canada: The disintegration of our institutions.* McGill-Queen's University Press.

Schaechter, A., Kinda, T., Budina, N., & Weber, A. (2012, July). *Fiscal rules in response to the crisis – toward the "next-generation" rules. A new dataset* (IMF Working Paper No. 12/187). International Monetary Fund. https://www.imf.org/external/pubs/ft/wp/2012/wp12187.pdf

Schertzer, R., McDougall, A., & Skogstad, G. (2016). *Collaboration and unilateral action: Recent intergovernmental relations in Canada* (IRPP Study No. 62). Institute for Research on Public Policy. https://irpp.org/wp-content/uploads/2016/12/study-no62.pdf

Scheve, K., & Stasavage, D. (2016). *Taxing the rich: A history of fiscal fairness in the United States and Europe.* Princeton University Press.

Scheve, K., & Stasavage, D. (2020). Economic crises and inequality in light of COVID-19. *American Political Science Association: Comparative Politics, 30*(2), 15–21.

Schuck, P. (2014). *Why government fails so often: And how it can do better.* Princeton University Press.

Schwab, K., & Malleret, T. (2020). *COVID-19: The Great Reset.* Forum Publishing.

Sen, A. (1973). *On economic inequality.* Clarendon Press.

Sen, A., Fitoussi, J.P., & Stiglitz, J. (2010). *Mismeasuring our lives: Why GDP doesn't add up.* New Press. http://www.tinyurl.com/y63bg5dj

Shand, D. (2013). External audit. In R. Allen, R. Hemming, & B.H. Potter (Eds.), *The international handbook of public financial management* (pp. 817–36). Palgrave Macmillan. https://link.springer.com/book/10.1057/9781137315304

Sharpe, T.P. (2013). A modern money perspective on financial crowding out. *Review of Political Economy, 25*(4), 586–606. https://doi.org/10.1080/095382 59.2013.837325

Sheffer, L., Loewen, P.J., Soroka, S., Walgrave, S., & Sheafer, T. (2018). Nonrepresentative representatives: An experimental study of the decision making of elected politicians. *American Political Science Review, 112*(2), 302–21. https://doi.org/10.1017/S0003055417000569

Shepherd, R.P. (2018). Expenditure reviews and the federal experience: Program evaluation and its contribution to assurance provision. *Canadian Journal of Program Evaluation, 32*(3), 347–70. https://doi.org/10.3138 /cjpe.43180

Simon, H.A. (1965). Administrative decision making. *Public Administration Review, 25*(1), 31–7. https://doi.org/10.2307/974005

Simon, H.A. (1983). *Reason in human affairs.* Stanford University Press.

Skidelsky, R. (2018). *Money and government: The past and future of economics.* Yale University Press. https://doi.org/10.2307/j.ctv6gqq16

Smart, M., & Jafry, S.H. (2022, 26 January). *Why won't Canada increase taxes on capital gains of the wealthiest families?* Finances of the Nation. https:// financesofthenation.ca/2022/01/26/why-wont-canada-increase-taxes-on -capital-gains-of-the-wealthiest-families/

Staples, D. (2018, 21 December). Albertans increasingly calling to chop equalization payments to Quebec. *Edmonton Journal.* https:// edmontonjournal.com/business/local-business/david-staples-albertans -increasingly-calling-to-chop-equalization-payments-to-quebec

Statistics Canada. (2019, 26 February). *Canadian Income Survey, 2017.* https:// www150.statcan.gc.ca/n1/daily-quotidien/190226/dq190226b-eng.htm

Statistics Canada. (2020, 20 October). *Impacts on indigenous peoples.* https:// www150.statcan.gc.ca/n1/pub/11-631-x/2020004/s7-eng.htm

Statistics Canada. (2021a). *Table 11-10-0055-01 High income tax filers in Canada* [Data table]. Last modified 12 November 2021 from https://doi .org/10.25318/1110005501-eng

Statistics Canada. (2021b). *Table 11-10-0134-01 (formerly CANSIM 206-0033) Gini coefficients of adjusted market, total and after-tax income* [Data table]. Last modified 23 March 2021 from https://doi.org/10.25318/1110013401-eng

Statistics Canada. (2021c). *Table 12-10-0011-01 International merchandise trade for all countries and by Principal Trading Partners, monthly (× 1,000,000)* [Data table]. Last modified 15 December 2021 from https://doi .org/10.25318/1210001101-eng

Statistics Canada. (2021d). *Table 14-10-0287-01 Labour force characteristics, monthly, seasonally adjusted and trend-cycle, last 5 months* [Data table]. Last modified 3 December 2021 from https://doi.org/10.25318/1410028701-eng

Statistics Canada. (2021e). *Table 14-10-0355-01 Employment by industry, monthly, seasonally adjusted and unadjusted, and trend-cycle, last 5 months (× 1,000)* [Data table]. Last modified 15 December 2022 from https://doi .org/10.25318/1410035501-eng

Statistics Canada. (2021f). *Table 17-10-0005-01 Population estimates on July 1st, by age and sex* [Data table]. Last modified 29 September 2021 from https://doi .org/10.25318/1710000501-eng

Statistics Canada. (2021g). *Table 36-10-0104 Gross domestic product, expenditure-based, Canada, quarterly (× 1,000,000)* [Data table]. Last modified 15 December 2021 from https://doi.org/10.25318/3610010401-eng

Statistics Canada. (2021h). *Table 36-10-0450-01 Revenue, expenditure, and budgetary balance – general governments, provincial and territorial economic accounts (× 1,000,000)* [Data table]. Last modified 9 November 2011 from https://doi.org/10.25318/3610045001-eng

Statistics Canada. (2021i, 23 March). *Canadian Income Survey, 2019.* https:// www150.statcan.gc.ca/n1/daily-quotidien/210323/dq210323a-eng.htm

Statistics Canada. (2021j, 26 November). Expenses of government classified by function, 2020. *The Daily.* https://www150.statcan.gc.ca/n1/daily -quotidien/211126/dq211126a-eng.htm

Statistics Canada. (2022a). *Table 11-10-0018-01 After-tax low income status of tax filers and dependants based on Census Family Low Income Measure (CFLIM-AT), by family type and family type composition* [Data table]. Last modified 9 August 2022 from https://doi.org/10.25318/1110001801-eng

Statistics Canada. (2022b). *Table 11-10-0135-01 Low-income statistics by age, sex and economic family type* [Data table]. Last modified 23 March 2022 from https://doi.org/10.25318/1110013501-eng

Statistics Canada. (2022c). *Table 36-10-0124-01 Detailed household final consumption expenditure, Canada, quarterly (× 1,000,000)* [Data table]. Last modified 29 November 2022 from https://doi.org/10.25318 /3610012401-eng

Statistics Canada. (2022d). *Table 36-10-0222-01 Gross domestic product, expenditure-based, provincial and territorial, annual (× 1,000,000)*

[Data table]. Last modified 8 November 2022 from https://doi.org /10.25318/3610022201-eng

Stevens, H., & Simpson, W. (2017). Toward a national universal guaranteed basic income. *Canadian Public Policy/Analyse de politiques, 43*(2), 120–39. https://doi.org/10.3138/cpp.2016-042

Stevenson, G. (2006). *Fiscal federalism and the burden of history.* Institute of Intergovernmental Relations. https://www.queensu.ca/iigr/sites /iirwww/files/uploaded_files/Stevenson.pdf

Stiglitz, J.E., Sen, A., & Fitoussi, J.P. (2009). *Report by the Commission on the Measurement of Economic Performance and Social Progress.* Commission on the Measurement of Economic Performance and Social Progress. https:// ec.europa.eu/eurostat/documents/8131721/8131772/Stiglitz-Sen-Fitoussi -Commission-report.pdf

Stoetzer, L.K., Giesecke, J., & Kluver, H. (2021). How does income inequality affect support for populist parties. *Journal of European Public Policy, 30*(1), 1–20. https://doi.org/10.1080/13501763.2021.1981981

Straubhaar, T. (2017). On the economics of a Universal Basic Income. *Intereconomics, 52*(2), 74–80. https://doi.org/10.1007/s10272-017-0649-8

Summers, L.H. (2014). U.S. economic prospects: Secular stagnation, hysteresis, and the zero lower bound. *Business Economics, 49*(2), 65–73. https://doi .org/10.1057/be.2014.13

Summers, L.H. (2018). Secular stagnation and macroeconomic policy. *IMF Economic Review, 66*(2), 226–50. https://doi.org/10.1057/s41308-018-0056-6

Sutcliffe, H. (2020, 11 August). COVID-19: The 4 building blocks of the Great Reset. *World Economic Forum.* https://www.weforum.org/agenda /2020/08/building-blocks-of-the-great-reset/

Sutherland, S.L. (1980). On the audit trail of the auditor general: Parliament's servant, 1973–1980. *Canadian Public Administration, 23*(4), 616–44. https:// doi.org/10.1111/j.1754-7121.1980.tb00320.x

Sutherland, S.L. (1986). The politics of audit: The federal Office of the Auditor General in comparative perspective. *Canadian Public Administration, 29*(1), 118–48. https://doi.org/10.1111/j.1754-7121.1986.tb00397.x

Sutherland, S.L. (2002). *The Office of the Auditor General of Canada – Government in Exile?* (Working Paper No. 31). School of Policy Studies.

Sutherland, S.L. (2006). The unaccountable Federal Accountability Act: Goodbye to responsible government? *Revue Gouvernance, 3*(2), 1–11. https://doi.org/10.7202/1039120ar

Taft, J. (2016). From change to stability: Investigating Canada's Office of the Auditor General. *Canadian Public Administration, 59*(3), 467–85. https://doi .org/10.1111/capa.12176

Taleb, N.N. (2007). *The black swan: The impact of the highly improbable.* Random House.

Talving, L. (2017). The electoral consequences of austerity: Economic policy voting in Europe in times of crisis. *West European Politics, 40*(3), 560–83. https://doi.org/10.1080/01402382.2016.1271600

Tasker, J.P. (2016, 19 December). *Ottawa, provinces fail to reach a deal on health spending*. CBC News. https://www.cbc.ca/news/politics/health-accord-meeting-1.3903508

Telford, H. (2003). The federal spending power in Canada: Nation-building or nation-destroying? *Publius, 33*(1), 23–44. https://doi.org/10.1093/oxfordjournals.pubjof.a004976

Tellier, G. (2019). *Canadian public finance: Explaining budgetary institutions and the budget process in Canada*. University of Toronto Press.

Tellier, G. (2022). The Canadian federal 1994–1996 program review: Appraising a success 25 years later. In E. Lindquist, M. Howlett, G. Skogstad, G. Tellier, & P. t'Hart (Eds.), *Policy success in Canada: Cases, lessons, challenges* (pp. 416–37). Oxford University Press. https://doi.org/10.1093/oso/9780192897046.003.0021

Tetlock, P. (2017). *Expert political judgment: How good is it? How can we know?* (Revised ed.). Princeton University Press.

Thaler, R. (1980). Toward a positive theory of consumer choice. *Journal of Economic Behavior & Organization, 1*(1), 39–60. https://doi.org/10.1016/0167-2681(80)90051-7

Thomas, P.E.J. (2020a, 2 April). *Parliament under pressure: Evaluating Parliament's performance in response to COVID-19*. Samara Centre for Democracy. https://www.samaracanada.com/democracy-monitor/parliament-under-pressure

Thomas, P.E.J. (2020b, 21 April). *Westminster Parliaments: Comparing four approaches to emergency lawmaking and scrutiny*. Samara Centre for Democracy. https://www.samaracanada.com/democracy-monitor/westminster-parliaments

Tiebout, C. (1956). A pure theory of local expenditures. *Journal of Political Economy, 64*(5), 416–24. https://doi.org/10.1086/257839

Tombe, T. (2020). Provincial debt sustainability in Canada: Demographics, federal transfers, and COVID-19. *Canadian Tax Journal, 68*(4), 1083–122. https://doi.org/10.32721/ctj.2020.68.4.fon

Tombe, T. (2021a, 23 February). *A new tool to understand equalization payments in Canada*. Finances of the Nation. https://financesofthenation.ca/2021/02/23/new-equalization-tool/

Tombe, T. (2021b, 26 November). *The effect of COVID on provincial finances*. Finances of the Nation. https://financesofthenation.ca/2021/11/26/covid-prov-fiscal/

Tooze, A. (2018). *Crashed: How a decade of financial crises challenged the world*. Viking.

Tooze, A. (2021). *Shutdown: How COVID shook the world's economy*. Penguin Random House LLC.

Tooze, A. (2022, 28 October). Welcome to the world of the polycrisis. *Financial Times*. https://www.ft.com/content/498398e7-11b1-494b-9cd3-6d669dc3de33

Treasury Board. (1981, May). *Guide on the program evaluation function – Program Evaluation Branch*. Government of Canada. https://www.tbs-sct.canada.ca/cee/pubs/guide1981-eng.asp

Treasury New Zealand. (2020). *Budget 2020*. https://www.treasury.govt.nz/publications/budgets/budget-2020

Trebilcock, M.J. (2014). *Dealing with losers: The political economy of policy transitions*. Oxford University Press.

Treisman, D. (2007). *The architecture of government: Rethinking political decentralization*. Cambridge University Press.

Trump, K.-S. (2017). Income inequality influences perceptions of legitimate income differences. *British Journal of Political Science, 48*, 929–52. https://doi.org/10.1017/S0007123416000326

United States. (2010). *Dodd-Frank Wall Street Reform and Consumer Protection Act*. Pub. L. No. 111–203, 124 Stat. 1376.

United States. (2022). *Inflation Reduction Act*. Pub. L. No. 117–169, 136 Stat. 1818.

Usher, D. (1980). How should the redistributive power of the state be divided between federal and provincial governments? *Canadian Public Policy/Analyse de politiques, 6*(1), 16–29. https://doi.org/10.2307/3550065

Van Parijs, P. (1991). Why surfers should be fed: The case for an unconditional basic income. *Philosophy and Public Affairs, 20*(2), 101–31. https://www.jstor.org/stable/2265291

Van Parijs, P. (2013). The Universal Basic Income: Why utopian thinking matters, and how sociologists can contribute to it. *Politics & Society, 41*(2), 171–82. https://doi.org/10.1177/0032329213483106

Veall, M.R. (2012). Top income shares in Canada: Recent trends and policy implications. *Canadian Journal of Economics, 45*(4), 1247–72. https://doi.org/10.1111/j.1540-5982.2012.01744.x

Venugopal, R. (2015). Neoliberalism as concept. *Economy and Society, 44*(2), 165–87. https://doi.org/10.1080/03085147.2015.1013356

Voitchovsky, S. (2005). Does the profile of income inequality matter for economic growth? *Journal of Economic Growth, 10*(3), 273–96. https://doi.org/10.1007/s10887-005-3535-3

Vollrath, D. (2020). *Fully grown: Why a stagnant economy is a sign of success*. University of Chicago Press.

von Weizsäcker, C.C., & Krämer, H.M. (2021). *Saving and investment in the twenty-first century: The great divergence*. Springer Cham. https://doi.org/10.1007/978-3-030-75031-2

Wall Street Journal. (1995, 12 January). Bankrupt Canada? *Wall Street Journal*, A14. https://www.proquest.com/docview/398559241

Wallner, J., & Boychuk, G. (2014). Comparing federations: Testing the model of market-preserving federalism on Canada, Australia, and the United States. In L. Turgeon, M. Papillon, J. Wallner, & S. White (Eds.), *Comparing Canada: Methods and perspectives on Canadian politics* (pp. 198–221). UBC Press.

Warren, M. (1999). What is political? *Journal of Theoretical Politics, 11*(2), 207–31. https://doi.org/10.1177/0951692899011002004

Warren, M. (2009, 26 June). Why is Kevin Page left twisting in the wind? *Globe and Mail*. https://www.theglobeandmail.com/opinion/why-is-kevin-page -left-twisting-in-the-wind/article1199505/

Weale, A. (1999). *Democracy*. St. Martins. https://doi.org/10.1007/978-1-349 -27291-4

Weaver, R.K. (1986). The politics of blame avoidance. *Journal of Public Policy, 6*(4), 371–98. https://doi.org/10.1017/S0143814X00004219

Weaver, R.K. (2020). Policy dynamics in federal systems: A framework for analysis. *Publius: The Journal of Federalism, 50*(2), 157–87. https://doi .org/10.1093/publius/pjaa003

Wehner, J. (2006). Assessing the power of the purse: An index of legislative budget institutions. *Political Studies, 54*(4), 767–85. https://doi.org /10.1111/j.1467-9248.2006.00628.x

Weingast, B.R. (1995). The economic role of political institutions: Market-preserving federalism and economic development. *Journal of Law, Economics, & Organization, 11*(1), 1–31. https://doi.org/10.1093/oxfordjournals.jleo. a036861

Weingast, B.R. (2009). Second generation fiscal federalism: The implications of fiscal incentives. *Journal of Urban Economics, 65*(3), 279–93. https://doi .org/10.1016/j.jue.2008.12.005

Wesley, J., Hyshka, E., Snagovsky, F., Carlson, N., Downe, P., & Mou, H. (2020, 28 October). *The politics of COVID-19 in Alberta* [Research brief]. Commonground. https://www.commongroundpolitics.ca/the-politics-of-covid19-in-alberta

White, S. (2000). Social rights and the social contract: Political theory and the new welfare politics. *British Journal of Political Science, 30*(3), 507–32. https:// doi.org/10.1017/S0007123400000211

White, S., Atkinson, M.M., Berdahl, L., & McGrane, D. (2015). Public policies toward Aboriginal Peoples: Attitudinal obstacles and uphill battles. *Canadian Journal of Political Science, 48*(2), 281–304. https://doi.org/10.1017 /S0008423915000281

Wiedemann, A. (2021). *Indebted societies: Credit and welfare in rich democracies*. Cambridge University Press. https://doi.org/10.1017/9781108975209

Wildavsky, A. (1974). *The politics of the budgetary process* (2nd ed.). Little, Brown.

Williams, B. (2005). *In the beginning was the deed: Realism and moralism in political argument.* Princeton University Press.

Williams, D. (2021, 14 December). *OECD predicts Canada will be the worst performing advanced economy over the next decade…and the three decades after that.* Business Council of British Columbia. https://bcbc.com/insights-and -opinions/oecd-predicts-canada-will-be-the-worst-performing-advanced -economy-over-the-next-decade-and-the-three-decades-after-that

Worldometer. (2021). *COVID-19 coronavirus pandemic: Canada.* Lasted updated 16 June 2021 from https://www.worldometers.info/coronavirus/country /canada/

Wren-Lewis, S. (2014). Comparing the delegation of monetary and fiscal policy. In G. Kopits (Ed.), *Restoring public debt sustainability: The role of independent fiscal institutions* (pp. 54–74). Oxford Scholarship Online. https://doi.org/10.1093/acprof:oso/9780199644476.001.0001

Wucker, M. (2016). *The gray rhino: How to recognize and act on the obvious dangers we ignore.* St. Martin's Press.

Wyplosz, C. (2013). Fiscal rules: Theoretical issues and historical experiences. In A. Alesina & F. Giavazzi (Eds.), *Fiscal policy after the financial crisis* (pp. 495–525). University of Chicago Press.

Yalnizyan, A. (2010, December). *The rise of Canada's richest 1%.* Canadian Centre for Policy Alternatives. https://policyalternatives.ca/sites/default /files/uploads/publications/National%20Office/2010/12/Richest%20 1%20Percent.pdf

Yared, P. (2019) Rising government debt: Causes and solutions for a decades-old trend. *Journal of Economic Perspectives, 33*(2), 115–40. https:// doi.org/10.1257/jep.33.2.115

Zucman, G. (2019, January). *Global wealth inequality* (NBER Working Paper No. 25462). National Bureau of Economic Research. http://www.nber.org /papers/w25462

Index

www.ingramcontent.com/pod-product-compliance
Ingram Content Group UK Ltd.
Pitfield, Milton Keynes, MK11 3LW, UK
UKHW040857140325
456137UK00002B/6